HAMLYN ALL-COLOUR

▶▶SCIENCE▶▶ ENCYCLOPEDIA

HAMLYN ALL-COLOUR

▶▶SCIENCE▶▶ ENCYCLOPEDIA

CONTRIBUTORS:
Edward Brace, Julia Brailsford, Judith Dresner,
William Gould, Keith Hitchin, John Illingworth,
Robin Kerrod, Peter Lafferty, Bill Lax,
Elizabeth Martin, John Scott, Stella Walker

HAMLYN

Photographic acknowledgements

All-Sport 31, British Airways 207, British Leyland 172 top, British Steel Corporation 20–21, Department of the Environment 90, Fleumer 196, G. Heilman 109 top, IBM UK Ltd 173, Japan Information Service 167, Kodak Ltd 165, Ministry of Agriculture, Fisheries and Food 166, NASA/Washington 213, National Coal Board, London 197, The Octopus Group Picture Library 218 top, Orion Press 73, Photri 109, Rex Features 206, Royal Navy Photographs 205, Clive Sawyer 122, Science Photo Library/CERN 186, S.P.L./Jerry Mason 170–171, Singer Company (UK) 172, Sony UK 160, V. Stapelberg 184, The Telegraph Colour Library 221, Timex Corporation 29, Thorn EMI/Ferguson 161, Woodmansterne Ltd/NASA 212, Woodmansterne Ltd/Nicholas Servain 218

Jacket: Science Photo Library/R. Folwell, bottom right, SPL/A. Hart-Davis, top right, SPL/NASA, centre, SPL/S. Summerhays, top left

Illustrations by: John Batchelor, Ralph Coventry, Gordon Davies, Peter Fitzjohn, Eric Jewell Associates, Linden Artists (Clive Spong, Craig Warwick), Ken Ody, Oxford Illustrators, Bill Stallion, Peter Thornley, Carlo Tora, Tudor Art Agency, Brian Watson, Whitecroft Designs, George Woodman

Most of the illustrations in this book have appeared previously in the following Hamlyn titles: *Hamlyn All-Colour World Encyclopedia, Hamlyn Colourfax: Fun with Science, Hamlyn Colour Encyclopedia of Transport, Hamlyn Encyclopedia of Space, Junior Science Encyclopedia, Microscopes and Microscopic Life, Modern World Encyclopedia, My Own Science Encyclopedia.*

This edition first published 1990 by
The Octopus Publishing Group Limited,
Michelin House, 81 Fulham Road, London SW3 6RB

ISBN 0 600 55736 7

Printed in Hong Kong

Contents

INTRODUCTION

Today's young people need a comprehensive introduction to the fascinating and fantastic world of science, and this book gives just that.

It is packed with hundreds of superb illustrations; it gives the historical background to many discoveries and inventions, and up-to-date information on some of the most recent scientific developments.

There is too a variety of safe and simple experiments that can easily be performed at home, and readers are shown how to make models and toys to demonstrate many scientific principles. There are Tables and "Factfinder" sections to help to make the book a source of easily understood and so easily remembered information.

Perhaps some young reader will find here the inspiration to go on and study one of these subjects in more and greater detail, and become one of those scientists of the future who one day will have their own place in a book like this.

The Elements Around Us

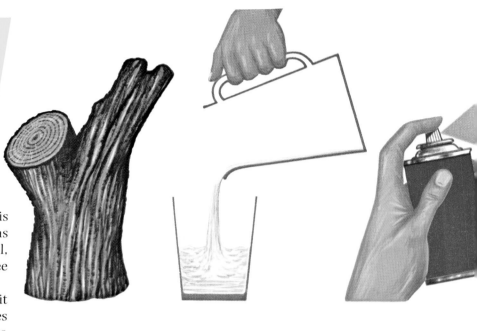

ATOMS AND MOLECULES

The stuff of which all things are made is called matter. It can be a solid such as wood or iron, a liquid such as water or oil, or a gas such as air or steam. These three forms are called states of matter.

If you take an ice cube and warm it gently in a saucepan it melts and becomes a liquid. As it becomes still hotter it boils to form steam, a gas.

Solids, liquids and gases

Solids have a fixed shape and a fixed size (or volume). It takes quite a lot of energy to change the shape of a solid. Its size will not change unless it is heated or cooled.

Liquids have a fixed volume too, but have the shape of whatever container they are poured into.

Gases do not have a fixed shape or a fixed volume. They expand to fill all the space in their container. So a gas leak in one room can quickly be detected by its smell throughout a house.

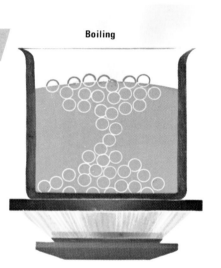

Boiling

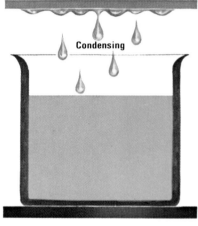

Condensing

Atomic theory

In ancient times, Greek philosophers thought that matter was made of vast numbers of very small particles called atoms. The word atom comes from a Greek word meaning 'unable to be divided'. The Greeks' ideas were revived by scientists, such as Boyle and Newton, in the seventeenth and eighteenth centuries. In 1803 an Englishman, John Dalton, worked out an atomic theory. Dalton said that all matter is made up of small particles called atoms, which cannot be split up.

Different materials behave in different ways because their atoms are different. For example, diamond is different from aluminium because it is made up of a different kind of atom.

Pure water   Salt solution

Top
Wood is an example of a solid. Water is a liquid: it can be poured and changes its shape. It is not so easy to draw a picture of a gas. The mist you see from a spray is very small drops of water, carried by the gas, which is invisible.

Above
As the molecules of a liquid are heated they move about more and more. Some of them escape from the surface of the liquid. This is called evaporation. A gas condenses when its molecules touch a cold surface. This is what happens when you see steam condensing back into water on a bathroom mirror.

Left
Prove that there can be spaces between atoms by a simple experiment. Take a measuring cylinder and fill it with water to a marked level. Now add salt. While the salt dissolves there is no increase in volume.

The atoms in a substance are usually joined together in groups called molecules. The way in which the atoms or molecules are packed together decides whether a substance is a solid, a liquid, or a gas.

Atoms and molecules attract one another. If they attract strongly they are packed close together and form a solid. In a solid the particles are fixed in position. This makes it difficult for a solid to change its shape or its size.

If the atoms or molecules do not attract so strongly, they can move about and form a liquid or a gas. As a solid is heated, the particles move to and fro, or vibrate. They vibrate more and more until they break away from each other. They then form a liquid. This is called melting. Ice melts into water.

The particles in a liquid can move around quite freely, but cannot escape from each other completely. They are much further apart than the particles in a solid, and so take up more space.

Heating a liquid makes its particles move even faster. Eventually they are moving so quickly that they can escape from the surface of the liquid, and form a gas. This is called evaporation. When the liquid gets hotter still the particles escape so quickly that the liquid bubbles. This is called boiling.

Right
Water in its three different states: ice, the solid; water, the liquid; steam, the gas.

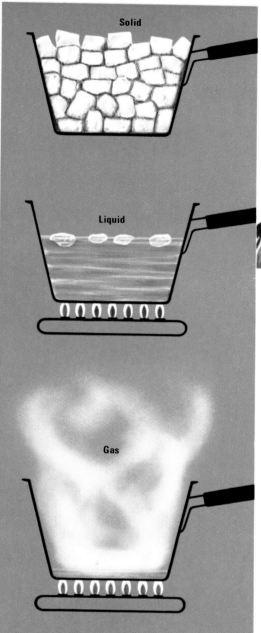
Solid

Liquid

Gas

Democritus

Above
Democritus (5th century BC) was an ancient Greek who believed matter was made up of atoms which moved about in empty space. He had no way of finding out whether this idea was true.

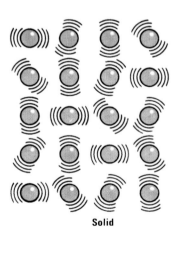
Solid

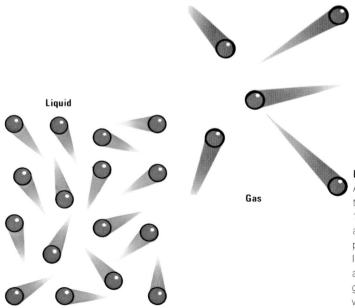
Liquid

Gas

Above
Take a glass of still water and place a drop of milk or ink carefully on the surface. After a time the milk or ink spreads through the water because of the movement of the atoms.

Left
Atoms are very small. One gram of the metal copper contains nearly 10,000,000,000,000,000,000,000 atoms. In a solid they have fixed positions about which they vibrate. In a liquid they move about but are still quite close together. In a gas they are far apart, and move very quickly.

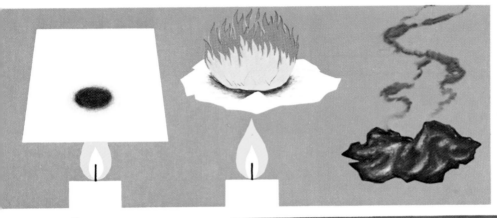

PHYSICAL AND CHEMICAL CHANGES

When ice is warmed it changes into water. This is called a physical change. In a physical change the material changes its appearance. It is easy to get the original material back again. If water is put in a refrigerator it freezes to ice. When warmed, ice quickly melts back to water. We say that the change from water to ice is the reverse of the change from ice to water. The change is a reversible change. Another example of a physical change is the change from water to steam when a kettle boils. When the steam cools it condenses back to water.

A quite different kind of change takes place when a piece of paper is heated. First it goes brown and becomes brittle. Then it bursts into flames and gives out a lot of heat. It ends up as ash. When the ash is

Right
The best known physical changes are the changes between solids, liquids, and gases. Water changes to steam at 100°C. When water is cooled below 0°C it changes to ice. Both these changes are reversible.

Above
The burning of a piece of paper is a chemical change. Paper and ash are quite different from one another. We say that they are different substances. Water, ice, and steam are just different states of the same substance.

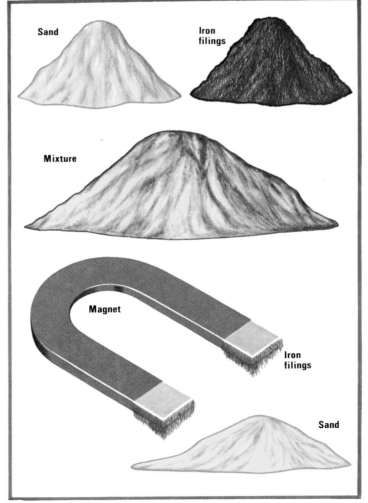

Right
A mixture of sand and iron filings can be separated with a magnet. The formation of the mixture is a physical change. The sand and the iron filings do not react chemically with each other.

cooled it does not change back into paper. A completely new substance has been made. A change of this kind is called a chemical change. In fact paper is changing slowly all the time. Very old paper is crumbly and yellow.

Everyday changes

Work out whether changes you see every day are physical changes or chemical changes. In hot weather butter becomes soft but if it gets cold the butter become hard again. The change is reversible and is an example of a physical change. When milk is left it turns sour and there is no way of getting fresh milk from sour milk. This change is not reversible. We say it is irreversible. It is an example of a chemical change.

If iron filings are mixed with sand the mixture looks grey. However the iron filings can easily be removed by using a magnet. If you look at the mixture with a magnifying glass you can still see the grains of sand and the small pieces of iron. No new substance has been formed. This is a physical change.

Shake some sugar and water together. The sugar dissolves in the water and the solution looks clear and colourless. You can get the sugar back again by letting all the water evaporate. Sugar crystals are left behind. This is a physical change.

Many of the changes that take place in nature are chemical. For example, inside a cow, grass is turned into milk. There is no way of turning milk back into grass. The changes that occur when food is cooked are also chemical. There is no way of changing chips back into raw potatoes.

Below left
Leave a solution of sugar in water in a saucer. After a few days the water evaporates away leaving the sugar crystals. This is a physical change.

Below
One of the most striking kinds of chemical change is burning. Chemists used to think that everything contained a substance called *phlogiston* which was given off when things burn. In the eighteenth century Lavoisier proved that there was no such thing as phlogiston and that when things burn they join with oxygen in the air. This experiment shows that things cannot burn without oxygen. When the oxygen has been used up the candle goes out.

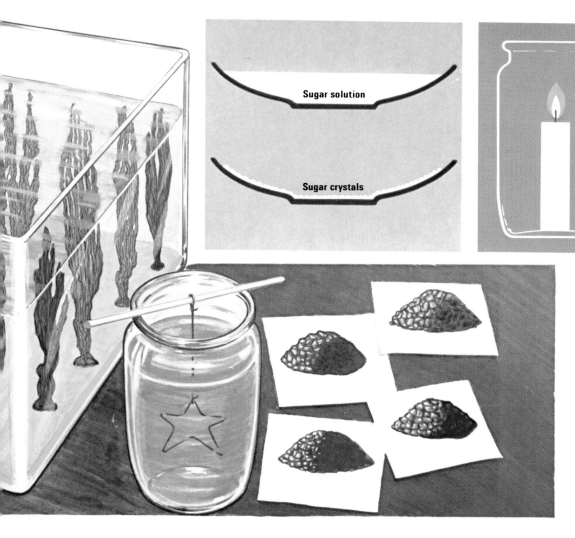

Sugar solution

Sugar crystals

Left
To make a chemical garden, put some sand in a tank and pour in waterglass solution. Drop in a few crystals, such as iron or copper sulphate, chrome alum or potassium dichromate. They will throw up 'shoots' in a few hours. To demonstrate another physical change, tie a tiny crystal of alum on a thread, suspend it in a jar of alum solution and watch the crystal grow.

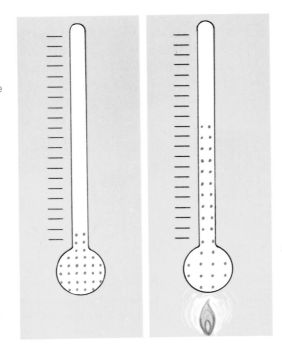

Right
A thermometer consists of a glass tube with a bulb at the bottom. There is mercury or alcohol inside the tube and bulb. As the liquid is heated it expands and needs more space. So it rises up the tube. We use a thermometer to measure temperatures. The level of liquid shows the temperature.

Below
This shows the temperature of the water layers in an ice-covered pond. Because water has its maximum density at 4°C, water at this temperature sinks to the bottom. This water can now only lose heat by conduction. Since water is a poor conductor it does not lose much in this way. Therefore in deeper water below the ice there should always be some water in which fish can live.

Below right
Water expands when it freezes. If you freeze a closed glass jar of water the glass will crack under the pressure of the expanding ice. This is why pipes have to be protected from cold.

EXPANSION

Most substances get bigger or expand when they are heated. If you pour hot water into a thick glass tumbler, the glass will often crack. The hotter inside of the glass expands more rapidly than the cooler outside. This cracks the glass.

Substances expand when they are heated because their atoms or molecules move about more rapidly. This makes them bump into their neighbours more frequently and push each other further apart. We cannot see the atoms and molecules doing this because they are too small. We see only the effects – the volume of the substance increases. Different substances expand by different amounts. The amount a substance expands when its temperature is raised one degree is called its coefficient of expansion. Pyrex glass has a very low coefficient of expansion. So Pyrex vessels do not crack easily from heat.

Solids

You can see many examples of expansion in everyday life. On hot days, telegraph wires sag because they have expanded. In winter they contract (become smaller) and they sag less. If they were put up on a hot day and stretched tight between their supports, the wire might break when it contracted on a cold winter's day.

Bridges with long steel girders have one end placed on rollers to allow for expansion. If both ends were firmly connected the bridge would buckle in hot weather.

Railway lines would also buckle in hot weather if expansion was not allowed for. This is done by using overlapping joints.

Sometimes expansion can be useful. If a glass stopper is stuck in a bottle neck you can use expansion to get it out. Dip a cloth in hot water and wrap it around the neck

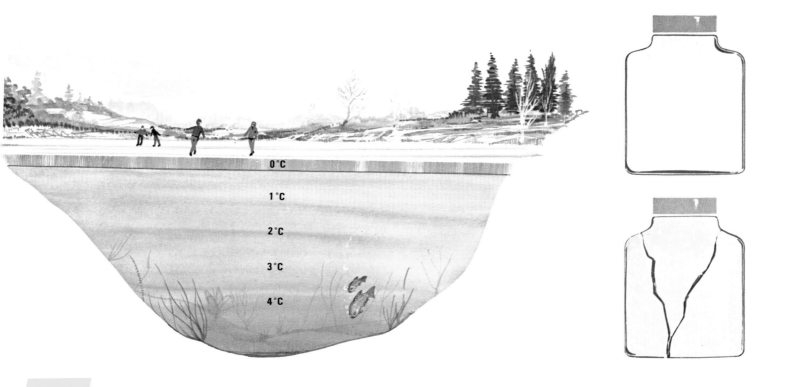

of the bottle. The neck will expand but the stopper will stay the same size. The stopper should now be loose.

Liquids

Liquids also expand when heated. You can see this by gently breathing on a thermometer. The mercury in the bulb is heated. Its atoms push themselves further apart and the liquid expands. It rises further up the tube.

Water has an unusual expansion. If you take some melting ice and heat it gently, it contracts or gets smaller until its temperature reaches 4°C. It then starts to expand again. This means that it takes up the least space and has its greatest density at 4°C.

Gases

Gases have a greater expansion than solids or liquids. Take a polythene bag with some air in it and firmly close one end. Dip the bag into a bowl of hot water and you will soon see it increase in size. This is because the air has expanded.

Motor car engines are driven by the expansion of gases. The gas expands when the fuel explodes. It pushes a piston down in a cylinder. The piston rotates the crankshaft. This is linked to the wheels, which move the car along.

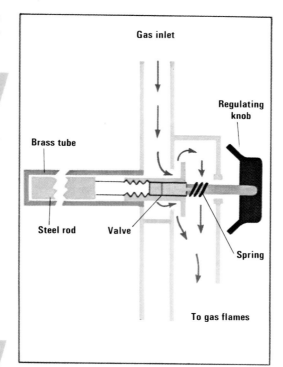

Left
Gas-oven thermostat. This is what you would see if you sliced one in half. The outside brass tube expands as the oven gets hot and pulls the steel rod with it. This closes the valve and the gas flow is cut off. When the oven cools, the brass case contracts pushing the steel rod back and opening the valve.

Above
As the bridge expands in hot weather and contracts in cold weather, the moveable end rolls backward and forwards on the rollers. If both ends were fixed the bridge would buckle in hot weather.

Left
A petrol engine in a car uses the expansion of gas. When the plug fires, the petrol and air mixture explodes and the gases expand, pushing the piston down.

Aristotle

Mendeleev

ELEMENTS AND COMPOUNDS

Elements

Wood, water, air, aluminium, paper, ash, oil, milk, sugar, and grass are some of the many millions of different substances. Over 2,000 years ago a famous Greek philosopher, Aristotle, thought that all substances were made up of four elements. These were earth, fire, water, and air. For example he thought that wood was made up of fire and earth because it burnt to an ash.

In the last 200 years people have discovered that the millions of different substances are made up of just over a hundred simple substances. These are also called elements. An element is a substance that cannot be split up into any more simple material.

Some elements are very common. One example is iron. Another is oxygen, which is a gas. It is invisible and is in the air we breathe.

Compounds

You have probably seen rust on old tin cans, iron railings, and car bodies. It is a red crumbly powder quite unlike the bright hard metal iron and the invisible gas oxygen. Rust is not an element because it is made of both iron and oxygen. Chemists call it iron oxide. Iron oxide is an example of a compound. It is

Above
Aristotle was a famous Greek philosopher born in 384 BC. He lived in Athens and wrote many books on natural science.

Above right
Dmitri Ivanovitch Mendeleev was a Russian chemist born in 1834. He made a table of the elements in which elements with the same properties were put into columns.

Thermometer (mercury)

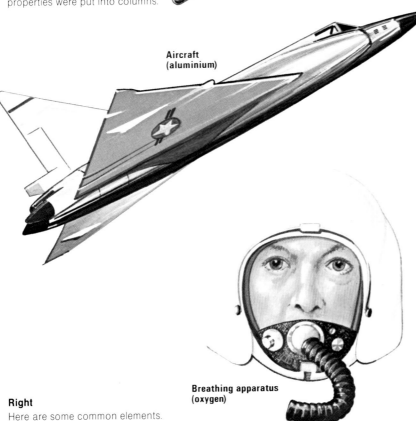

Aircraft (aluminium)

Breathing apparatus (oxygen)

Right
Here are some common elements. Mercury is the silvery liquid you see in thermometers. Aluminium is the silvery metal used in milk bottle tops. It is used for aircraft because it is a light material. Oxygen is an invisible gas. It is necessary for breathing. Sulphur is a yellow element. When it is a powder like this it is called flowers of sulphur. It used to be called brimstone.

Brimstone (sulphur)

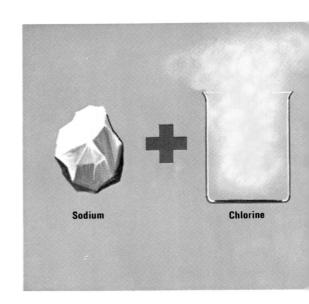

Sodium + **Chlorine**

formed from the two elements iron and oxygen. The change from iron and oxygen to rust (iron oxide) is an example of a chemical change. The rust is quite different from the elements from which it is made.

There are other substances besides elements and compounds. They are called mixtures. If powdered iron is mixed with sand the grains of sand and iron can be seen in the mixture. The iron can easily be separated from the sand. No new substance has been formed. The mixing of iron and sand is a physical change. Dental fillings are a mixture of the elements mercury, tin, silver, and zinc. Air is a mixture of gases, consisting mainly of nitrogen and some oxygen.

All elements are made up of millions and millions of small particles called atoms.

Iron is made up of a lot of atoms, called iron atoms. These are different from the oxygen atoms and this makes iron quite different from oxygen. When iron and oxygen form the compound rust the iron atoms join with oxygen atoms to give small groups of atoms. These groups are called molecules. The smallest particle in an element is an atom. The smallest particle in a compound is a molecule.

The most common compound on the earth is water. Water is made up of two elements. One is oxygen. The other is hydrogen, a very light invisible gas. Water molecules are made up of hydrogen atoms and oxygen atoms. Not all compounds are as simple as water. Some have large molecules made up of many atoms.

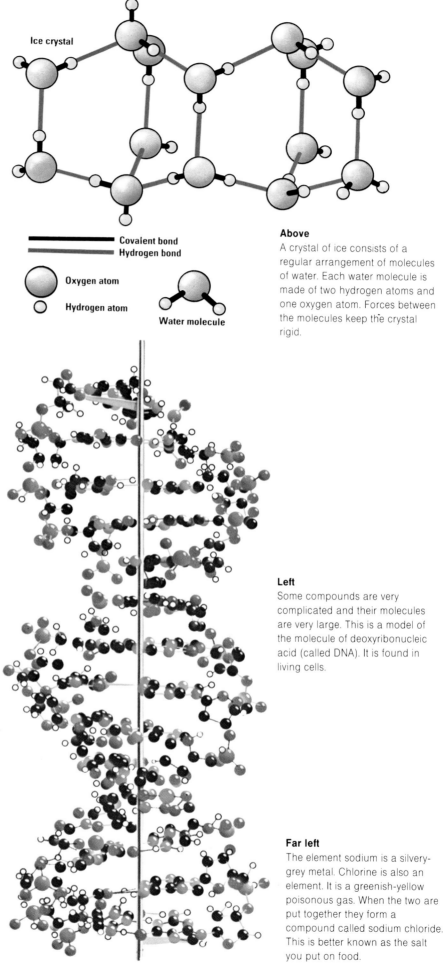

Ice crystal

| | Covalent bond |
| | Hydrogen bond |

Oxygen atom

Hydrogen atom

Water molecule

Above
A crystal of ice consists of a regular arrangement of molecules of water. Each water molecule is made of two hydrogen atoms and one oxygen atom. Forces between the molecules keep the crystal rigid.

Left
Some compounds are very complicated and their molecules are very large. This is a model of the molecule of deoxyribonucleic acid (called DNA). It is found in living cells.

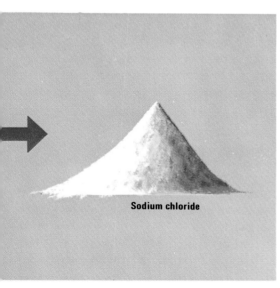

Sodium chloride

Far left
The element sodium is a silvery-grey metal. Chlorine is also an element. It is a greenish-yellow poisonous gas. When the two are put together they form a compound called sodium chloride. This is better known as the salt you put on food.

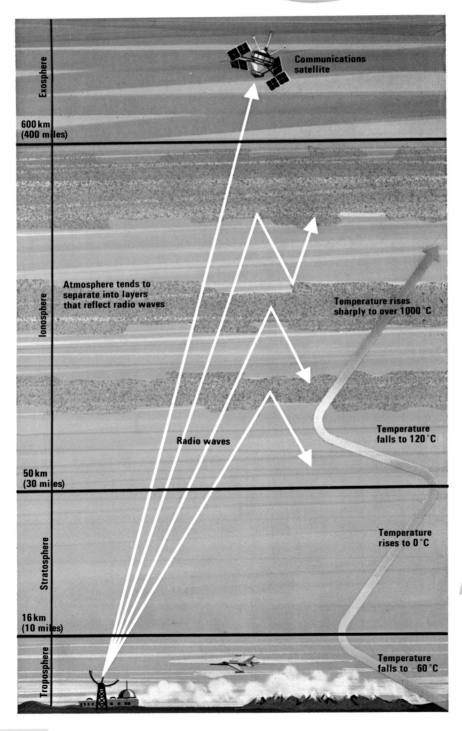

Other gases 1%

Oxygen 21%

Nitrogen 78%

Right
The proportions of gases in the atmosphere. It is easy to see that nitrogen makes up most of the atmosphere.

Below
The layers of the atmosphere. Notice how narrow the troposphere is.

Exosphere

600 km
(400 miles)

Communications satellite

Ionosphere

Atmosphere tends to separate into layers that reflect radio waves

Temperature rises sharply to over 1000 °C

Radio waves

Temperature falls to 120 °C

50 km
(30 miles)

Temperature rises to 0 °C

Stratosphere

16 km
(10 miles)

Troposphere

Temperature falls to -60 °C

THE ATMOSPHERE

The atmosphere is a layer of gases surrounding the earth. It extends out into space for about 800 km. It is held there by the pull of the earth's gravity. Most of it lies within 16 km of the earth's surface. Above this level the amount of gas slowly decreases with height until there is very little left. This marks the beginning of outer space.

The atmosphere protects the earth from extremes of heat and cold, and from dangerous rays from the sun. It stores and carries water and gases which are necessary for life.

Nitrogen is the main gas in the atmosphere. It also contains oxygen and small quantities of argon and carbon dioxide. Plants take in carbon dioxide from the air and give out oxygen. Humans and other animals do the opposite. Oxygen allows burning to take place; without it things will not catch fire. Water vapour, which forms rain, is also present in the atmosphere in varying amounts. Other gases are present in tiny quantities.

Dust occurs in the atmosphere. It include tiny particles of soot (carbon), cosmic dust from the breaking up of meteorites, salt particles from evaporated seawater, and the spores of plants (by which plants reproduce). Particles of water vapour can collect around these tiny particles to form raindrops.

The lower part of the atmosphere is called the troposphere. Here the air nearer the earth's surface is warmer than that higher up. This is because at lower levels the air is warmed more by the heat coming from the earth than by that coming directly from the sun. The troposphere is where our weather is formed. Above the troposphere lie other layers, such as the stratosphere and ionosphere. In these layers the temperature does not decrease with height.

Atmospheric pressure

Atmospheric pressure is the force that the weight of air above the earth exerts on the earth's surface. This also decreases with height because the higher you climb, the less air there is above you to exert pressure. At sea level the atmosphere exerts a

16

Left
The gases of the atmosphere are vital to all life. People must carry an artificial atmosphere about with them if they wish to explore airless regions. This diver wears a pressurised suit and helmet which is connected to an air supply by a pipe line.

Below left
When people and animals breathe they use up oxygen in the air. But plants replace the lost oxygen by taking in the carbon dioxide which people and animals breathe out and using sunlight to change it and water back into oxygen and plant food. This is the process called photosynthesis.

Below
The high and low pressure belts around the earth and the pattern of the winds. In the Northern Hemisphere winds veer to the right of their path and in the Southern Hemisphere they veer to the left, because of the spin of the earth. This is why the winds do not blow directly from high to low pressure.

pressure of about 1 kg per square cm (14.7lb per square inch or 1013.2 millibars – a unit of pressure). To get an idea of this force, lift a weight of 1 kg (just over 2lb) and try to imagine this weight pressing on every square cm of your body. We do not feel this weight because the liquids in our bodies exert an opposing pressure.

Pressure varies from place to place as well as at different heights. Winds, which are a flow of air, blow from areas of high pressure to areas of low pressure. High pressure tends to develop over cold areas; low pressure over hot areas.

Certain winds, which blow regularly, have names. These winds, together with sea currents, were vital to early explorers, whose sailing ships had to depend on them for movement. They had to keep courses set by the regular winds and currents, otherwise they ran the risk of being becalmed.

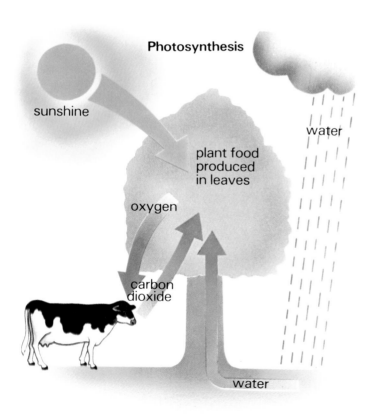

Photosynthesis

sunshine

water

plant food produced in leaves

oxygen

carbon dioxide

water

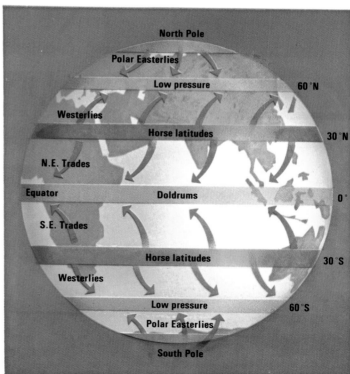

North Pole

Polar Easterlies

Low pressure — 60°N

Westerlies

Horse latitudes — 30°N

N.E. Trades

Equator — Doldrums — 0°

S.E. Trades

Horse latitudes — 30°S

Westerlies

Low pressure — 60°S

Polar Easterlies

South Pole

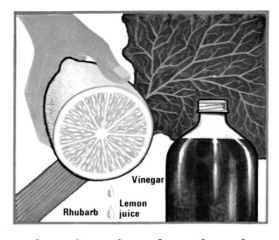

Right
Acids are present in vinegar, lemon juice and rhubarb leaves.

Far right
Some animals and plants use acids and alkalis to defend themselves.

Bee

Wasp

Nettle

Ant

Vinegar

Rhubarb

Lemon juice

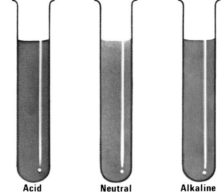

Right
The best known indicator is called litmus. Litmus turns red in acids and blue in alkalis.

Acid   Neutral   Alkaline

Right
All acids contain hydrogen. Their molecules have hydrogen atoms in them. Hydrochloric acid is a strong acid made of hydrogen and chlorine. It is also called hydrogen chloride. Caustic soda is a strong alkali. Alkalis contain oxygen atoms and hydrogen atoms and are often called hydroxides. Caustic soda is sodium hydroxide. When hydrogen chloride is mixed with sodium hydroxide they change to give sodium chloride and water. Both these new compounds are neutral. Sodium chloride is common salt.

Below
Many different salts exist and some of them are coloured. Here are some useful coloured salts. Chrome alum is used in dyeing and tanning leather. Copper sulphate kills fungi. Potassium dichromate is the orange substance used in the breathalyser test for drivers. Iron sulphate is used in making ink.

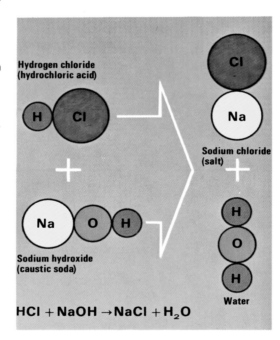

Hydrogen chloride (hydrochloric acid)

H   Cl

Cl

Na

Sodium chloride (salt)

Na   O   H

Sodium hydroxide (caustic soda)

H

O

H

Water

HCl + NaOH → NaCl + H₂O

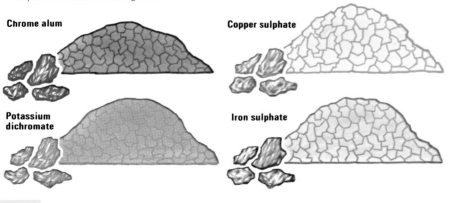

Chrome alum

Copper sulphate

Potassium dichromate

Iron sulphate

ACIDS, ALKALIS AND SALTS

There are millions of chemical compounds. Each is slightly different from the others. However, there are groups of compounds which behave in some similar ways. One such group is called the acids.

Sulphuric acid is used in car batteries. It is a dangerous poisonous liquid which attacks many materials and burns the skin. Acids like this are called strong acids. They are said to be corrosive.

Not all acids are so dangerous. Some familiar liquids are acids, such as vinegar and lemon juice. All acids have a sharp taste. Some plants and animals use acids as weapons. The stings of ants, bees, and nettles are acids. The gas that animals breathe out is carbon dioxide. When this dissolves in water an acid is formed. It is a very weak acid and is not corrosive. Soda water is water with a lot of carbon dioxide in it.

Another important kind of compound is called a base. If a base dissolves in water it is an alkali. Alkalis are often dangerous and attack the skin.

Wood ash contains an alkali. People used to mix wood ash with water so that the alkali was dissolved out and separated from the ash. The water was then boiled away in an iron pot and the alkali was left. Because of the way it was made this alkali is called potash. Potash is now made in a different way. Large amounts are used for making soap. Other alkalis come from lime and wasp stings. Saliva is a weak alkali.

Compounds that are not acids or alkalis are said to be neutral.

The colour of many flowers and fruits depends on whether the soil contains an acid or an alkali. Blue hydrangeas can produce pink flowers if planted in alkaline soil. Other substances change colour when an acid or alkali is added. They are called indicators. They can be used to indicate whether a liquid is acidic or alkaline.

You can make indicators yourself. Any fruit or vegetable which has a dark colour is worth investigating. Try boiling some red cabbage in water, and strain off the coloured liquid when it is cool. If you add a drop of vinegar to this solution, it will go red. If you then add a little soap, which is a weak alkali, the solution will turn blue.

Solutions of indicators can also be made from fresh beetroot, dark red rose petals, and blackcurrants. Once you have made an indicator, test different liquids.

Salts

When an acid is mixed with an alkali a chemical change takes place and two new compounds are formed. One of them is always water. The other is called a salt. The salt we eat is sodium chloride and it is often called common salt. Many other salts exist. Examples are washing soda (sodium carbonate), Epsom salts (magnesium sulphate), and limestone (calcium carbonate).

Below
Testing for acids and alkalis. Acids taste sour; alkalis taste brackish. Acids turn litmus red; alkalis turn litmus blue. Acids react with metals; alkalis react with fats. Acids neutralize alkaline solutions (turning them purple if they contain litmus); alkalis neutralize acid solutions (turning them purple if they contain litmus). Note: only taste food acids (lemon, etc.); others are often poisonous. Many alkalis are dangerous and should not be tasted.

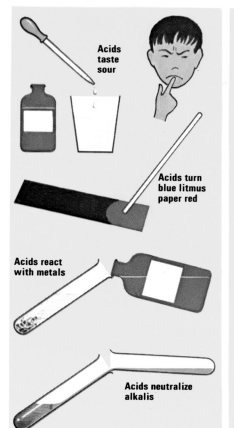

Acids taste sour

Acids turn blue litmus paper red

Acids react with metals

Acids neutralize alkalis

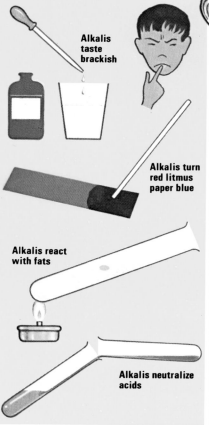

Alkalis taste brackish

Alkalis turn red litmus paper blue

Alkalis react with fats

Alkalis neutralize acids

MAKE A FIRE EXTINGUISHER
Ask an adult to help you do this. Carbon dioxide is widely used in home fire extinguishers. It can put out fires because it is heavier than air. The heavy gas pushes the air away from what is burning. But nothing can burn without the oxygen in air, so the fire is put out. You can prove this for yourself. To represent a small fire, use a candle in a tin. Make some carbon dioxide in a large bottle by adding vinegar to one or two tablespoons of baking soda. The vinegar makes the soda fizz and gives off carbon dioxide. Carefully "pour" the carbon dioxide gas from the bottle, through a rolled-up paper tube, into the tin. You will find that the candle soon goes out. The heavy carbon dioxide gas pushes the air out of the tin and snuffs out the flame.

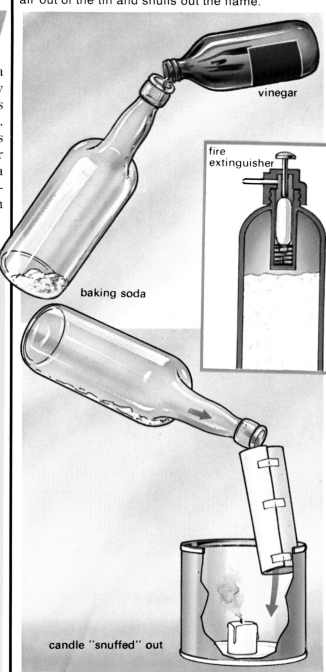

vinegar

fire extinguisher

baking soda

candle "snuffed" out

19

Left
A wide variety of items are made of metal. Steel is used to make girders and tools. Aluminium is also important in making machinery, aircraft bodies, and kitchen utensils. Copper and brass are used in electrical fittings and cables. Copper is used in coins, together with such metals as zinc and nickel. Mercury is used in thermometers and other instruments.

METALS

There are two kinds of elements, metals and non-metals. They can be told apart by their physical properties. Mixtures of metals are called alloys. These usually have some of the properties of each of their components. For example brass is an alloy

Wooden spoon | Metal spoon

Hot water

Right
Switch an electric hand-torch on, then carefully unscrew the base and see if the light has gone out. Put a large circle of paper or polythene between the base, and the batteries and the case, then screw the base up again. The bulb does not relight, because paper does not conduct electricity, but if you used a piece of aluminium kitchen foil instead, the bulb would relight as the metal allows electricity to pass through it.

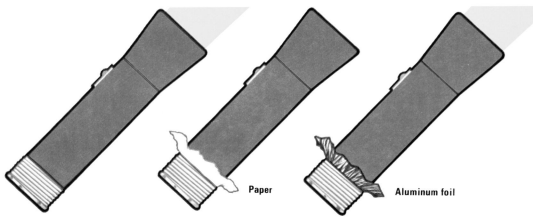

Paper

Aluminum foil

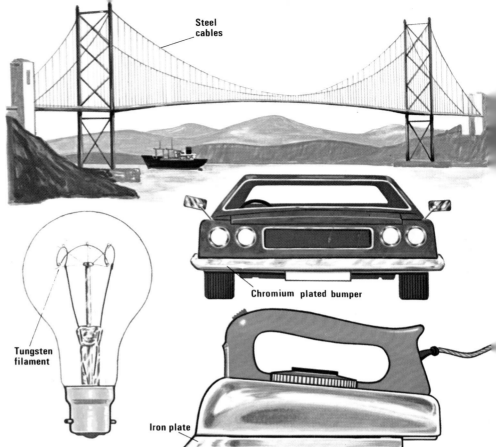

Steel cables

Tungsten filament

Chromium plated bumper

Iron plate

of copper and zinc.

Probably the best test for a metal is its appearance. A polished metal has a shiny look called its lustre. Gold, aluminium, and even the liquid metal, mercury, are shiny. Some non-metals can be polished, such as sulphur, or carbon, especially in the form of diamond, but do not have the same kind of "sheen". Another very simple test for a metal is to suspend a piece. It will give a ringing sound like a bell when it is hit sharply. We say that metals are sonorous.

Simple experiments show that heat and electricity can pass easily through metals. They do not do so through non-metals. Because of this metals are said to be good conductors of heat and electricity. Most non-metals are insulators.

Physical properties

The most valuable property of metals is their strength. Many can be forged or hammered into any shape or made into wire. The non-metals are brittle.

The way metals are used depends on these physical properties. Lustrous metals like gold or chromium are used for ornaments or protective plating. Bells are often made of bronze, an alloy of copper and tin which is very sonorous. Two of the best

conductors are aluminium and copper. So saucepans, which must heat up quickly, can be made of either metal. Most electrical equipment uses metals to conduct electricity. Copper wires carry electric currents long distances. Another metal, tungsten, is used for the heat-resistant filament in a light bulb.

The cheapest metal is iron. This is used, sometimes protected by concrete, to give strength to large structures such as sky-scrapers and blocks of flats.

Iron mixed with carbon is called steel. It can be made in almost any shape, and is tough and springy. Steel is used for swords, car bodies, machinery, and thousands of other products. For strong light aeroplanes, alloys containing aluminium and magnesium are used.

Most non-metallic elements, or compounds, do not have these properties. They are often useful because of this. Saucepan handles are often made of wood or plastic, which are insulators. Porcelain or glass can be used to protect wires carrying electricity.

Many metals are expensive, but their strength and other properties make them extremely valuable. So there is a constant search for new alloys which might have more interesting and useful physical properties. Scientists who study metals are called metallurgists.

Above

Very strong bridges are built using steel or iron. This is a suspension bridge.

The steel on a car is usually protected by the very lustrous metal, chromium, at points where paint would get worn away quickly. The fine filament of a light bulb carries an electric current and glows white hot. This is made of the metal tungsten.

An electric iron must have a metallic base, to become warm quickly. The top and handle must be made of an insulator, like plastic, to keep cool.

Top left

A furnace in a modern steel works. Steel is one of the most vital materials of our time. It is an alloy of iron with carbon and small amounts of other substances.

Above left

Stand a wooden spoon and a large metal spoon at the same time in a bowl of hot water. Then touch their handles. The metal spoon becomes hot long before the wooden one, because metal conducts heat, whilst wood is an insulator.

Far right
Wood, cotton, and sugar are organic chemicals. They contain carbon. Iron, brick, and salt are inorganic chemicals. They do not have any carbon in them.

Right
Polyethylene is used to make plastics. It is made from the gas ethylene, which has molecules which contain six atoms. In polyethylene the carbon atoms join to form molecules containing thousands of atoms.

Wood

Cotton

Sugar

CARBON

If you hold a shiny tin lid in a candle flame it becomes coated with a black powder called soot. Soot is a very important element called carbon.

Soot is just one of the many forms in which carbon is found. The lead in an ordinary pencil contains a form of carbon called graphite. When wood is burned without air it turns into a form of carbon called charcoal.

Soot and diamonds consist of carbon. They look and feel quite different because the atoms of carbon in them are joined together in different ways

Atoms of carbon can link up with atoms of other elements to form compounds. Carbon forms more compounds than all the other elements put together. All plants and animals contain carbon compounds. So they are found in wood, sugar, and cotton, from plants, and candle wax and meat, from animals. The carbon compounds in living organisms are called organic compounds.

Substances that do not contain carbon, such as oxygen, glass, and brick, are called inorganic compounds.

Right
Graphite and diamond are both forms of carbon. They are different because of the arrangement of the carbon atoms. Graphite has layers of atoms; this makes it soft and slippery and it does not let light through. Diamond has a quite different arrangement which makes it very hard and transparent to light.

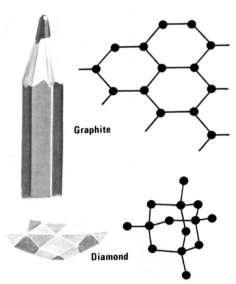

Graphite

Diamond

Right
Models of molecules of methane, which is found in North Sea gas, and butane, which is used in lighter fuel and in camping stoves. The large black balls are carbon atoms and the small white ones are hydrogen atoms.

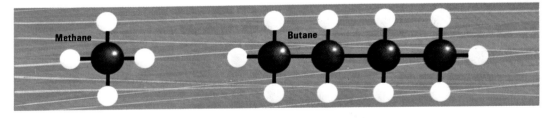

Methane

Butane

Right
A model of a molecule of octane, which is in petrol.

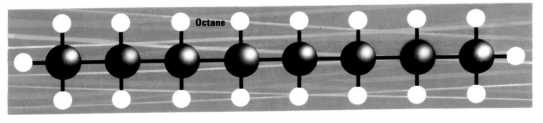

Octane

22

Iron

Brick

Salt

Hydrocarbons

Some carbon compounds, such as wood and cotton, are made up of large complicated molecules. The simplest organic compounds are made of combinations of carbon and hydrogen. Such compounds are called hydrocarbons.

If one atom of carbon joins with four atoms of hydrogen they form a molecule of the gas methane. This gas is used for cooking and heating.

Another hydrocarbon is butane, the liquid used as lighter fuel. A molecule of butane contains four carbon atoms and ten hydrogen atoms. One of the most important fuels is petrol, a mixture of hydrocarbons. It contains octane with eight carbon atoms and eighteen hydrogen atoms.

All these hydrocarbons have the atoms joined together in long chains. Some carbon compounds contain atoms that are linked together in rings.

By heating carbon compounds under pressure, many important materials can be made, such as plastics and artificial fibres.

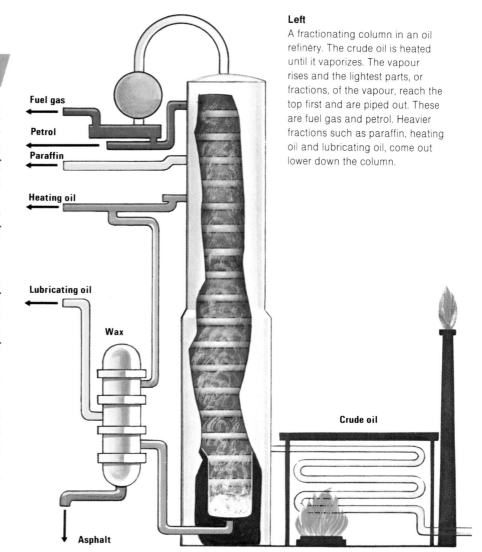

Fuel gas

Petrol

Paraffin

Heating oil

Lubricating oil

Wax

Asphalt

Crude oil

Left
A fractionating column in an oil refinery. The crude oil is heated until it vaporizes. The vapour rises and the lightest parts, or fractions, of the vapour, reach the top first and are piped out. These are fuel gas and petrol. Heavier fractions such as paraffin, heating oil and lubricating oil, come out lower down the column.

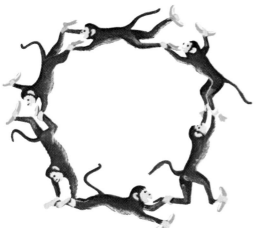

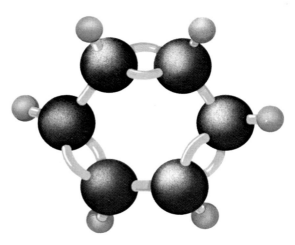

Left
A model of a molecule of benzene. Each hydrogen atom is linked to a carbon atom by one bond. Each carbon atom is also linked to one carbon atom by a single bond and another carbon atom by a double bond. Think of the carbon atoms as six monkeys and the hydrogen atoms as six bananas. Each monkey uses one paw to hold a banana and three others to hang on to the other free paws in the ring.

The elements of the earth and the life it now supports

1 hydrogen H 1									
3 lithium Li 7	4 beryllium Be 9								
11 sodium Na 23	12 magnesium Mg 24								
19 potassium K 39	20 calcium Ca 40	21 scandium Sc 45	22 titanium Ti 48	23 vanadium V 51	24 chromium Cr 52	25 manganese Mn 55	26 iron Fe 56	27 cobalt Co 59
37 rubidium Rb 85	38 strontium Sr 88	39 yttrium Y 89	40 zirconium Zr 91	41 niobium Nb 93	42 molybdenum Mo 96	43 technetium Tc 99	44 ruthenium Ru 101	45 rhodium Rh 103
55 caesium Cs 133	56 barium Ba 137	57 lanthanum La 139	72 hafnium Hf 178	73 tantalum Ta 181	74 tungsten W 184	75 rhenium Re 186	76 osmium Os 190	77 iridium Ir 192
87 francium Fr 223	88 radium Ra 226	89 actinium Ac 227						

58 cerium Ce 140	59 praseodymium Pr 141	60 neodymium Nd 144	61 promethium Pm 145	62 samarium Sm 150	63 europium Eu 152
90 thorium Th 232	91 protactinium Pa 231	92 uranium U 238	93 neptunium Np* 237	94 plutonium Pu* 242	95 americium Am* 243

atomic number →

atomic weight (of most stable isotope to nearest whole number) →

name
symbol

elements found in life chemicals

other elements

*man-made elements

						2 helium He 4
5 boron B 11	6 carbon C 12	7 nitrogen N 14	8 oxygen O 16	9 fluorine F 19	10 neon Ne 20	
13 aluminium Al 27	14 silicon Si 28	15 phosphorus P 31	16 sulphur S 32	17 chlorine Cl 35	18 argon Ar 40	

	29 copper Cu 66	30 zinc Zn 65	31 gallium Ga 70	32 germanium Ge 73	33 arsenic As 75	34 selenium Se 79	35 bromine Br 80	36 krypton Kr 84
nickel Ni 59								
palladium Pd 106	47 silver Ag 108	48 cadmium Cd 112	49 indium In 115	50 tin Sn 119	51 antimony Sb 122	52 tellurium Te 128	53 iodine I 127	54 xenon Xe 131
platinum Pt 195	79 gold Au 197	80 mercury Hg 201	81 thallium Tl 204	82 lead Pb 207	83 bismuth Bi 209	84 polonium Po 210	85 astatine At 210	86 radon Rn 222

64 gadolinium Gd 157	65 terbium Tb 159	66 dysprosium Dy 163	67 holmium Ho 165	68 erbium Er 167	69 thulium Tm 169	70 ytterbium Yb 173	71 lutetium Lu 175
96 curium Cm* 245	97 berkelium Bk* 249	98 californium Cf* 249	99 einsteinium Es* 251	100 fermium Fm* 253	101 mendelevium Md* 256	102 nobelium No* 253	103 lawrencium Lw* 257

Cubit rod

One cubit

1 metre
= 100 centimetres

Metre rule

Above

The ancient unit called a cubit is based on the distance between the point of a man's elbow and the tip of his middle finger. From recorded measurements of the pyramids we know that the Egyptians took the cubit as about 53 centimetres.

Above right

A metre contains 100 centimetres and each centimetre contains ten millimetres. Atomic scientists use even smaller metric units. One thousandth of a millimetre is called a micrometre (or a micron). One thousandth of a micrometre is called a nanometre. One thousandth of a nanometre is called a picometre; this is one millionth of a millionth of a metre.

Measurement

LENGTH

When we talk about a length we always compare one measurement with another. If you say you are taller than someone else you mean that the distance from the soles of your feet to the top of your head is greater than that distance on the other person. If you wanted to find out if you were taller than a pen friend in another town it would not be possible to compare your heights by standing side-by-side. Instead you would both use a scale such as a ruler or a tape measure to compare heights. In this case, you would each compare your own height with a standard length – a foot or metre. It would be impossible to use this method if the standard of length in one place was different from the standard in the other. So it is most important to make sure that the standard length is the same everywhere.

Yards and metres

The imperial or British system of measurement of length was based on the yard but in 1963 the yard was defined in terms of the metre.

There is a legendary tale that the yard was originally the distance from the tip of King Alfred's nose to the tip of his fingers when his arm was stretched out.

The first accurate standard yard was made in 1878. It was a bronze bar exactly one yard long kept by the government. This was called a primary standard. From it, lengths a yard long were measured onto other rods. These rods, kept in laboratories throughout the country, were called secondary standards. However, in 1960 the British standard yard was found to be contracting by a tiny amount – about one millionth of an inch each year. So it was decided to abandon this type of standard of length. In 1963 the yard was defined in terms of the metre, 1 yard being equal to 0.9144 metre. The metre is the standard unit of length used in European countries. It was originally defined, in 1791, as one

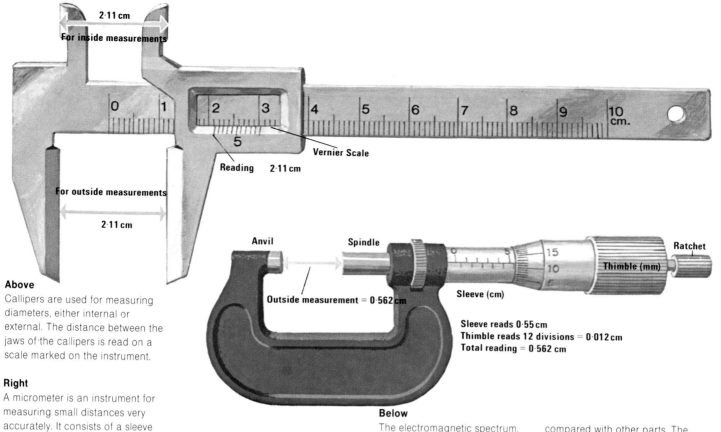

For inside measurements

2·11 cm

Vernier Scale

Reading 2·11 cm

For outside measurements

2·11 cm

Anvil **Spindle** **Ratchet**

Thimble (mm)

Outside measurement = 0·562 cm **Sleeve (cm)**

Sleeve reads 0·55 cm
Thimble reads 12 divisions = 0·012 cm
Total reading = 0·562 cm

Above

Callipers are used for measuring diameters, either internal or external. The distance between the jaws of the callipers is read on a scale marked on the instrument.

Right

A micrometer is an instrument for measuring small distances very accurately. It consists of a sleeve which rotates on a screw inside it. As the sleeve is rotated it moves forward until the tip of the micrometer just touches the object being measured. The width of the object is then given on the scale.

Below

The electromagnetic spectrum. Radio waves have much longer wavelengths than light waves which in turn have greater wavelengths than X-rays and gamma rays. The visible part of the spectrum is very narrow compared with other parts. The diagram at the bottom of the page shows the speed of light. It takes the time shown for an electromagnetic wave to travel between London and the places in the diagram.

ten-millionth of the length of the meridian through Dunkirk in France.

In 1927 the metre was redefined as the length of a platinum-iridium bar kept in Paris. This bar was also found to vary in length by tiny amounts. So in 1960 a new type of definition was internationally agreed. This is based on the wavelength of the light emitted by atoms. This length never varies; the same atom under the same conditions always emits light of identical wavelength. The atom chosen is an isotope of the gas krypton. The metre is now defined as 1,650,763.73 wavelengths emitted by this atom under certain conditions.

Astronomers sometimes use another method of measuring lengths when discussing the distance of stars. This is the light-year and is an enormous distance. It is the distance travelled by light in one year. Light travels at a velocity of 300 million metres per second. As there are about 31.5 millions seconds in a year, one light year is 9,460 million million metres or about 6 million million miles.

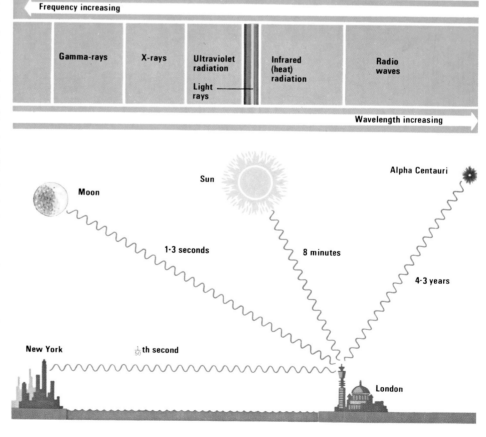

Frequency increasing

| Gamma-rays | X-rays | Ultraviolet radiation | Infrared (heat) radiation | Radio waves |

Light rays

Wavelength increasing

Moon

Sun

Alpha Centauri

1·3 seconds

8 minutes

4·3 years

New York

$\frac{1}{50}$th second

London

TIME

In ancient times, before clocks were invented, people knew that the seasons came and went at regular intervals. The sun also rose and set regularly creating night and day. Far back in prehistory, people realized that time could be measured using these regular events. The length of time between the appearance of two summers was called a year. The time between one sunrise and the next was called a day. Another way of measuring time was by noting the occurrence of a new moon. This happens at regular intervals of about 30 days. When someone said "many moons have passed" he or she meant that the moon had waxed and waned many times. The word month comes from the word moon.

We now know that these regular events are due to movements of the earth and moon. The moon waxes and wanes as it moves round or orbits the earth. A day is the time taken for the earth to spin round on its own axis. Whilst the earth is spinning on its own axis it is also travelling around the sun. A year is the time that it takes for the earth to make one complete circuit of the sun. It actually takes us $365\frac{1}{4}$ days to travel completely round the sun. So every fourth year we have a leap year of 366 days. The extra day occurs as the 29th February. This avoids the calendar getting out of step with the movements of the earth and sun.

A day is divided into 24 equal divisions of an hour. Each hour is divided into 60 minutes and each minute into 60 seconds.

THE EARTH'S ORBIT

It takes the Earth 365 days, 5 hours, 48 minutes and 46 seconds to complete each orbit around the Sun. The Earth travels around the Sun at a speed of 106 000 kph (66 000 mph)

As the Earth moves around the Sun, it is also spinning on its own axis, taking about 24 hours to complete an entire revolution. As the Sun's rays shine steadily from one direction, the spin of the Earth has the effect of creating day and night on the Earth's surface.

THE SEASONS

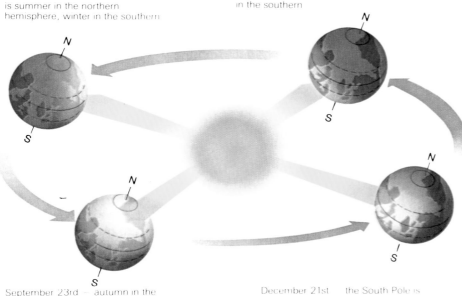

June 21st — the North Pole is tilted towards the Sun and it is summer in the northern hemisphere, winter in the southern

March 21st — spring in the northern hemisphere and autumn in the southern

September 23rd — autumn in the northern hemisphere and spring in the southern hemisphere

December 21st — the South Pole is tilted towards the Sun. It is summer in the southern hemisphere

Measuring devices

One of the first devices used to measure time was a sundial. As the earth spins round on its axis a shadow cast by the sun gradually moves round. This movement was mapped out and used for telling the time. Other methods of measuring time depend on processes that occur at regular rates. A simple example is the burning down of a candle. If you have two similar candles you can make a candle clock. Measure the time it takes for the first candle to burn down a measured distance. It may take say 3 hours to burn 3 cm. You now know that 1 cm is burned in one hour. Mark your second candle with 1 cm marks. If you now light your second candle you will be able to tell how much time has passed by seeing how many marks have disappeared. Another regular process used to measure time is the passing of sand through a small hole. An egg timer works in this way. A larger

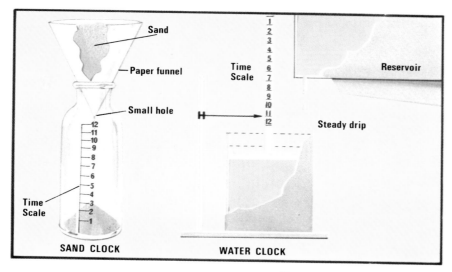

Sand
Paper funnel
Small hole

Time Scale
12
11
10
9
8
7
6
5
4
3
2
1

Time Scale

SAND CLOCK

Time Scale
1
2
3
4
5
6
7
8
9
10
11
12

H →

Reservoir

Steady drip

WATER CLOCK

version of the egg timer is called an hour glass.

The next regular process used to measure time was the swing of a pendulum. This is a weight at the end of a stick or string. Pendulums of the same length will always take the same time to swing from one side to the other, no matter how far they travel. To obtain different periods of swing you need pendulums of different lengths. A pendulum about 25 cm long swings both ways in a second. A 1-metre pendulum takes roughly twice as long (about 2 seconds). The pendulum of Big Ben in the Houses of Parliament, London is 4 metres long. It takes 4 seconds to swing back and forth.

The clocks that scientists use to measure time are based on the vibrations of atoms. These vibrations are very regular and atomic clocks are correct to one second in 3,000 years. Quartz digital watches measure time by counting the atomic vibrations of a quartz crystal.

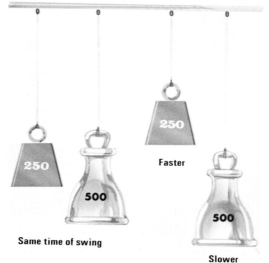

Same time of swing

Faster

Slower

Above left
Devices for measuring time depend on processes that occur at a constant rate. The sand clock depends on sand falling through a small hole. The water clock depends on water dropping from one level to another and raising a float.

Above
An early eighteenth-century sundial in the Science Museum in London.

Left
You can prove for yourself that the time of swing of a pendulum does not depend on how far it travels. Tie a weight to the end of a string and hang it from a hook on the wall. Make it swing gently and time five swings. Now time another five much bigger swings and you will find that the time is the same. Try changing the weight, you will find this does not alter the time of swing. It is the length that controls the time. Shorten the string and the time is reduced, lengthen it and it increases.

Above left
A quartz digital watch keeps time by counting the atomic vibrations of a small quartz crystal.

Left
In watches and small clocks the pendulum is replaced by a hairspring. This makes a balance wheel rotate backwards and forwards. The balance wheel is kept in motion by the impulse it receives from the mainspring through the escape wheel.

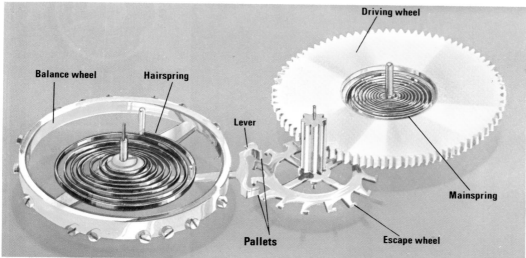

Driving wheel

Balance wheel

Hairspring

Lever

Mainspring

Pallets

Escape wheel

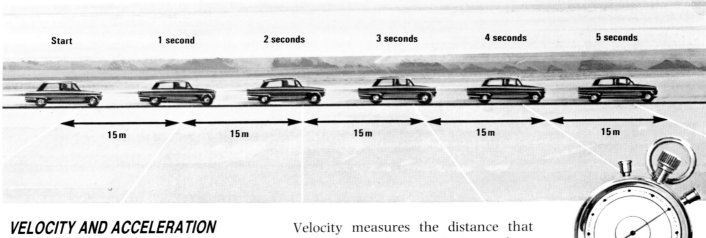

15 m   15 m   15 m   15 m   15 m

VELOCITY AND ACCELERATION

Imagine two towns that are 60 miles apart. Two cars drive the distance between these towns. One goes all the way at 60 miles per hour (mph) and the other goes at 30 mph. Obviously the one that travels faster will get there more quickly.

Velocity

When we say that a car moves at 60 mph we mean that it takes it one hour to travel a distance of 60 miles. Therefore it gets from one town to the other in one hour. The second car only travels at 30 mph so that in one hour it has gone thirty miles. It takes two hours to go the sixty miles. We say that the speed or velocity of the first car is greater than that of the second car. In one hour the first car travels 60 miles whereas the second car only travels 30 miles.

Velocity measures the distance that something moves in a certain time, or how fast it moves. Besides miles per hour velocity is also measured in metres per second or kilometres per hour.

It is quite easy to work out how fast something moves. If a car travels 100 miles in four hours how far does it travel in one hour? The answer is 100 divided by four, or 25 miles. In other words the car's velocity is 25 mph.

Next time you travel by car you can work out the average speed for the journey. Find out from the mileometer how far you have travelled. Velocity is equal to distance divided by time, so divide this distance by the length of time you have been travelling. A motorway journey of 110 miles may take two hours. The average speed is 55 mph. For a town journey you may only go 20 miles in 1 hour so your velocity is 20 mph.

Look at the speedometer during these journeys. Sometimes it may read 60 mph,

Above
This car is moving along the road and a watch is used to measure the time taken to cover a certain distance. After 1 second it has moved 15 metres. After two seconds it has moved another 15 metres, making 30 metres altogether. You can see that every second it moves 15 metres. Its velocity is always the same. It is 15 metres per second (about 34 mph).

Below
Animals show a wide difference in the speeds at which they can travel. A snail can move at about 1 millimetre per second (3.9 yards per hour). The fastest land animal is the cheetah which has been known to move at 26 metres per second (60 mph) over short distances. A racehorse can gallop at 18 metres per second (about 40 mph). The fastest speed ever measured for a man running was 11.8 metres per second (almost 27 mph).

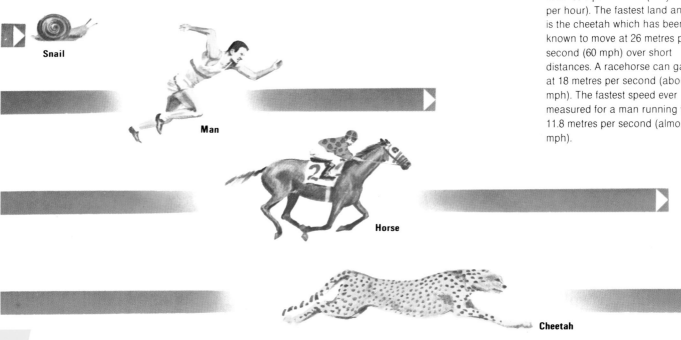

Snail

Man

Horse

Cheetah

| Start | .1 second | 2 seconds | 3 seconds |

Above

This car starts off and after one second it has covered 3 metres. After two seconds it has covered another 6 metres, making 9 metres altogether. After three seconds it has gone another 12 metres, making 21 metres altogether. You can see from the diagram that as time goes by the car is moving faster and faster. This is acceleration.

Far right

Most ordinary cars can reach a speed of between 70 and 100 mph, but cars powered by jet engines can go much faster. In 1983 the British driver Richard Noble raised the world land speed record to 633.4 mph in his car, *Thrust 2*, seen here.

sometimes 30 mph. It may even read 0 mph when you are stuck in a traffic jam. This is because the speed of the car is changing all the time. The speedometer shows how fast the car is moving at any point. The speed of a car over a whole journey is the average speed.

Acceleration

When a car is standing still it does not have any velocity at all. As it starts to move it goes faster and faster. This is called acceleration. If a car goes from 0 miles per hour to 50 miles per hour it has accelerated. A racing car can move from 0 miles per hour to 50 mph very quickly. An old car may take much longer to reach this speed. The racing car has more acceleration. Acceleration is the rate at which something changes its speed. The opposite of acceleration is called deceleration – the rate of slowing down.

Right

The boat *Bluebird* was driven at 328 mph by Donald Campbell in 1967. It reached this speed on the run in which it crashed – killing its driver.

Bluebird

Pick up a brick in one hand and a block of wood of about the same size in the other. The brick will feel heavier. It has more weight than the wood. The earth is pulling the brick with a larger force. It does this because the brick has more mass than the block of wood. In other words the total amount of matter in the brick is greater than in the wood.

We can see and feel that different materials have different masses even if they are the same size. The mass of a cube of gold would be nearly twenty times the mass of an ice cube of the same size.

Density

The lightness or heaviness of a substance for a given volume is called density. It depends on how tightly the molecules in the substance are packed.

We say that brick has greater density than wood. The stony particles of brick are heavy and are packed more tightly than the fibres of wood.

Imagine a lift. When the lift is empty, its density is low. As the lift begins to fill with people its density increases until it is full. It is then that its density is greatest. Its size has remained the same thoughout but its mass has increased.

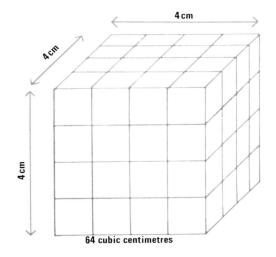
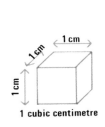

64 cubic centimetres

1 cubic centimetre

Density is the mass of a certain volume of material. If a cube is 1 centimetre by 1 centimetre by 1 centimetre it has a volume of 1 cubic centimetre (1 cm^3). 1 cm^3 of water weighs 1 gram. We say its density is 1 gram for every cm^3. This is written 1 g per cm^3. 1 cm^3 of lead weighs 11.3 grams so its density is 11.3 g per cm^3. The molecules of air are not very tightly packed and so its density is very low, about 0.0012 g per cm^3.

Imagine a piece of material to be made up of little cubes of the same size. If you know how many of these cubes there are and the weight of just one of them, you can work out the weight of the piece. The number of small 1 centimetre cubes is the total volume of the piece.

Above
The small cube measures 1 centimetre on all its sides. Its volume is 1 cubic centimetre. If its mass is 2 grams then the density of the material is 2 grams per cubic centimetre. The large block measures 4 centimetres along all its sides. Its volume is $4 \times 4 \times 4 = 64$ cubic centimetres. You can see that it could be made up of 64 small cubes. Its density is 2 grams per cubic centimetre, in other words every cubic centimetre has a mass of 2 grams. Therefore the total mass of the block is $64 \times 2 = 128$ grams.

Left
People sometimes weigh their suitcases on a spring balance. At first the density of the case is low because the space is not very tightly packed. As more clothes are put in they are packed more tightly. The density is greatest when the case is full. The mass is then greatest, although the volume is the same. The heavier the case is, the more the scale pointer moves.

Equal weights of different material may have different volumes.

If you have a pair of old balance scales, put an iron kilogram weight on one side. Measure a kilogram of sugar on the other. You can see that a kilogram of sugar has a much larger volume than 1 kg of iron. This is because sugar has a much lower density than iron. Measure kilograms of other materials and see how their volumes vary. The smaller the volume for a given weight, the greater the density.

Materials less dense than water can float. Icebergs which have a density less than that of water can float in it. Steel ships have an overall density of less than 1g per cm³ because their insides contain so much air. They can therefore float in water. A piece of solid steel does not float. People are about the same density as water so they can float or swim without sinking.

The density of a material is very important. We would not want to use a very dense material to make an aeroplane because it would make the plane too heavy. So an alloy, or mixture of metals is used. The alloy consists mainly of aluminium because it is not very dense. Other metals in the mixture give it strength. Model aeroplanes are made of balsa wood which also has a very low density. Lead is used as the sinker on the end of a fishing line because it is very dense.

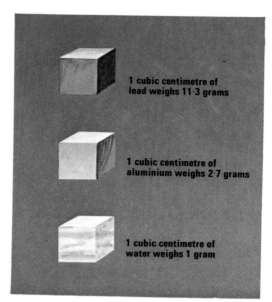

1 cubic centimetre of lead weighs 11·3 grams

1 cubic centimetre of aluminium weighs 2·7 grams

1 cubic centimetre of water weighs 1 gram

Left
Weigh some objects that look the same size. If they have different weights then they have different densities.

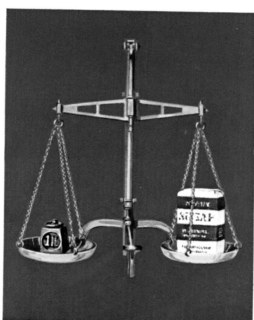

Left
Find objects of different sizes that have the same weight. Materials of different densities have different volumes for the same weight. For example, a kilogram of feathers or foam rubber would have a much larger volume than the same weight of iron.

Left
Some materials sink in water because their densities are greater than the density of water. Others will float. This shows that they are less dense than water.

Hot   Cold   Warm

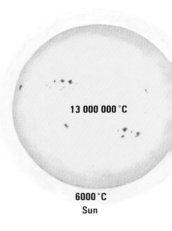

13 000 000 °C

6000 °C
Sun

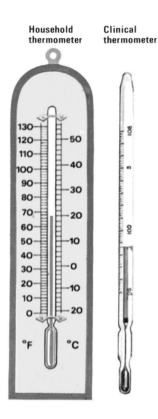

TEMPERATURE

Temperature is a measure of how hot or cold something is. On a cold day the temperature of the air is low and on a hot day the temperature is high. Ice has a lower temperature than boiling water. The temperature of the sun is very high.

We can measure temperature by many methods. One way is to touch things with our hands and judge how hot or cold they are. This method is not accurate enough for scientists because the skin is not sensitive enough to notice very small changes in temperature. For accurate measurements we use thermometers. Ordinary thermometers use the fact that liquids get bigger or expand when they get hotter. If we can see how much a liquid has expanded then we can find its rise in temperature.

There are many different types of thermometers. The common ones are filled with either alcohol or mercury. Alcohol is better than mercury in very cold countries because it has a lower freezing point. It can be used in conditions where mercury would freeze. Mercury thermometers are often used in laboratories for measuring high temperatures. Alcohol has a low boiling point. If an alcohol thermometer were put into hot water the alcohol would boil and the thermometer would burst.

A special type of thermometer is used to take your temperature when you go to the doctor. It is called a clinical thermometer. It is made so that the highest temperature it reached still shows after it has been removed from your mouth.

Centigrade scale

To get a standard scale of markings or graduations on a thermometer two fixed points must first be found. These points are temperatures which are easily obtained. The upper fixed point is the temperature of steam from boiling water. The lower fixed point is the temperature of melting ice. In the centigrade scale (°C) the difference between these two points is divided into 100 parts or degrees. The temperature of melting ice is 0°C and the temperature of

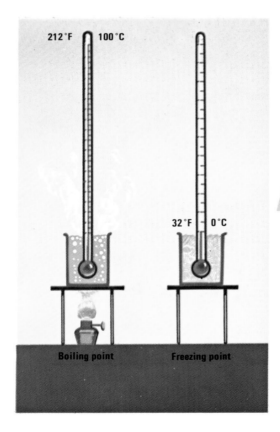

212°F   100°C

32°F   0°C

Boiling point   Freezing point

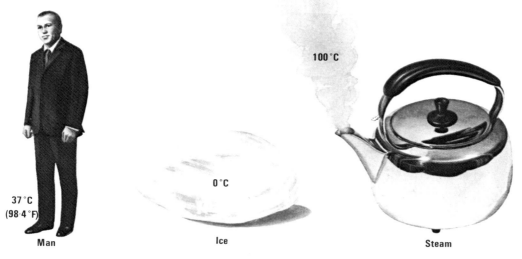

100°C

0°C

37°C
(98·4°F)

Man

Ice

Steam

Left
Here you see many familiar things all of which are at different temperatures.

Below
Lord Kelvin (1824–1907) was a brilliant scientist and engineer. His former name was William Thomson. He is famous for his work on electricity, magnetism, and heat. He invented a scale of temperature based on the fact that it is impossible to get below a temperature of about −273°C. Scientists now use a temperature scale, the Kelvin scale, in which this temperature is the zero and the freezing point of water is 273.15 kelvins. One kelvin is equal to 1°C.

steam from boiling water is 100°C. This scale is also called the Celsius scale, after a Swedish scientist.

Fahrenheit scale

On the Fahrenheit scale the ice point is 32°F and the upper fixed point is 212°F. Today, most people, including scientists, use the centigrade scale. The Fahrenheit scale is much less important.

There is a difference between heat and temperature. Imagine a red-hot sewing needle and a kettle full of boiling water. The temperature of a red-hot needle is many times higher than that of boiling water. However there is less heat in the needle than in the kettle full of water. You could prove this by dropping a red-hot needle into a kettle of cold water. It would hardly raise the temperature at all and certainly not make the kettle boil.

The amount of heat in a body does not only depend on its temperature. It also depends on how much matter it contains.

Kelvin

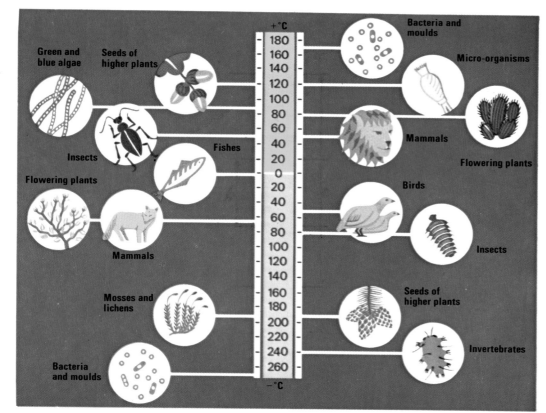

Left
The extreme limits of temperature at which animals, plants, and bacteria can survive. Life can exist between the temperatures of −273°C to +170°C. Mammals can only exist between −65°C to +50°C.

MEASURING THE WEATHER

A BAROMETER

You will need: jam jar ● balloon ● elastic band ● straw ● glue

A barometer measures the air pressure. When the air pressure rises, it usually means that better weather is on the way. When the air pressure falls, rain can usually be expected. To make a barometer, stretch a piece of rubber from a balloon over the neck of a jam jar and keep it tightly in place with an elastic band. Glue the end of a straw to the middle of the piece of the rubber. This becomes your pointer.

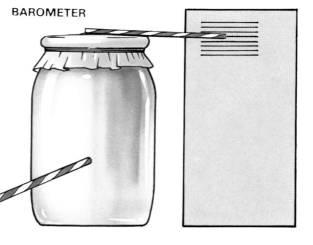

BAROMETER

When the pressure of the atmosphere goes down, the pressure of the air trapped inside the jar pushes up the rubber. The tip of the pointer dips down. When the outside air pressures goes up, it presses down the rubber, and the tip of the pointer rises.

A RAIN GAUGE

You will need: large can ● jam jar ● funnel ● rain

When rain does come, measure the amount of rainfall with a rain gauge. Use a large can – a 5 l (8 pt) plastic emulsion paint can, washed out, is ideal. You could measure the rainfall in the can with a rule marked in centimetres or inches. But it is better if you use a separate jar which you calibrate first.

Pour water into your rain gauge can to a depth of 5 cm (2 in). Then pour the water from the can through a funnel into a narrow straight-sided jar. On the outside of the jar, mark the surface level of the water and label this 5 cm (2 in). Divide the depth of water into equal parts, and make this your scale. Put your can in the open, away from overhanging trees or buildings. When it next rains, pour the water from the can into the jar, and read the amount of rainfall from the scale.

RAIN GAUGE

A HYGROMETER

You will need: wooden stand ● cotton reel ● straw ● human hair ● drawing pin ● sticky tape ● card

It often rains when the air is humid, or contains a lot of moisture. You measure humidity with a hygrometer.

Ask an adult to make a wooden stand like the one shown. Find a long, blond human hair (blond hair is particularly stretchy) and fasten the hair with sticky tape to the top of the stand. Run the hair over the cotton reel.

Stick the card to the stand under the cotton reel. Pin the straw on to the card making sure it moves freely. Pin the straw nearer one end and tie the hair round near the other end. The hair will be longer when the air is wet than when the air is dry. As the humidity changes, the hair will stretch or shrink, moving the straw down or up.

You can roughly calibrate, or put a scale on, your hygrometer by noting the readings when it is near a radiator (dry, low humidity), or when it is draped with a hot wet towel (wet, high humidity).

HOW WATERY IS SNOW?

You will need: jam jar ● snow

When there's been a heavy snowfall, it's hard to imagine what'll happen to all that water. But there is less water in a mound of snow than you might think.

Next time it snows, collect some in a glass jar. Fill it up, but don't pack it tightly. When the snow melts you'll see that you haven't got a lot of water. The snow was really ice crystals with air between them.

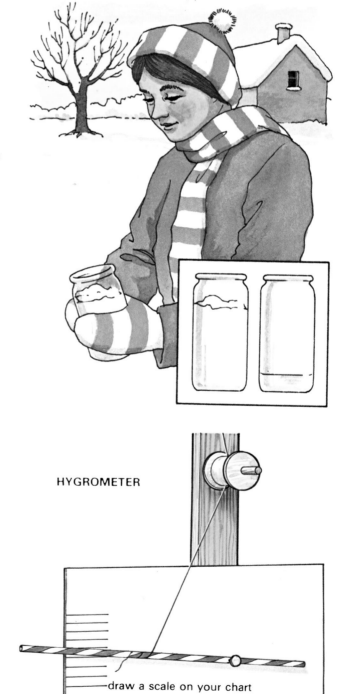

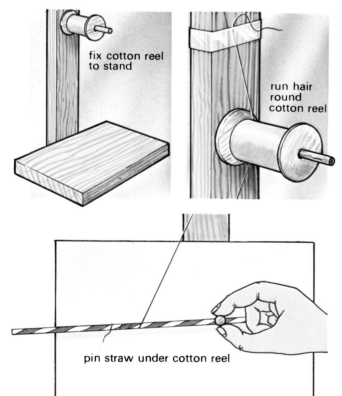

fix cotton reel to stand

run hair round cotton reel

pin straw under cotton reel

HYGROMETER

draw a scale on your chart

Right

Inertia enables you to tell the difference between a raw egg and a hard boiled egg, without cracking them. Spin each egg in water. The hard boiled one will stay spinning longer. The raw one will wobble and fall over. To double-check, spin them again, then catch them suddenly, and immediately let them go again. The hard boiled egg will stay still but the raw one will begin to spin round again on its own. The reason for this difference is that the contents of the egg have a greater inertia when they are liquid. They resist spinning in the first place, but once they are in motion they keep on moving for a time, even after the shell has been brought to a stop.

Hard boiled egg spins

Raw egg wobbles

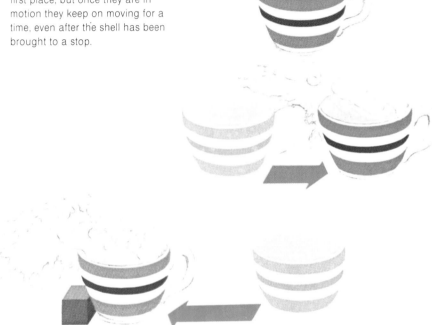

FORCES

We know that objects that are not moving do not start moving by themselves. For example a football will not move unless it is kicked. Things that are at rest seem to want to stay there.

Balance a postcard on your fingertip with a coin on it. If you flick the postcard away quickly, the coin will stay on your finger. You may have seen a similar trick with a tableful of plates. Some people can pull away the tablecloth so that the plates stay on the table. The plates do not want to move. It is better not to try this particualr trick – it takes a lot of practice.

There are other examples of things wanting to stay in place. Look at people standing in a bus. When the bus starts they tend to fall backwards. This is because they were stationary and their bodies want to stay like that. If the bus stops with a jerk everyone falls forward. There is nothing to stop them so they keep on moving. If someone runs into you, you can feel how their body does not want to stop moving.

Inertia

Generally, things do not want to move if they are at rest. Nor do they want to stop once they are moving. This tendency of something to stay at rest or stay moving is called inertia. An empty tea trolley has very little inertia. It is easy to get it moving and it is easy to stop it once it has started. When you load a trolley with heavy things

Above

Liquids show the effects of inertia dramatically. Pull sharply on a still cup of water. Some of the water will splash out or be left behind because its inertia tries to keep it in the same place. Slide a cup of water along steadily towards a barrier. When it hits the barrier, the cup will stop but the water will keep on moving in the forward direction and will splash out.

Left

Balance a card with a coin on it on top of a glass. Ask someone to put the coin in the glass without touching either. The trick is to flick the card away quickly so that the coin drops into the glass. If you flick the card the coin does not move with it. This is because its inertia tries to keep it in the same place.

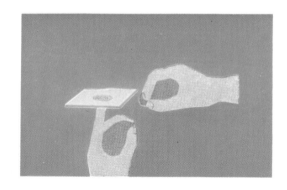

its inertia is much greater. It is more difficult to start and stop because it has more mass.

To start and stop things you need to pull or push them. These pulls and pushes are known as forces. If you hold two magnets close together you can feel them pull or push against each other. This is an example of a force.

A force is needed to start a body moving and to slow down a moving body. In other words the force overcomes the inertia of the body.

Sir Isaac Newton gave an explanation of force, motion, and inertia. He said that an object will stay at rest unless it is acted on by a force. He also said that if an object is moving at a constant speed it will continue to do this unless it is acted on by a force.

A bullet fired from a gun gradually slows down and falls to the ground. This happens because air pushes against the bullet as it moves. In outer space, where there is no air, the bullet would continue moving. This is why a space ship outside the earth's atmosphere can move without fuel. Its rockets are only necessary to allow the ship to change velocity – that is, to slow down (decelerate), to speed up (accelerate) or to change direction. Newton suggested that the bigger the force, the more the acceleration (or deceleration) produced.

Above
It takes more force to throw a cricket ball than a tennis ball because the cricket ball has more mass.

Left
Objects falling towards the ground move faster and faster. This is because they are accelerated by the force of gravity (see page 40). People used to think that if two objects were dropped from the same height the heavier one would reach the ground first. An Italian scientist called Galileo showed that this is not true. All objects fall at the same rate. He is supposed to have tested this by dropping stones from the leaning tower of Pisa – but this is probably only a myth. The heavier object has a bigger force pulling it to the ground. It also has more mass and therefore more inertia. So it only falls at the same rate as the lighter object.

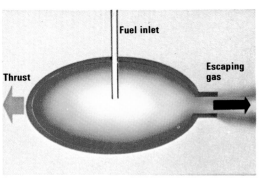

Left
Newton showed that whenever there is a force on an object there is always an equal and opposite reaction. This is how rockets work. Hot gas is forced out of the back of the rocket. The equal force on the rocket (the reaction) pushes it forward.

Left
Balance a card with a coin on it on the tip of your finger. Flick the card away, leaving the coin sitting on your finger. Because of its inertia, the coin tends not to move.

Right
Not all objects fall at the same rate. A coin will reach the ground faster than a small piece of paper. This is because the air holds the paper up. If you put the paper on the coin they both reach the ground at the same time.

Right

The earth pulls objects towards it because of an attraction called gravity. The force of gravity always pulls towards the centre of the earth.

GRAVITY

If you lift a brick and let go of it, it falls to the floor. What causes this to happen? Bricks do not move sideways without being pushed or pulled. They do not move upwards unless they are thrown or something is pulling them. For the brick to move downwards there must be some force pushing it or pulling it towards the ground. You can feel this force if you hold anything in your hand or try to lift anything off the floor. It is called weight.

Gravitational force

The first person to discover why things have a weight and why they fall to the ground was Sir Isaac Newton. It is said that one day he was sitting in his mother's orchard when he saw an apple fall from a tree. This started him thinking why such a thing should happen. His explanation was that the earth and the apple pull each other together. The earth attracts the apple and the apple attracts the earth. The earth is very large and is not affected by the pull of the apple. The apple, being much smaller, is pulled down towards the earth. This force attracting things through space is called gravity. It is this force that holds everything on the earth's surface and causes them to have a weight.

Isaac Newton also realized that the force of gravity between things gets smaller as they get further apart. People high up in an aeroplane do not weigh as much as they do on the ground. This is because they are further from the earth and so the pull of gravity on them is weaker. We do not usually notice this change in weight because it is so small.

Astronauts in a rocket notice that the pull of gravity begins to get weaker as they go further from the earth. They can eventually float around the cabin. They can also do this in orbit around the earth because the pull of the earth is balanced by the centrifugal force (see page 44).

As a spacecraft goes further from the earth towards the moon it begins to be affected by the gravity of the moon. The gravity on the surface of the moon is less than the gravity on the earth. A woman who weighs 60 kilograms on earth would weigh 10 kilograms on the moon. She would be able to throw things much further and jump much higher because the force pulling her down would be smaller.

The weight of things also depends on

Newton

Above

Sir Isaac Newton was one of the greatest scientists who ever lived. He was born in 1642 in Woolsthorpe in Lincolnshire and went to Cambridge University where he studied science and mathematics. He died in 1727.

Right

A field of zero gravity (0g) can be created for a few seconds by flying an aircraft in a particular path called a ballistic trajectory. When the aeroplane is flying on this path, the centrifugal force balances the pull of gravity, with the result that any objects inside the plane become weightless. Part of an astronaut's training to deal with weightlessness involves such flights. While they are weightless, people can fly, or swim about inside the cabin.

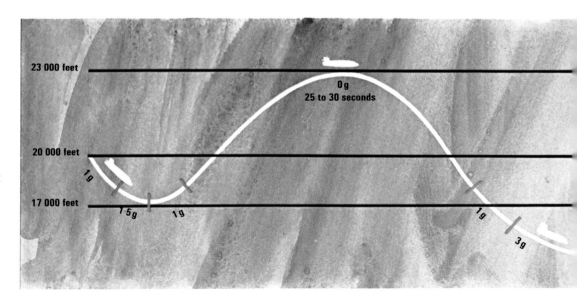

Kilometres   Kilograms

20 000	6
15 000	8
10 000	14
5 000	31
4 000	36
3 000	46
2 000	57
1 000	75
0	100

Left

A cricket ball weighs more than an apple because it has more matter in it. This means it has a higher mass than the apple. In space the cricket ball would have no weight at all because there would be no gravity to pull it. In spite of this it would still have the same mass. This is the difference between weight and mass. Weight is a force which varies from place to place. Mass is the amount of matter and it does not vary.

Far left

As we go further from the surface of the earth the effect of gravity becomes weaker and things weigh less.

Below

A spring balance measures the weight of an object, that is, the pull of gravity on it. The extension of the spring is proportional to the load hanging on it. A beam balance compares the masses of two objects. When the beam is level, the pull of gravity is the same on both sides of the balance. The force of gravity on the moon is only about one-sixth of the force on earth. If you were to weigh an object on the moon, this could not be detected on a beam balance. But on a spring balance the object would register only one-sixth of its weight on earth.

how big they are and on what they are made of. What weighs more, a kilogram of lead or one of feathers? Many people without thinking say a kilogram of lead weighs more. Of course this is a trick question because they both weigh the same, but people think of feathers as being lighter than lead. If you hold a cricket ball in one hand and an apple in the other the cricket ball weighs more although they are almost the same size. This is because the stuff (or matter) of which cricket balls are made is more tightly packed than the matter of which apples are made. Scientists say that the cricket ball has a greater density than the apple. Lead has a greater density than feathers.

The total amount of matter in anything is called the mass. The cricket ball has more mass than the apple although they look the same size. A kilogram of feathers has the same mass as a kilogram of lead. However, the size of the pile of feathers would be much greater than the size of the piece of lead.

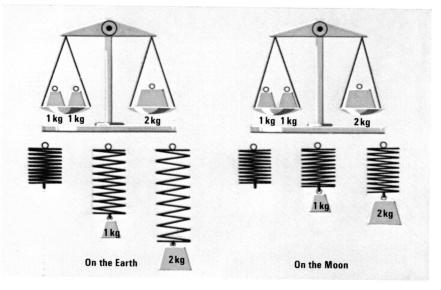

1 kg   1 kg   2 kg   1 kg   1 kg   2 kg

1 kg

2 kg

1 kg

2 kg

On the Earth   **On the Moon**

Archimedes

FLOATING

If your throw a stone and a cork into a pond, the stone sinks and the cork floats.

If you gently lower a piece of wood into water you will find that it feels lighter and lighter until finally it appears to have no weight at all. It is now being supported by the water instead of your hand. The support from the water is called an upthrust, because the water is pushing up against the bottom of the wood. When the upthrust is equal to the weight of the wood, it floats.

There is also an upthrust against things that do not float. Lower a brick into water and it will seem to become less heavy. But an ordinary brick will not float.

Archimedes' principle

Archimedes, an ancient Greek scientist, was the first to study upthrusts. He found that the upthrust was equal to the weight of fluid displaced. This is known as Archimedes' principle. It means that if an object pushes aside (displaces) one kilogram of water then there will be an upthrust equal to one kilogram acting on the object.

Suppose that a brick and a block of wood of the same size are put into water so that they are both totally covered. Because they are the same size, they both displace the same weight of water. This means that the upthrust on each of them is the same. The upthrust on the wood is greater than its weight so it rises to the surface and floats. The brick sinks because the upthrust on it is smaller than its weight.

Whether a substance will float in water or not depends on its density. Density is the weight of the substance divided by its volume. If its weight is greater than the weight of an equal volume of water it will sink. If its weight is less than the weight of an equal volume of water it will float. The brick has a greater density than water and sinks. Wood floats because the density of wood is less than that of water.

It is possible to float one liquid on

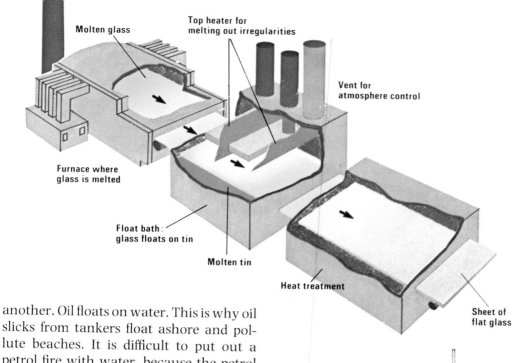

Molten glass

Top heater for
melting out irregularities

Vent for
atmosphere control

Furnace where
glass is melted

Float bath:
glass floats on tin

Molten tin

Heat treatment

Sheet of
flat glass

another. Oil floats on water. This is why oil
slicks from tankers float ashore and pollute beaches. It is difficult to put out a
petrol fire with water, because the petrol
floats on the top of the water and keeps
burning.

Oil and petrol float because they are less
dense than water. Mercury sinks because
its density is thirteen times greater than
water.

A ship floats because it has a large
volume of air in its hull, giving it an overall
density less than water. If a ship is badly
holed by a rock or a torpedo, water floods
in. This increases its density and it may
sink.

Things can also float in air, for example,
airships and balloons. This is because they
are filled with helium which is less dense
than air.

Ballast tanks empty

Ballast tanks full

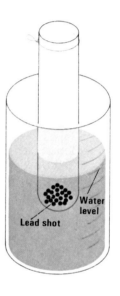

Water
level

Lead shot

Above
This experiment shows that a
floating body displaces a weight
of water equal to its own weight.
Read the water level in a
measuring cylinder (graduated in
cm³). Float a weighted test tube
in it. Read off the new water level.
The difference in the two levels
gives the volume. This is the
weight of the water displaced,
because one cm³ of water weighs
one gram. Take out the weighted
test tube, dry it and weight it. Its
weight should be the same as the
weight of water displaced. Try it
again with different weights in the
test tube.

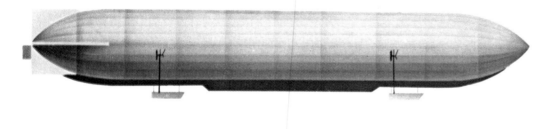

CENTRIFUGAL FORCE

If you swing a bucket of water over your head fast enough the water will not come out. When anything is spun round in a circle there is a force acting on it directly outwards from the centre of the circle. This is called the centrifugal force. It happens because the object wants to continue to move in a straight line.

The force depends on the speed with which the object is going round. The greater the speed of rotation is, the greater the force.

You can feel centrifugal forces pushing you outwards when a car takes a bend quickly, and on roundabouts in fair grounds. On roundabouts the force may be so strong, that you have to hold tightly to stay on. The same effect occurs on the 'Wall of Death'. As you spin round you are pushed outwards against the wall. Because you spin very rapidly the force is great enough to stop you falling.

When a bucket of water is swung round quite quickly, a centrifugal force pushes the water into the bucket. If, when the bucket is above your head, this force is greater than the weight of the water, the water will not fall out.

Centripetal force

There is another force, equal, but opposite in direction, to the centrifugal force, called the centripetal force. This is the force acting towards the centre of the circle, that keeps the bucket moving in a circle. If there was no centripetal force the bucket would fly off in a straight line.

When you swing the bucket, you can feel a pull in your arm. This is what provides the centripetal force. The centrifugal force acts outwards from the centre, while the centripetal force acts towards the centre.

If you swing the bucket more slowly you will find out what happens to these forces. The slower the swing the smaller the force. So now there is less centrifugal force pushing the water into the bucket. If this force is less than the weight of the water, then the water will begin to fall out. At the same time, the centripetal force, the pull in your arm, gets less.

The centrifugal force balances the force of gravity in the solar system. The earth

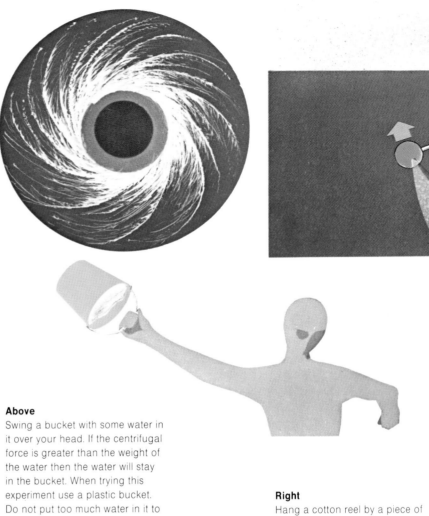

Above
Swing a bucket with some water in it over your head. If the centrifugal force is greater than the weight of the water then the water will stay in the bucket. When trying this experiment use a plastic bucket. Do not put too much water in it to begin with, otherwise you may get very wet.

Right
Hang a cotton reel by a piece of string. Tie it on firmly. As you spin the cotton reel faster and faster it will rise higher and higher until it flies round in a horizontal circle. This is because the centripetal force is gradually overcoming the weight of the cotton reel.

and the sun are both very large masses. So there is a large force of gravity between them (see page 40). Since they do not crash into each other there must be another force pulling them apart. This is the centrifugal force caused by the earth travelling in its orbit round the sun.

These two forces oppose each other in the solar system. The force of gravity acts as the centripetal force. Opposing this is the centrifugal force caused by the motion of the planets round the sun. The planets do not have air resistance to slow them down, so they keep moving round.

In the same way the moon and the artificial satellites orbit the earth. The gravitational attraction between the earth and the moon or the satellites is balanced by their centrifugal forces.

Right
The spin drier depends on centrifugal force. As the clothes are rotated the clothes themselves and all the moisture they contain are thrown outwards by the centrifugal forces. The clothes cannot move outwards beyond the wire cage. The water flies out through the holes, leaving the clothes drier.

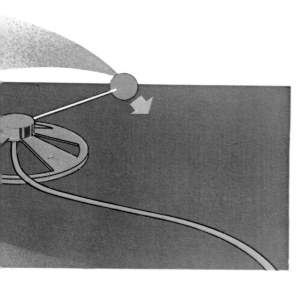

Left and far left
A rotary garden spray and a catherine wheel are examples of centrifugal force causing a fine spray of matter to fly outwards, forming a disc.

Right
An orbiting body must travel just fast enough for the centrifugal force (tending to shoot it off into space) to balance the gravitational force (tending to draw it back to earth).

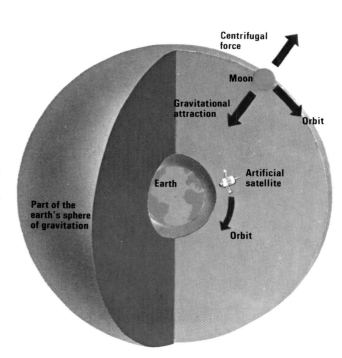

Centrifugal force

Moon

Gravitational attraction

Orbit

Earth

Artificial satellite

Orbit

Part of the earth's sphere of gravitation

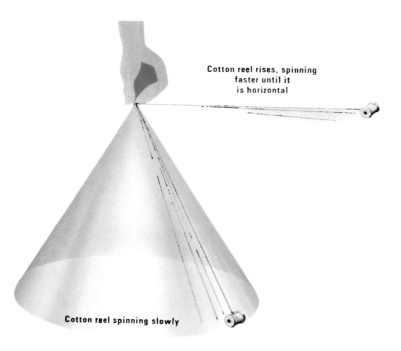

Cotton reel rises, spinning faster until it is horizontal

Cotton reel spinning slowly

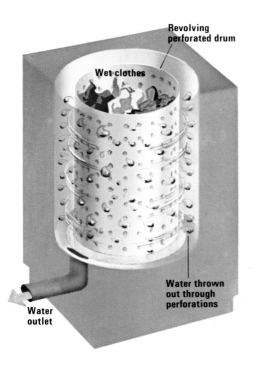

Revolving perforated drum

Wet clothes

Water thrown out through perforations

Water outlet

Right
To escape from the earth's gravity, a space ship has to go into orbit round the earth. It must accelerate until the centrifugal force due to its circular motion is greater than the force of gravity pulling it towards the earth. The speed which has to be reached is called the escape velocity. The force of gravity on the moon is much lower, so the escape velocity from the moon is also lower.

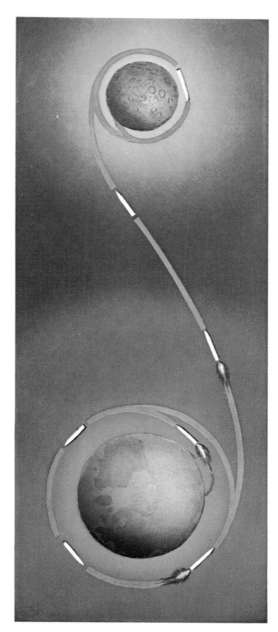

Axis of spin

ROTATION

If you spin a coin on a table it will have two kinds of motion. Firstly it will move across the table, and secondly it will spin round and round on its own axis. These two motions are quite separate. In the same way, when a golf ball is flying through the air it is both spinning and changing its position.

Spinning objects have special properties. The most important of these is that they tend to resist any change in the direction of the spin. You can feel this by doing a simple experiment with the front wheel of a bicycle. Lift the wheel off the ground and spin it round. Now move the handlebars from side to side. You can feel a force that tries to stop you. This is the inertia of the wheel resisting a change in the direction of the axis of the spin. In the case of the bicycle wheel the axis is the wheel axle. This inertia of spinning objects is called gyroscopic inertia.

Gyroscopes

A gyroscope is a small heavy wheel mounted so that it can move about any axis. This is called a universal mounting. The wheel will always tend to keep spinning in the direction in space in which it started spinning.

The principle of the gyroscope is used in the gyro-compass. This device is used in ships and aircraft. A wheel is kept spin-

Above
Prop a bicycle up so that it will not fall over sideways. Spin the wheel and try to change the direction of the axis of spin. You will feel the inertia of the wheel trying to stop you.

Above right
You can make a small top by tracing a round coin on a piece of thick paper. Cut out the circular shape. Make a small hole in the centre and push through it a used match sharpened at one end. By giving the top a quick flick it should spin quite easily on a table or smooth floor.

Right
When a top is spinning fast, the stick rotates vertically (1). As it slows down it tips over and the stick moves in the shape of a cone (2). As it comes to a stop and the edge touches the ground, it will roll around in the opposite direction (3).

Below
Some ships use gyro-stabilizers. The heavy gyroscope mounted in the hull helps to cut down the rolling motion of the ship.

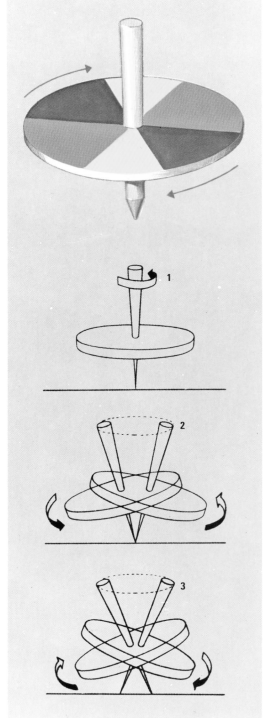

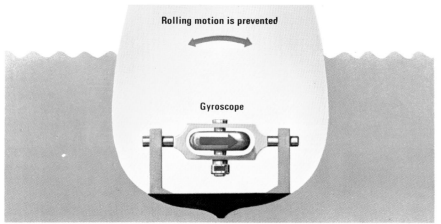

Rolling motion is prevented

Gyroscope

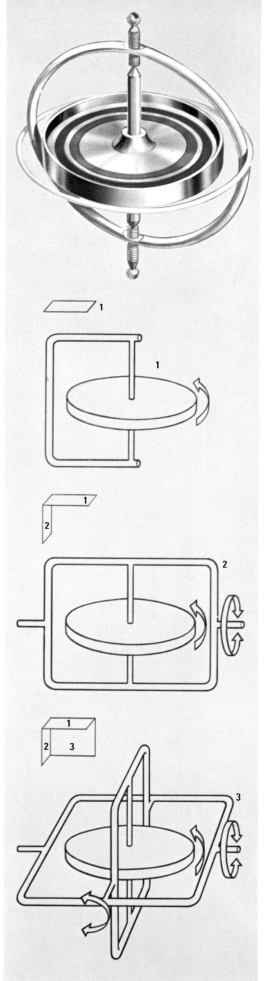

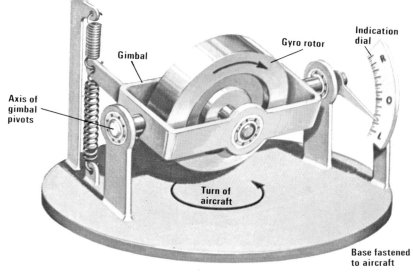

Gimbal

Gyro rotor

Indication dial

Axis of gimbal pivots

Turn of aircraft

Base fastened to aircraft

Above

The rate-of-turn indicator in an aircraft. A spinning wheel called a gyro-rotor is in a mount held by fixed springs. When the aircraft turns, the gyroscope turns with it and experiences a force which is greater when the rate of turn is greater. This force is indicated on a scale which shows the rate of turn.

Above left

You can start a toy gyroscope spinning using a piece of string. It has exactly the same properties as the gyroscopes on large ships.

Left

This gyroscope's mounting gives it three degrees of freedom. The disc rotates about a vertical axis (1). This is suspended to rotate about a horizontal axis (2). The outer frame rotates about a horizontal axis at right angles to both the other axes (3). Gyroscopes have many uses in moving vehicles, from sailing ships to rocket ships.

ning electrically with a compass mounted over it. The spinning wheel of the gyroscope, because of its inertia, is unaffected by the motion of the ship. It will therefore always point to true north.

A similar device is the gyro-pilot. This is an instrument for steering a ship automatically. It is set to the course of the ship. Any change of course is detected by the gyro-pilot because it stays pointing in its original direction. The gyro-pilot sends a message to the motor controlling the rudder. The rudder then brings the ship back on course again.

This property of spinning objects is called spin stabilization. A frisbee spins rapidly while it is moving through the air. It is the spin that keeps it in the air. If it did not spin, it would not stay horizontal and so would not travel far.

You may have seen circus performers spinning plates on the tips of long sticks. The plates remain horizontal because they are stabilized by their spin. The plates do not want to change the direction of the axis of their spin. Once they start slowing down, the spin stabilization gets much less and they soon fall off the stick. The skill of the juggler is to keep each stick moving so that it keeps the plate spinning. A spinning top stays balanced for the same reason. It is stabilized by its spin.

The earth is also spinning round on its axis. This keeps the axis pointing in one direction in space, just as the spinning of a gyroscope keeps it pointing in its original direction.

Below
Pushing on the end of a spanner,
which acts as a lever, increases
the force that pushes on the nut at
the other end. This tightens the
nut.

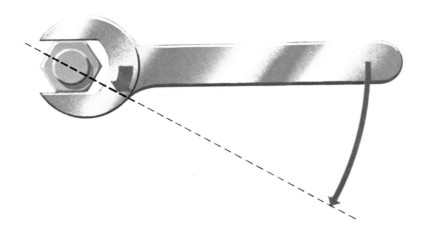

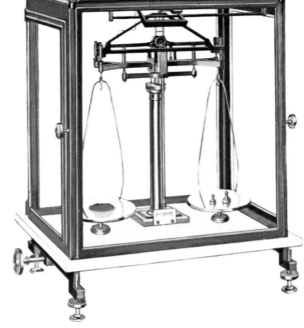

LEVERS

Place a 30 cm ruler on a table with a pencil under it. You will find that the ruler only balances when the pencil is underneath the 15 cm mark. Now place one coin on the 0 mark and another on the 30 cm mark. The ruler will still balance. You will also find that one coin on the 7.5 cm mark is balanced by one on the 22.5 cm mark. The ruler is balanced by equal weights or forces at equal distances from the centre.

What happens if you try to balance one coin at the 0 mark with coins at the 22.5 cm mark? You will find that for it to balance you will need two coins at this 22.5 cm point. If the distance from the centre is halved, the weight or force must be doubled.

Moments

These coins are trying to turn or rotate the ruler. This tendency of a weight or force to rotate an object is called a moment. From the ruler experiment you can see that the moment does not only depend on the size of the force. It also depends on the distance that the force is from the point of balance (the 15 cm mark). The point of balance is called the fulcrum.

The moment of a force is equal to the force multiplied by its distance from the fulcrum. When the ruler is balanced, the

moments of the two forces must be equal in order to cancel each other out. In the last case we had one coin 15 cm from the centre. This gives a moment of $1 \times 15 = 15$ units. The other side had two coins 7.5 cm from the centre, giving a moment of 2×7.5 which also equals 15 units. That is why the ruler balanced. Try different weights and distances to see what happens.

Moments are used in a simple balance, like an old pair of kitchen scales. Weights are put on a pan on one side to balance the food to be weighed on the other side. The distances from the centre, or fulcrum, are the same. So when the correct weight is

Above
Jewellers use balances such as these to measure weights of substances very accurately. They place weights to the value that they want on one side, and measure out the gold on the other side until the scales are balanced.

Left
Ask an adult's permission before doing this experiment. Push a hot nail through the middle of a slow-burning candle. Balance it between two glasses. Light both ends and watch it see-saw up and down. As one end of the candle drips it becomes lighter and moves up. At the next drip from the other end, that moves up, and so on. If you make riders for your see-saw, use tinfoil, not paper, as this could catch fire. Place the see-saw on a metal tray to prevent the dripping candle from doing any damage.

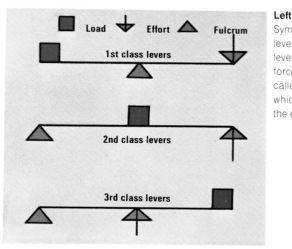

Left
Symbols for the three classes of levers. The point of a balance of a lever is called the fulcrum. The force which is to be moved is called the load and the force which is trying to move it is called the effort.

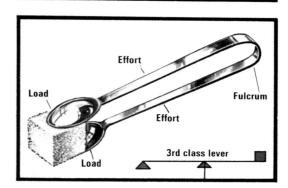

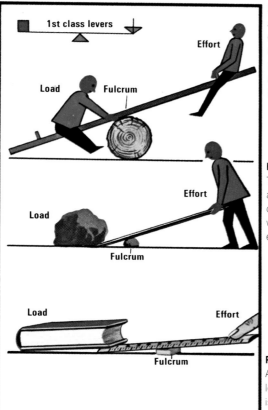

Left
All of these, the seesaw, the crowbar, and the ruler, are acting as levers. A large load is being moved by a smaller effort. These are examples of the first class of levers.

Right
The wheelbarrow, nutcrackers, and bottle opener are all examples of the second class of levers in which the load is between the effort and the fulcrum.

Right
An example of the third class of levers is the sugar tong. The effort is between the fulcrum and the load.

put in the pan, the moments on both sides of the balance are equal. The system is said to be in equilibrium.

A lever also uses moments. You can often prise a rock out of the ground by using a crowbar. You put a stone under the crowbar near the rock. The stone acts as a fulcrum. Then you push down at the other end of the crowbar, which is a greater distance from the fulcrum than the rock. In this way, you produce a greater moment than you could by trying to roll the rock out of the ground.

The weight of the rock is called the load.

The force with which you push down is called the effort. When the moment of your effort is greater than the moment of the load, the rock moves.

There are three classes of levers. One is like the crowbar, in which the fulcrum is between the load and the effort. In the second class, the fulcrum is at one end, the effort at the other, and the load is in between the two. An example of this is a wheelbarrow. In the third class, the fulcrum is at one end, the load at the other, and the effort in between. Sugar tongs are an example of this class.

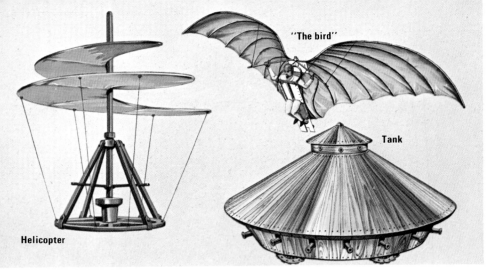

"The bird"

Tank

Helicopter

Leonardo da Vinci

Above
Leonardo da Vinci, who lived in Italy from 1452 to 1519, was a musician, painter, and sculptor as well as being an engineer. He attempted to design several complicated machines including an aeroplane.

Below
The knife and the claw hammer both show how loads are overcome by using levers. They are simple machines.

MACHINES

Levers and pulleys

A machine is any device that overcomes a force at one place by enabling a force to be applied somewhere else. A knife is a very simple example of a machine. When you push on the knife, you produce a cutting force in the blade. Another example is a claw hammer, which is used to pull out nails. Both of these machines are levers.

Another type of machine is a pulley. A simple pulley enables a heavy load to be lifted up by pulling downwards. It is much easier to lift something heavy, such as the engine from a car, by pulling downwards. We can use the natural downward pull of gravity on the weight of our bodies.

If a large load can be raised using a small effort, this is an advantage. The mechanical advantage, as it is called, is equal to the load divided by the effort. The greater the load that can be raised for a given effort, the greater is the mechanical advantage.

However we cannot get something for nothing. Pulleys allow us to lift a large weight by using a small force. But we have to move the rope much further down-

wards than the weight moves upwards. So the effort we apply moves much further than the load. In fact the work we do raising a weight with a pulley is not less than the work we would do lifting the weight directly. Work, in physics, is defined as the force applied to anything, multiplied by the distance through which the thing moves. To raise a car engine weighing 100 kilograms a distance of 2 metres might require an effort of 50 kilograms applied to a pulley rope. This effort would have to move 4 metres. We say that the work done by the effort is the same as the work done on the load.

In practice the figures would not work out quite like this because no machine is 100 per cent efficient. That is, not all the work put in as effort can be used to raise the load. Some work is lost in friction (see page 52). The efficiency of a machine is the work actually applied to the load divided by the work put in as effort. It is usually multiplied by 100 so that it can be expressed as a percentage. The efficiency is never greater than 100 per cent and in practice is always much less.

Screws and gears

Another machine in which the effort moves a larger distance than the load is the screw. Again, large forces are produced by smaller ones. For every turn of the screwdriver the screw moves only a small distance into the wood, overcoming very large friction forces as it does so. Imagine how difficult it would be to insert a screw into wood without a screwdriver.

The same principle is used in the car jack. In this device a large turn on the handle lifts the car a very small distance.

Gears are also machines and they can operate in two ways. They can make large forces from small ones and they can make small forces from large ones.

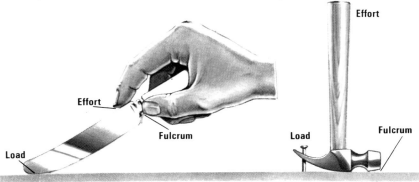

Effort

Effort

Fulcrum

Load

Load

Fulcrum

HEAVE TWO

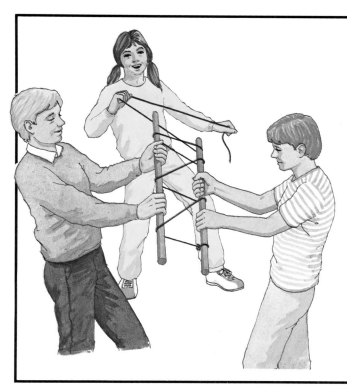

You will need: clothes line ● 2 broom handles ● 2 friends
Find out how strong you are. Give each of your friends a broom handle to hold. Tie a clothes line (or a piece of rope) to one of the handles, and wrap the rope around both the handles several times, as shown. Ask your friends to pull on the handles, while you pull on the end of the rope. Your friends will not be able to pull the handles apart. Indeed, you will be able to pull them together, no matter how hard your friends try to stop you.

This trick does not work because of your strength. It works because you have made the broom handles and rope into a pulley system – a simple device that magnifies effort, or pull. A pulley will help you to lift a heavy load with a little effort. In this case, you overcome the big pull of your two friends (the heavy load) with a little pull (the effort).

In the construction industry people use a pulley system to lift enormous objects with little effort. This system is called a block and tackle, and forms the major part of a crane.

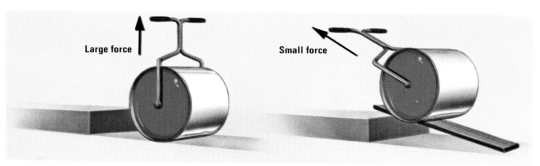

Large force

Small force

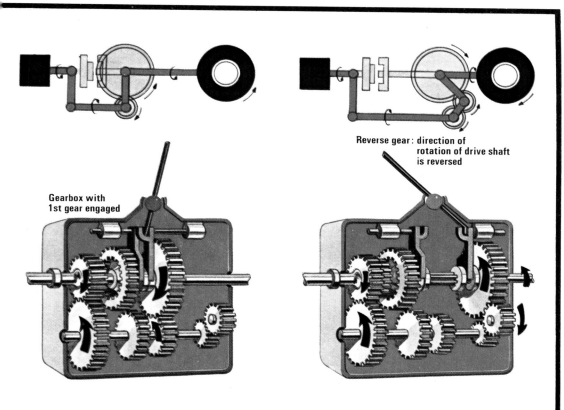

Reverse gear: direction of rotation of drive shaft is reversed

Gearbox with 1st gear engaged

Above

There are two simple ways of lifting a garden roller up a step. One way is simply to pick it up. This would certainly be difficult and might be dangerous. A better way would be to roll it up a strong plank. The inclined plane of the plank is a machine. It enables a force (the weight of the roller) to be overcome by a smaller force (the force needed to pull it up a plank). The work is not less, because the roller has to travel a greater distance.

Left

Gears in a car carry forces from the engine to the wheels. They also change the size of the forces depending on the load. When the car is starting or climbing a hill the engine has to turn quickly although the wheels are only turning slowly.

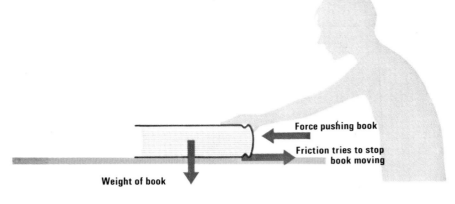

Force pushing book

Friction tries to stop book moving

Weight of book

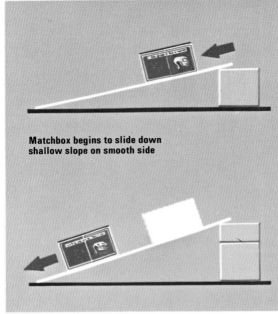

Matchbox begins to slide down shallow slope on smooth side

Above right
You can do experiments on friction by using a piece of wood or stiff cardboard to make a slope. Put a matchbox on the wood and tilt it slowly until the box begins to slide. Does it make any difference if the matchbox is put on its edge? If the edge is rough you will find that you have to tilt the slope further.

Above
Put a book on the table and try pushing it along. Friction tries to stop it moving. Now pile some more books on top of the first one and try again. It is more difficult to push the pile of books because they are heavier. There is more force pushing the book against the table. This makes the friction greater.

FRICTION

Rub your finger on a smooth polished surface. Now do the same on a piece of stone or brick. Do you feel any difference? You will notice that in the second case there appears to be some force trying to stop your finger moving. This force is called friction. Friction tends to stop two surfaces moving over each other.

The friction is greater for some surfaces than for others. It is easy to slide on a highly polished floor or on ice but it is difficult to slide on a rough surface. Friction is usually greater between two rough surfaces than between two smooth ones.

There are some ways in which friction is very useful. For example the brakes on a bicycle work by friction. Rubber blocks rub against the rim of the wheel and stop it moving. Another use is in walking. If there were no friction between the soles of our shoes and the ground we would slip as soon as we tried to walk.

Heat caused by friction

If you rub you hands together for a few seconds you will notice that they begin to get warm. Friction causes heat. Some-

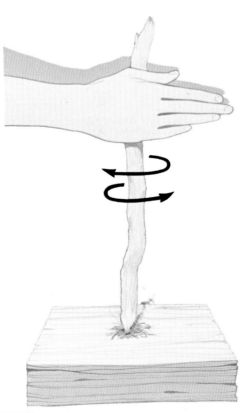

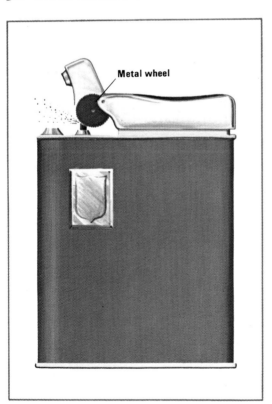

Metal wheel

Left
Friction always causes heat. This is an old method of making fire. The pointed stick is twisted very quickly in a piece of wood and becomes hot. This sets the dry grass alight.

Right
This is a more modern method of making fire, but it still uses friction. When the lighter is pressed the metal wheel turns and rubs against the flint. The flint is a small piece of a special metal called cerium. Very small pieces of flint are thrown off. The friction caues so much heat that these pieces are white hot. These are the sparks which set the gas alight.

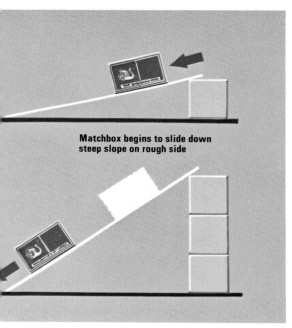

Matchbox begins to slide down steep slope on rough side

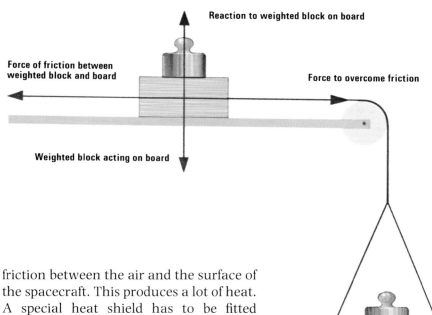

Reaction to weighted block on board

Force of friction between weighted block and board

Force to overcome friction

Weighted block acting on board

times this is useful. If you are cold you rub your hands together to make them warm. People used to start fires by rubbing dry sticks of wood together until the friction gave enough heat to produce a flame. Nowadays we often make a flame by striking a match. Rubbing the match on a rough surface gives enough heat to set fire to the chemicals on the end of the match.

Sometimes the heat made by friction can be harmful. When a spacecraft re-enters the earth's atmosphere there is friction between the air and the surface of the spacecraft. This produces a lot of heat. A special heat shield has to be fitted around the craft to protect the astronauts.

When a motor car engine is running there are many moving metal surfaces. These would cause a lot of friction if they rubbed together. So oil is used in the engine. The oil forms a film between the metal surfaces so that they do not rub together. This stops the engine getting too hot.

Another way of lessening friction is to use rollers. There is much less friction when you roll something along than when you slide it. Large objects can be moved along by pushing them along on rollers.

Above
This is a laboratory experiment to measure the force of friction between two surfaces; in this case between the board and the block. The friction equals the total weight of the pan and its load, divided by the total weight of the block and its load. You can study how this varies: a) for different weights on the block; b) for different surfaces, by using a variety of blocks.

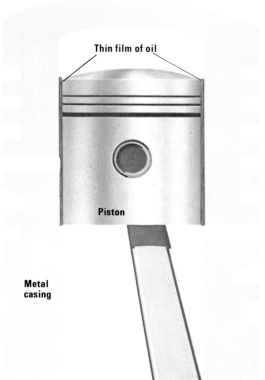

Thin film of oil

Piston

Metal casing

Left
Oil reduces friction because it forms a very thin film which keeps the surfaces in a motor car engine apart.

Right
Ball-bearings reduce friction. To test this, take two cans with lip edges and try rotating one on top of the other. Take some small marbles or ball-bearings. Place them round inside the edge between the two cans. Now try rotating the cans again and feel how much easier it is.

SPRINGS AND ELASTICITY

If you were asked to name an elastic material you would probably say rubber. A rubber band can easily be stretched and snaps back into shape again. If you squeeze a piece of rubber to make it smaller, it goes back to its original size when you let go.

Inelasticity

Scientists think of a substance as being elastic if it easily recovers its shape and size after these are changed. Rubber is elastic but so also are steel and glass. Putty and plasticine are not elastic because they do not go back to their original shape. They are said to be inelastic. Copper and aluminium are less elastic than steel and glass but more elastic than putty and plasticine.

Compression

To change the size of anything a force has to be applied to it. The more force is applied the more the thing changes its size or shape. When you pull an elastic band, you stretch the band and make it longer. Squeezing a piece of rubber makes it smaller. This is called compression. You can bend a wooden ruler by a small amount. Bending is a mixture of stretching and compressing. If you bend the ruler downwards, the top face is stretched and the bottom face is compressed.

The elastic properties of materials were investigated by an English scientist, Robert Hooke (1635–1703). He was one of the greatest scientists of the seventeenth century. He invented the balance spring for regulating the workings of watches.

One way of finding out how elastic things are is by bouncing them. If you drop a marble on to a hard floor it bounces quite high. The faster it hits the floor, the higher it will bounce. If you make a ball of plasticine of the same size as the marble you will find that it does not bounce at all. It is simply flattened. This is because plasticine is inelastic. As the marble hits the floor it is squashed slightly out of shape. Because it is elastic it regains its original shape and bounces. However it does not bounce to the same height as it

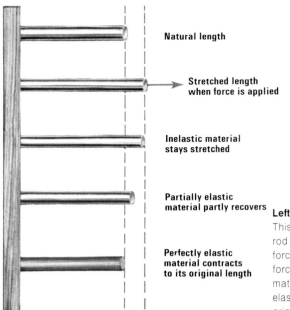

Natural length

Stretched length when force is applied

Inelastic material stays stretched

Partially elastic material partly recovers

Perfectly elastic material contracts to its original length

Left
This shows what happens when a rod is stretched by a force. This force is called the load. When the force is taken away, inelastic materials stay stretched. Perfectly elastic ones go back to their original length. Partly elastic things have a small permanent change in their size.

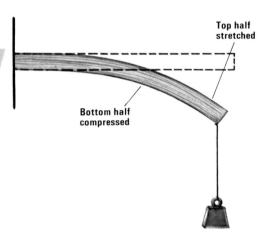

Top half stretched

Bottom half compressed

Left
When a weight is hung on a beam it bends. The top half of the beam is being stretched. The bottom half is being compressed.

Below
Coil springs are used in the spring balance for measuring weight. The spring stretches by an amount that depends on the weight. For example a weight of 10 grams stretches the spring twice as a weight of 5 grams. The weight is shown by a pointer moving over a scale.

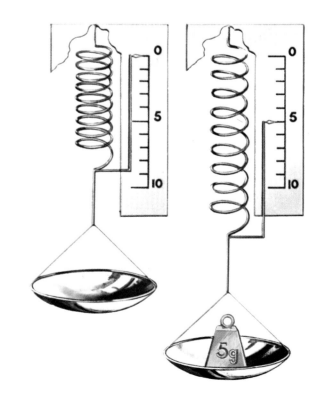

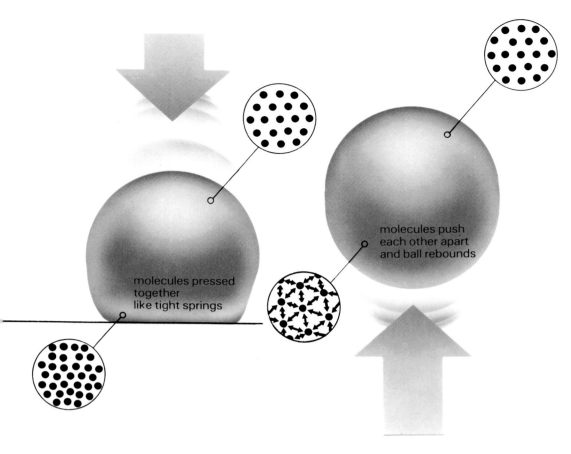

molecules pressed
together
like tight springs

molecules push
each other apart
and ball rebounds

Left

Inside a rubber ball, millions of
rubber molecules are packed
together. Between the molecules is
a force that acts like a spring.
When the ball hits the ground, the
lowest part is compressed and the
molecules are pressed towards
each other. The forces between
them push the molecules apart
again. The molecules at the
surface of the ball push on the
ground, sending the ball back up
into the air – that is, it bounces.

was dropped from. Some of its energy has been lost in the bounce.

Elastic materials are used in many ways. When a piece of wood is bent it easily springs back to its original shape. This elasticity is used in the bow and arrow. It is also used in springboards in swimming pools. Steel springs have many uses. They are found in mattresses, chairs, clocks, watches, and the suspension of railways engines and some cars. The suspension of a car improves the journey by absorbing shocks and bumps. This is helped by air-filled tyres. If air is compressed into a small space it is very springy. When a car goes over a bump the tyres are distorted but they quickly go back to their original shape.

Left and below

Here are just three of the many
ways that springs are used.
Mattresses use coil springs which
are compressed when someone
lies on the bed. Leaf springs are
used in the suspension system of
some cars. They are made of
several strips of steel joined
together, and work by bending.
The spring in a clock is a flat coil
which is wound tightly. It then
unwinds to drive the mechanism.

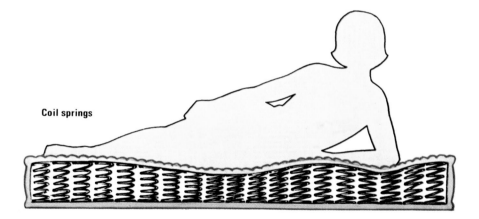

Coil springs

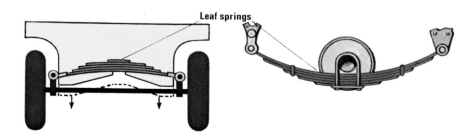

Leaf springs

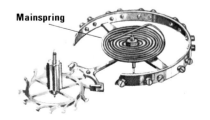

Mainspring

SURFACE TENSION

SIMPLE EXPERIMENTS

Put a clean dry needle on a piece of blotting paper which is floating on a glass of water. The paper eventually sinks to the bottom but the needle stays on the surface of the water. Fill a glass as full as you can with water. You will see that the surface of the water bulges over the glass at the top.

These experiments show that the surface of the water seems to have a skin, rather like that of a blown-up balloon. The skin is made up of the layer of molecules on top of the water. They are being pulled into the centre of the liquid by the other molecules. The surface therefore shrinks and this makes it strained. The strain is known as surface tension.(It is important to understand that the water does not really have a skin like hot milk. It is only the top layer of molecules behaving like one.)

Here are four more experiments to try.

SOAP RINGS

You will need: wire ● red thread ● soap solution

Bend the end of the wire into a ring. Tie red thread loosely across the ring. Dip the ring into soapy water. If you break the soap film on one side of the thread, the thread is pulled by the film. This is because the remaining soap film is under strain and is trying to make itself as small as possible. Now tie a loop in the thread and break the film inside the loop. You will find that it is pulled into a circle by the strain in the surface. The soap film that is left is again trying to shrink.

MOVING MATCHES

You will need: a bowl of water ● dead matches ● soap ● blotting paper

Arrange some matches like spokes, on a bowl of water. Dip a piece of soap in the centre. The matches will move outwards. Dip a piece of blotting paper in the centre and they will be drawn inwards again.

The soap causes a thin soap film to spread across the surface. This reduces the surface tension. The surface tension is greater round the edges of the soap film, so the matches are pulled outwards. Blotting paper is not solid, but is filled with tiny cracks. Water rises up the cracks, pulled by surface tension. This is known as capillarity. The blotting paper draws water up into it by capillarity. The pull on the water increases the surface tension at the centre and pulls the matches inwards.

Trees and plants have fine tubes running through them. They pull water up by capillarity.

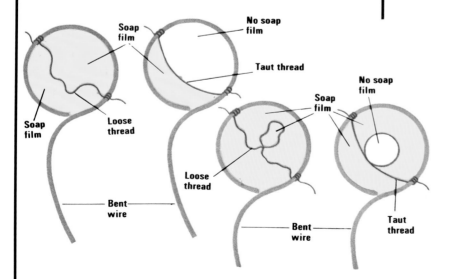

Soap film

No soap film

Taut thread

Loose thread

Soap film

No soap film

Soap film

No soap film

Loose thread

Taut thread

Bent wire

Bent wire

MAGIC BOATS

You will need: a plastic tray ● cardboard or plastic foam ● soap

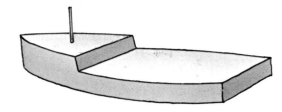

Make your launch from thick cardboard or plastic foam packing. Wood is too heavy. Cut a notch in the stern (rear) of the launch, and wedge into it a small piece of soap. Fill a plastic tray with water. Place your launch in the water, and it will speed away.

The boat is not really propelled by the soap. The surface tension of the water does the work. It pulls around anything floating on water. The soap reduces the surface tension at the rear of the boat, which stops the surface forces pulling there. So the forces working at the front win, dragging the boat along.

Soap and detergents lower the surface tension of water. In this way they increase the cleaning power of water by allowing it to come into greater contact with dirt and grease on the surfaces to be washed.

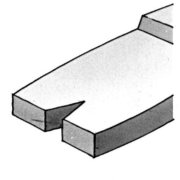

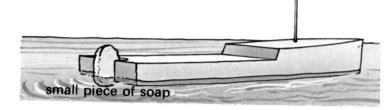

small piece of soap

WATER RISES

Take a glass and fill it with a coloured liquid, like blackcurrant or orange juice. Put two plastic straws into the glass. One of the straws should be fat and the other thin. You will see that the liquid rises further up the thin straw than the thick straw.

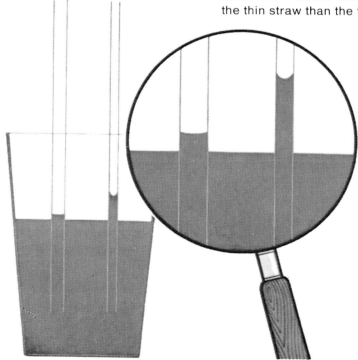

PRESSURE

Pressure is the force acting on a certain area. Your feet sink into loose sand when you stand on it. If you lie on sand you do not go down very far. In each case the force acting on the sand is the same weight, the weight of your body. When the force acts on an area the size of your feet, the pressure is high. When the force acts on an area the size of your whole body, the pressure is lower.

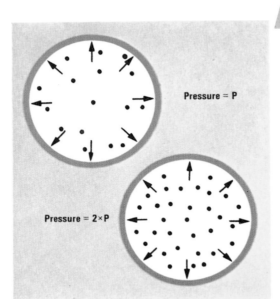

Below right
Gases exert a pressure. A gas has many millions of small molecules all moving about. The pressure of the gas is caused by molecules bouncing off the walls of the container. There are so many molecules that they exert a steady pressure. If twice as much gas were put into the container there would be twice as many molecules. So the pressure would double.

Below
Hang two objects close together on long threads and blow between them. You might expect them to blow apart. In fact they swing closer together because, by blowing between them, you reduce the air pressure on the insides. The higher, normal air pressure on the outsides pushes them towards each other.

High and low pressure

A sharp knife cuts better than a blunt one. This is because there is much less area on the cutting edge if the blade is sharp. So the pressure is higher.

A liquid presses on every side of anything that is put in it. The pressure is caused by the weight of liquid. Pressure increases with depth. So the pressure at the bottom of the ocean is much greater than near the surface. Deep-sea divers have to wear special suits to prevent their bodies being crushed.

The earth is surrounded by a layer of air, called the atmosphere. We live at the bottom of this layer. The air above presses down on us with a force of 1 kg on every sq cm (14.7 lb on every sq in). This is called the atmospheric pressure. If you hold out your hand, there is a force of nearly 10 kg (22 lb) pressing down on it. You can't feel it, because an equal force is pressing up on the other side of your hand, and the two balance out.

Nature tries to make pressures equal everywhere. A bicycle pump compresses the air inside it. This makes the pressure of the air inside the pump greater than the

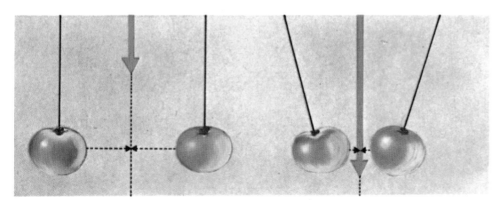

Right
Barometers measure atmospheric pressure and are used for weather forecasts. A mercury barometer is very simple. It measures how much mercury the atmosphere can hold up. As the pressure changes the height of the mercury changes. An aneroid barometer is more complicated. It is a sealed metal box with thin walls. There is no air inside it and the sides are held apart by a spring. As the pressure outside increases or decreases, the sides of the box go closer together or further apart. The movement of the top of the box moves levers which move a pointer over a scale.

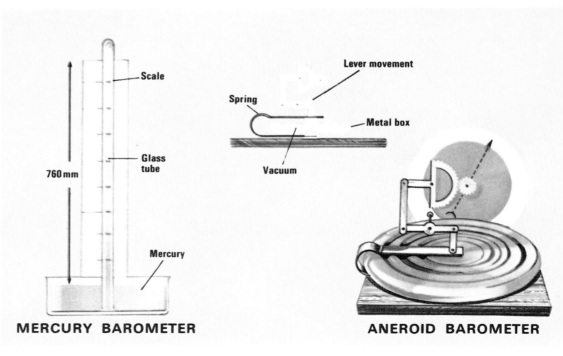

MERCURY BAROMETER

ANEROID BAROMETER

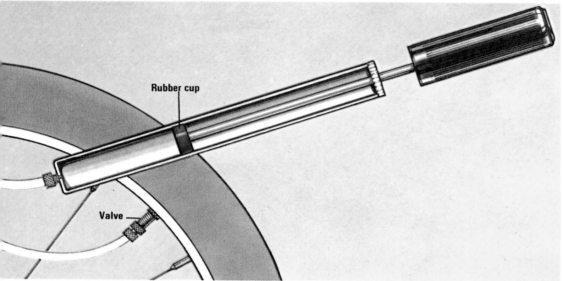

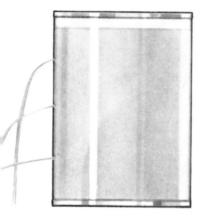

pressure of the air in the tyre. So air moves into the tyre.

A bicycle pump works by increasing the pressure. You suck up liquids through a drinking straw by reducing the pressure. When you suck a straw you take air out of the straw. To make the pressure the same as it was before, the atmosphere pushes liquid from the glass up the straw into your mouth. You can keep drinking by continuing to suck. This keeps the pressure in your mouth lower than atmospheric pressure. A vacuum cleaner works on the same principle. A fan makes the pressure in the cleaner lower than the

pressure outside. So air rushes in, taking with it the dirt on the floor.

As you climb above sea level the pressure of the atmosphere decreases. This is because at great heights there are fewer air molecules around. People who climb very high mountains such as Everest have to take their own oxygen with them. There is not enough air for them, and so they breathe from oxygen cylinders. The cabins of aircraft which fly very high also have to take their air supply with them. If they did not, then the cabin would not stay at atmospheric pressure. The cabin is said to be pressurized.

AIR PRESSURE TRICK

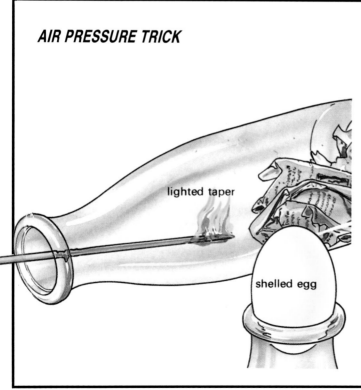

lighted taper

shelled egg

Ask an adult to help you do this.
You will need: shelled boiled egg ● clean milk bottle ● newspaper ● lighted taper

Clean out and dry a milk bottle, which has a neck slightly smaller than an egg. Drop some pieces of crumpled-up newspaper into the bottle and set them alight with a taper. Stand the bottle upright and push the egg into the neck.

The bottle greedily starts to swallow the egg whole! After a while you will notice that the burning paper goes out. Soon the egg stops moving.

The trick works because of air pressure. Before the paper in the bottle starts to burn, the pressure of the air trapped inside by the egg is the same as the air pressure outside. When the paper starts burning, it begins to use up the oxygen in the air inside the bottle. So the pressure in the bottle starts to fall. The air outside is now at a higher pressure, and starts to push the egg into the bottle. This continues until the paper stops burning, showing that all the oxygen inside the bottle has been used up. Then the pressure inside won't fall any lower and the egg stops moving.

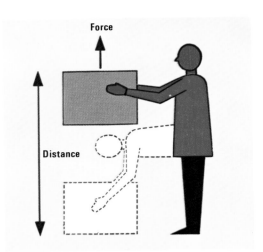

Force

Distance

Below and right
If you lift a box you exert a force on it to overcome the force of gravity. You also move this force through a certain distance. In other words you do work on the box. If you push the box along the ground you also exert a force on it to overcome the friction between the ground and the box.

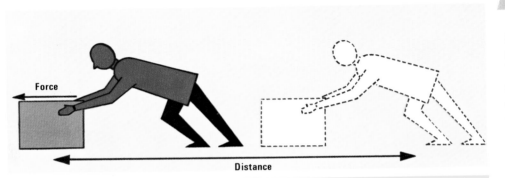

Force

Distance

Below right
If you take a weight on one end of a piece of string and tie the other end to a fixed point you have a pendulum. If you pull the weight to one side you are doing work because you are lifting it against the force of gravity. You have increased the potential energy of the weight. Now let it go. As it moves it first increases its speed until it reaches the bottom of the swing. It is then moving fastest and all its potential energy has changed to kinetic energy. As it goes up the other side it slows down again and its kinetic energy turns back to potential energy. This picture shows a number of photographs taken of a pendulum so that you can see how it moves during one swing.

Far right
Two toys that use the energy stored in a twisted elastic band. Wind the cotton reel tractor up by turning the match "key". It will drive itself along the floor gripping with the toothed tread. Make up a "magic rolling tin" as in the picture. When you roll it along the floor the heavy nut will cause the elastic to twist up. When you let go it will roll backwards, apparently of its own accord, but it is really the hidden elastic unwinding.

Energy

WORK AND ENERGY

A man carrying sacks of potatoes up some stairs is doing work. The amount of work that he does depends not only on the weight of the sacks but also on the height to which they are carried. One man carrying a sack to a height of 12 metres is doing twice as much work as a man who carries a similar sack up 6 metres. Also a man who carries a 20 kilogram sack up 6 metres has done twice as much work as a man who only carries a 10 kilogram sack up to the same height. So work involves both force and distance. The work done equals the force used multiplied by the distance for which the force is used. According to this idea work is only done when a force moves.

Potential and kinetic energy

Strictly speaking if you hold a heavy book above your head no work is done on the book because it has not moved. However some work is done by the contraction and expansion of your muscles. If you lift a weight on to a shelf you have to do work to put it there. This work is not wasted. The weight has more energy than it had when it was on the floor. This stored energy is called potential energy. If the weight falls from the shelf it loses this potential energy. It falls faster and faster and gains a new kind of energy called kinetic energy. Kinetic energy is the energy due to the motion of a body.

If the weight drops on to some sand or soft soil it makes a hollow where it falls. The kinetic energy has been used up in doing work to move the soil. The energy of a body is its ability to do work. Energy is never lost but it can be changed or converted from one form to another.

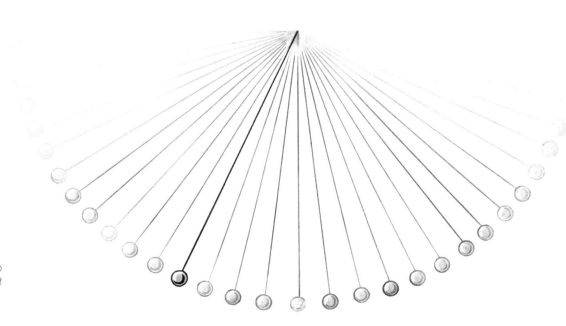

Other forms of energy

What happens if a falling weight hits a hard floor? Where does its energy go? Some of the kinetic energy is used in making a noise. Some of it may be used to knock the weight out of shape. The remainder is turned into another form of energy, which we call heat. The weight gets slightly hotter. You can show how kinetic energy is turned into heat by hitting a small piece of metal with a hammer a number of times. The metal quickly becomes quite hot.

Of course hitting things is not the best way to make them hot. Burning things is a much better way of producing heat. When coal burns, heat is given out. We say that the coal is a source of energy. The energy is stored in the coal and when the coal burns it forms new chemicals. These have less energy than the coal. The rest of the energy has been converted into heat. The heat from coal can be used to make steam which drives a steam engine. In turn the steam engine can be used to do work.

You also use up a fuel when you do work such as lifting a weight or pushing something. The fuel is the food you eat. Chemical changes in the food provide the energy. The energy stored in things like food, coal, petrol, and gas is called chemical energy.

There are other forms of energy. For example when things burn they give out light as well as heat. Part of the energy is converted into light energy. In an electric fire heat and some light are produced from electrical energy.

Left
When the arrow is released the potential energy of the bent bow is changed to kinetic energy of the moving arrow.

Watt

Top
James Watt (1736–1819) was a Scottish engineer and inventor. He designed an efficient steam engine with many improvements shortly after such machines had been invented.

Above
A steam engine made in 1788 by James Watt.

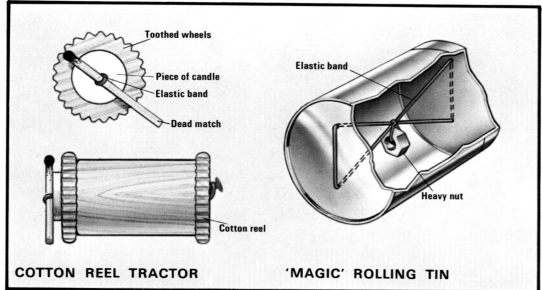

Toothed wheels
Piece of candle
Elastic band
Dead match
Cotton reel

Elastic band
Heavy nut

COTTON REEL TRACTOR   **'MAGIC' ROLLING TIN**

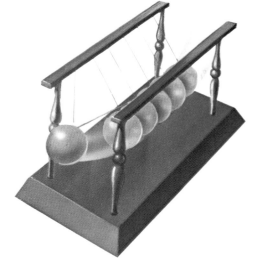

Above

One of the ways in which we get energy from the sun. Sunlight is necessary for plants to grow. The plants are eaten by animals which are used for human food. This gives us energy to do work.

Far right

Newton's cradle. When the ball at one end strikes the line of stationary balls, its energy is transmitted along the line and the ball at the other end flies up. With highly polished steel balls on fine supporting threads, very little energy is lost and the movement continues for a long time without anyone touching the cradle.

Below right

The energy in this powerful laser beam is sufficient to bore a hole through a thick aluminium plate. LASER stands for Light Amplification by Stimulated Emission for Radiation (see page 108).

Below

In an electric toaster the electric current passes through special wires. These get hot just like the element in an electric fire. Electrical energy is converted into heat energy.

CONSERVATION OF ENERGY

Imagine a car is moving along the road and the driver has to stop quickly. She applies the brakes – that is, she applies a force to the wheels to stop them going round. If the car is moving at 70 mph it takes more force to stop it than if it moves at only 30 mph. Now think of a lorry moving at 70 mph. It takes more force to stop a lorry than to stop a car moving at the same speed. This is because the lorry is heavier than the car. We say that the car and the lorry have momentum.

Momentum depends not only on the speed of a thing but also on its mass. A lorry travelling at 70 mph has more momentum than a car travelling at 70 mph. A car travelling at 70 mph has more momentum than if it travels at 30 mph. The momentum of anything is its mass multiplied by its velocity.

Law of conservation of momentum

Scientists have found out that when things collide their total momentum is unchanged. This is called the law of conservation of momentum. Suppose you are sliding on ice and you catch hold of someone as you are going past them. You will both move together but your combined speed will be less than your original speed. This is because your original momentum is being shared between two people.

The law of conservation of momentum is one of the important principles in physics. There is a similar law concerning energy. It says that energy is neither created nor destroyed but is simply changed from one form to another. It is called the law of conservation of energy.

Coal is burned in a power station and gives heat. This is used to produce steam for driving a turbine. The turbine turns a generator and gives electricity. In an electric fire the electrical energy is converted into heat. In this way the chemical energy in the coal has been used to provide heat energy in the electric fire. However, all the chemical energy in the coal does not reach electric machines. Some of the energy is lost along the way. For example, in the turbine and generator, friction in the moving parts causes heat. Some of the electrical energy is used in warming the wires and cables carrying the electric current. This energy is not used for any useful purpose. However the important thing is that no energy is really lost overall. It is just converted to other forms.

In prehistoric times heat and light energy from the sun was used by growing trees and plants. These eventually changed to fuels such as coal, oil, and natural gas. When we burn these fuels, we release the energy that reached the earth from the sun many years ago. This is stored in the fuel as chemical energy.

Over the last fifty years people have discovered and developed a new source of energy called nuclear energy (see page 192).

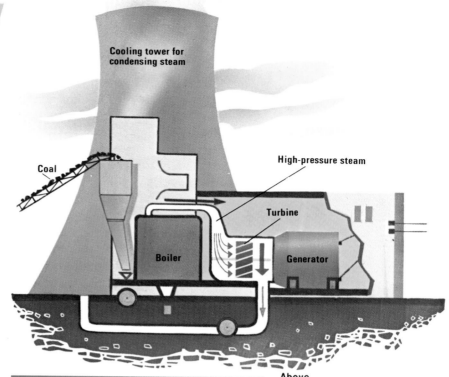

Above
A thermoelectric power station uses thermal (heat) energy from coal or oil to make electricity. The fuel is used to heat the steam that drives the turbines for the generator. In a hydroelectric power station the turbines are driven by a constant flow of water. They use the potential energy of the water behind a dam or in a waterfall (see page 154).

Left
A coal truck in a modern mine. The energy in coal, which is stored as chemical energy, is burned in power stations and gives heat originally obtained from the sun.

Below
There is a difference between power and energy. It would take a long time for the man to lift all these sacks on to the back of the lorry. The fork-lift truck does the job very quickly. Both would use the same amount of energy in doing the job but the machine is more powerful and does it quicker. Power is the amount of work that can be done in a given time.

CONDUCTION AND INSULATION

If you coat a knife blade with butter and hold the knife tip near a flame the butter will quickly melt. It melts at the tip first and then begins to melt further and further from that end. This is because the heat of the flame passes down the length of the blade. The passage of heat through a solid substance, like the knife, is called conduction.

The movement of the atoms and molecules within the solid causes conduction. When the molecules near the flame are heated they vibrate (move back and forth) more rapidly. As they vibrate faster, their energy increases. They jostle the molecules next to them and these too move more rapidly. Eventually all the molecules in the solid are vibrating faster and so have more energy. This energy is heat. As it passes down the blade, the temperature of each part of the knife increases.

Good and bad conductors

Some solids are better conductors of heat than others. Metals such as copper, alumi-nium, and silver are good conductors. Non-metals, including glass, wood, rubber and plastic do not conduct well. These bad conductors are called insulators.

Materials, such as copper, that are good conductors of heat are usually also good conductors of electricity. Good heat insulators are often good electrical insulators too.

When the knife was held in the flame, the handle did not get hot because most knife handles are made of insulating substances. So are saucepan handles, but saucepans are metal or enamel so that heat can easily pass from the cooker into the pan.

Most liquids are bad conductors. Milk can be kept cool in summer by putting the bottle into a bucket full of cold water. Gases such as air are also very bad heat conductors. Woollen clothing stops heat being lost from the body because there is air trapped between the strands of wool. The layer of air between two jumpers, or the pockets of air in the holes of a string vest, will make the conductivity even less. This insulation keeps out cold air and prevents heat being lost from the wearer's body.

Below

This experiment is explained in the text. It shows the way in which heat passes slowly down the metal blade. DO NOT TRY THIS EXPERIMENT UNLESS AN ADULT IS PRESENT.

Left

When we do not want heat to travel, we use insulators. Wooden spoons are used in cooking because a metal one would soon get hot. Pipes are lagged with cloth to stop them freezing in winter. Insulation in the roof of a house keeps in the heat.

Good conductors are used when heat has to flow easily. Insulators are used to make the flow of heat as small as possible.

A car radiator is made of metal. The water inside it cools the engine, and therefore gets hot. The metal conducts away this heat. A rubber hot-water bottle filled with hot water will keep warm for a long time. The small amount of heat which passes through the bottle heats the bed. The bed stays warm because hot air is trapped between the blankets. Another example of insulation is the lagging on pipes, hot water tanks, and boilers. It reduces the loss of heat from a hot water system. It also prevents the water in pipes from freezing during a cold winter.

Left
Double glazing is used to keep houses warm. It is a double layer of glass with air trapped between the panes. Since air is a bad conductor it reduces the loss of heat from the house and saves money spent on fuel bills.

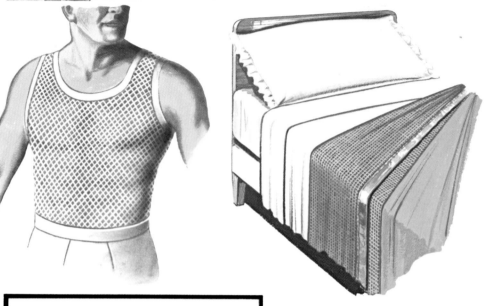

Below
A vacuum does not conduct at all. This is because there are no molecules there to carry the heat. A vacuum flask is used for keeping things hot or cold. A glass bottle inside the flask has double walls. All the air is removed from between the walls to leave a vacuum. The walls are silvered to stop heat loss by radiation.

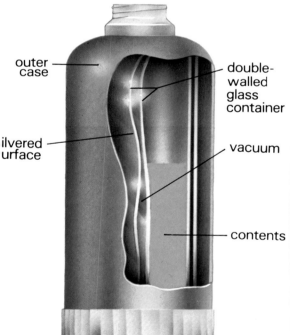

outer case

double-walled glass container

silvered surface

vacuum

contents

Above
The string vest and the cellular blanket both use the fact that air is a bad conductor. A cellular blanket is placed between two other blankets on the bed and traps a layer of air. It keeps the bed warm because it stops heat being lost.

Left
ONLY DO THIS EXPERIMENT WITH AN ADULT PRESENT. Many people will not believe you if you tell them you can boil water in a paper dish, but you can. The reason is that the water conducts the heat away from the paper and stops it from getting hot enough to burn. If you try this experiment, make sure that your dish is quite strong and will not collapse when you put water in it. Be careful not to let the dish boil dry because then it will catch alight.

CONVECTION

If you watch a saucepan of water being heated you will see ripples of water breaking the surface. These are caused by hot water rising from the bottom. Its place is taken by colder water from the top. This is called convection. It is the passage of heat by movement of the material itself. In conduction movement of heat takes place without any movement of the material.

Convection occurs in gases as well as liquids. Carefully heat a metal rod (not so hot that it burns your fingers) and hold it in the air. Put your other hand a little above it and you can feel the warm air rising from the hot rod. If you put your hand below it you will not feel any warmth.

Convection takes place because gases and liquids get bigger or expand when they are heated. This expansion makes them less dense than the surrounding material. So they rise and their place is taken by the dense colder fluid from above. These movements of material are called convection currents. The currents can be quite strong. Place a small paper windmill above an electric light and watch it spin around. This is how a flickering flame effect is made in some electric fires.

Because of the way convection works, a glass of water cannot be cooled by standing it on a block of ice. The water at the

bottom becomes colder and colder. It also becomes more and more dense and therefore stays at the bottom. The warmer water at the top has no chance of cooling because it always stays at the top.

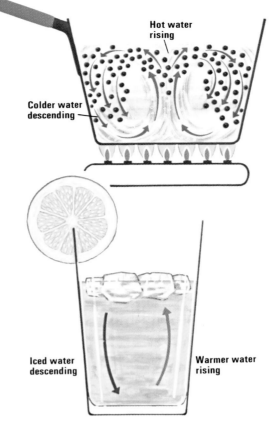

Hot water rising

Colder water descending

Iced water descending

Warmer water rising

Left
When a liquid is heated, convection currents are set up in it. The warmer water rises to the top and the cooler water sinks to replace it until that too is heated and rises. The ripples show the movement of the water. A similar effect takes place when cooling a glass of water with ice. Ice cools the water at the top which falls to the bottom of the glass. Its place is taken by warmer water from the bottom.

Below left
There are two types of electric convection heater for rooms. In the natural convection heater the cold air enters the bottom. It is heated by passing over an element, and the warm air rises out of the top. The natural convection current keeps the air circulating. In the fan heater, which can be much smaller, a fan sucks in cold air from the back and blows it over the heating elements.

Below
Ventilation in a coal mine. The fire heats the air which expands, becomes less dense, and rises out of the shaft. Fresh air comes in the other shaft to ventilate the mine.

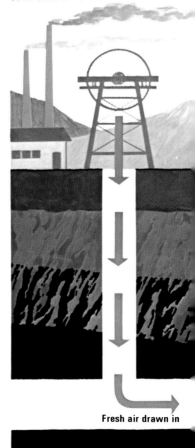

Fresh air drawn in

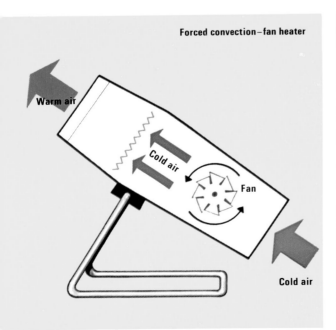

Forced convection – fan heater

Warm air

Cold air

Fan

Cold air

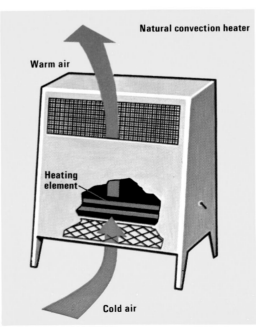

Natural convection heater

Warm air

Heating element

Cold air

Convection currents

In the early days of coal mining, the mines were ventilated by convection currents. Two shafts were sunk and a fire lit at the bottom of one of them. As the heated air rose out of this shaft fresh air was drawn into the other one, thus ventilating the mine.

Convection heaters work on the principle that hot air rises. Cold air from near the floor is taken in and heated. It rises by convection to come out of the top of the heater. A stream of warm air constantly emerges from the heater. Fan heaters and hairdriers transfer heat by convection. Air is heated by an electric element and blown out by a fan. Heat is being transferred by the movement of air so convection is taking place. When a fan is used, it is called forced convection.

Convection currents take place in the atmosphere. The land is heated to a higher temperature than the sea during the day. Air over the land becomes warmer, rises, and its place is taken by cooler air from the sea. So there is usually a breeze towards the land during the day. At night the land cools down more quickly than the sea so the sea is warmer than the land. A convection current takes place the other way. The air over the sea is heated, rises and cool air from the land takes its place.

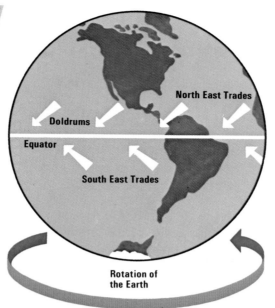

Left
The trade winds are streams of cool air taking the place of warmer air. They are on a slant because of the spin of the earth. Along the equator is an area known as the doldrums. Here sailing ships were often becalmed because there were no winds to blow them along. The only movement of the air was upwards by convection.

Below
The formation of land and sea breezes by convection currents. Breezes in the opposite direction, but much higher up, complete the circulation.

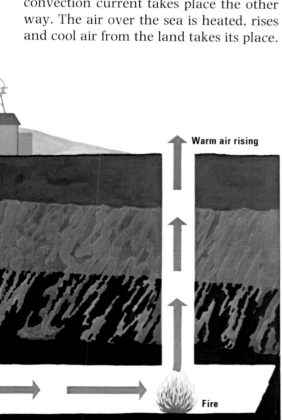

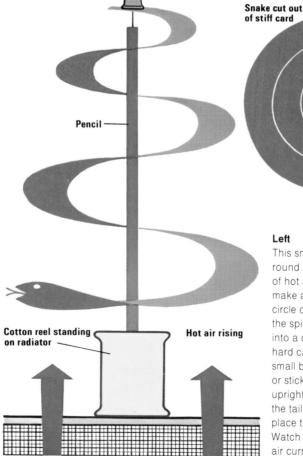

Left
This snake windmill is driven round by the convection currents of hot air rising from a radiator. To make a snake, draw a spiral on a circle of card as above. Cut along the spiral and pull it out a little, into a coil. Attach the tail to a hard cap, such as a thimble or a small bottle top. Sharpen a pencil, or stick a needle in it. Hold it upright in a cotton reel. Balance the tail on the sharp point and place the windmill on a radiator. Watch it spin round as the rising air currents flow along the spirals.

RADIATION

If you stand in the sunshine on a fine day you will feel warm. But if the sun is suddenly hidden by a cloud you will no longer feel its warmth. This means that the sun can warm you without heating the air. Heat is travelling without using the material between you and the sun. Also there is no air beyond the earth's atmosphere. So the sun's heat must be able to pass through a vacuum (a space which has no particles in it). This way of transferring heat is called radiation. It is the way that energy travels across empty space.

This is also how heat is passed from the bar of an electric fire. If you stand in front of an electric fire you will feel warm. If you move to one side, you will feel cooler. Once again the heat is being passed without using the air. Heat radiates from the fire in straight lines, just like light from a torch. If you put your hand in front of a torch you can block the light. In exactly the same way someone standing between you and an electric fire blocks the heat and stops it from reaching you.

Radiant heat and light

Radiant heat and light are very similar. They are both electromagnetic waves.

Radiation is not only emitted by extremely hot things, such as the sun and

Below
A solar furnace which was built in the French Pyrenees to make use of the sun's radiation. No longer in operation, it had a 10 metre wide reflector consisting of 3,500 small mirrors that focused the sun's rays to a point. At the focus a temperature of over 3,000°C was reached.

Above right
By holding tins of four different colours filled with hot water to your cheek you will find out which radiates the most heat. The black radiates the most, next is the brown, next the white, and finally the shiny surface radiates the least.

Right
In the bathroom the heated towel rail is silvered because it is only to heat the towels. It is not needed to heat the room by radiation. In the sitting room the radiator is painted a dark colour to enable it to radiate the maximum amount of heat.

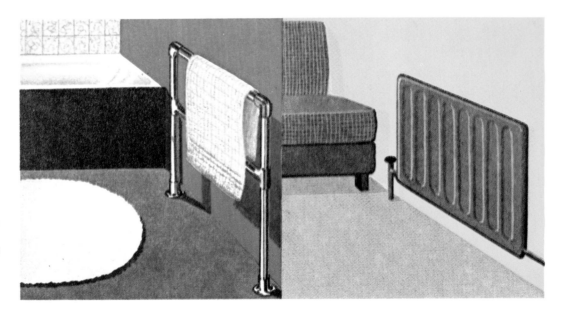

electric fires. It can also be emitted by cooler objects. If too much heat is allowed to radiate from a teapot then the tea gets cold quickly. Putting a tea cosy over it reduces the radiation loss.

Some surfaces are better radiators of heat than others. Try this experiment with an old baked bean tin. Scrape off the label and paint one half black. Leave the other side shiny. Fill the can with hot water and hold the back of your hand first near the black side and then near the shiny side. You will find that your hand is warmer when held opposite the black side. This is because a black surface is a good radiator of heat. A polished surface is a bad radiator. Repeat the experiment with another can whose sides are painted white and brown. Generally, a darker surface radiates more heat than a lighter one.

From these experiments you will understand why a silver teapot with highly polished sides will not lose much heat by radiation, whereas a brown or black teapot will lose much more.

As well as radiating heat, surfaces can also reflect and absorb heat. When it falls on a surface, heat is partly reflected and partly absorbed, just like light. Good radiating surfaces are also good absorbers of radiation. Bad radiating surfaces tend to reflect heat instead of absorbing it.

People who live in hot countries do not want their clothes to absorb heat. They therefore wear white clothes and hats which reflect the heat. Spacecraft have highly polished surfaces to reflect away the radiated heat from the sun.

The sun radiates both heat and light to the earth. You can see the light rays which are radiated but you cannot see the heat rays. You can only feel them as they warm you up.

Left
In hot countries people keep cool by wearing light-coloured clothes and living in white painted houses. This reduces the amount of heat absorbed.

Left
Firemen wear suits with highly polished surfaces so that the heat from the fire is reflected and not absorbed. This helps the firemen to keep cool as they fight a fire.

Water and ice at 0°C

Salt solution and ice at -10°C to -20°C

Far left
Here is one way of producing a low temperature. Mix some crushed ice with water. Its temperature is 0°C. If you stir in some salt the mixture become colder. Its temperature falls to between −10°C and −20°C. Before refrigerators were invented mixtures like this were used for freezing ice cream.

LOW TEMPERATURES

It is fairly easy to produce high temperatures. Making things colder is more difficult. One way of producing low temperatures is by evaporating liquids. You can demonstrate this by wetting your hand and waving it around. Your hand will feel colder. This is because the water is turning into a vapour. When water boils it needs heat to change into a vapour. In the same way the water on your hand needs heat to evaporate. This heat is taken from your hand and so it feels colder. The faster the liquid evaporates the more heat is taken away. Try the same experiment with methylated spirits or after-shave lotion which both evaporate more quickly than water.

Refrigerants

Inside a refrigerator there are tubes containing either a liquid with a very low boiling point or a gas that can easily be changed into a liquid under pressure. It is called the refrigerant. Some examples are ammonia, ethyl chloride, and Freon. The refrigerant is first compressed to a high pressure in one part of the refrigerator. At this high pressure the refrigerant's mole-cules are pushed close together so it is a liquid. The compressed liquid is passed through a valve into a region of low pressure. At this low pressure the liquid changes back into a vapour. This fast evaporation takes heat from the inside of the refrigerator, just as the water evaporating took heat from your hand. The refrigerant is compressed to turn it back to a liquid and used again. The heat passes out through the back of the refrigerator.

Many domestic refrigerators use evaporation to cool food and make ice.

A slightly different method is used to produce very low temperatures. It depends on the fact that if a gas expands quickly it cools. When you pump up a bicycle tyre you are compressing the air. You have probably noticed that the pump gets hot when you do this. The opposite happens when a gas at high pressure is suddenly changed to low pressure. The gas gets slightly colder.

This slight fall in temperature is called the Joule-Kelvin effect after its discoverers James Prescott Joule and Lord Kelvin. Using this effect, it is possible to cool gas so much that it becomes a liquid. Oxygen changes from a gas to a liquid at −183°C. Nitrogen gas changes to liquid at −195.8°C.

These are very low temperatures, but even lower temperatures can be produced.

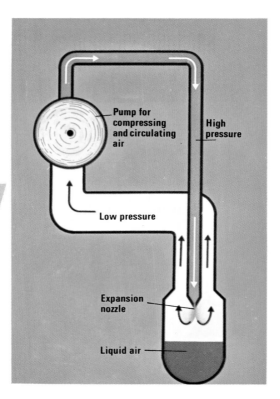

Pump for compressing and circulating air

High pressure

Low pressure

Expansion nozzle

Liquid air

Left
This shows how liquid air is made. The air is compressed and then allowed to expand through a nozzle. This cools it slightly. The cold air is used to cool the air coming into the nozzle and this is cooled even more when it expands. Eventually the temperature becomes so low that the air changes to a liquid.

Far right
Absolute zero is the temperature at which there is no movement of atoms. Scientists often use the Kelvin scale of temperature. On this scale, absolute zero is 0 kelvin. The freezing point of water is 273.15 kelvins and the boiling point is 373.15 kelvins.

Hydrogen forms a liquid at a temperature of −259.14°C and helium at −268.9°C. It requires a great deal of energy to maintain these low temperatures.

Absolute zero

The temperature of anything depends on how fast the atoms or molecules are moving about. If they are moving very quickly the temperature is high. If they are moving slowly the temperature is low. At the lowest temperature the atoms and molecules are not moving at all. It is called absolute zero and is −273.15°C. Scientists have produced temperatures that are only a millionth of a degree above absolute zero, but they have never reached it.

Above absolute zero atoms move

At absolute zero atoms are still

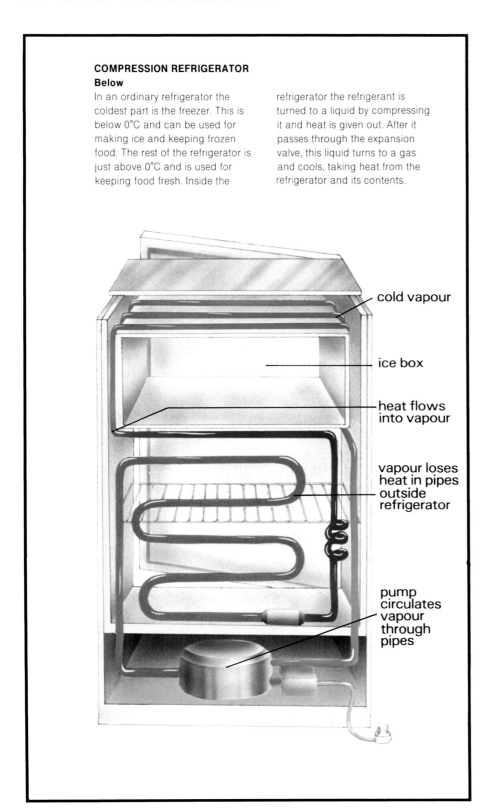

COMPRESSION REFRIGERATOR
Below
In an ordinary refrigerator the coldest part is the freezer. This is below 0°C and can be used for making ice and keeping frozen food. The rest of the refrigerator is just above 0°C and is used for keeping food fresh. Inside the refrigerator the refrigerant is turned to a liquid by compressing it and heat is given out. After it passes through the expansion valve, this liquid turns to a gas and cools, taking heat from the refrigerator and its contents.

cold vapour

ice box

heat flows into vapour

vapour loses heat in pipes outside refrigerator

pump circulates vapour through pipes

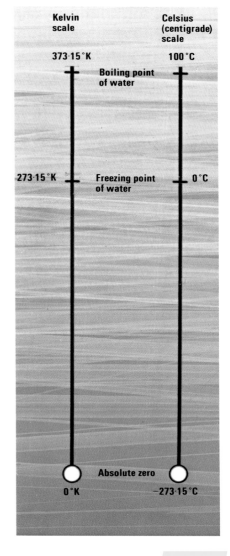

Kelvin scale   Celsius (centigrade) scale

373·15°K   100°C   Boiling point of water

273·15°K   0°C   Freezing point of water

Absolute zero

0°K   −273·15°C

71

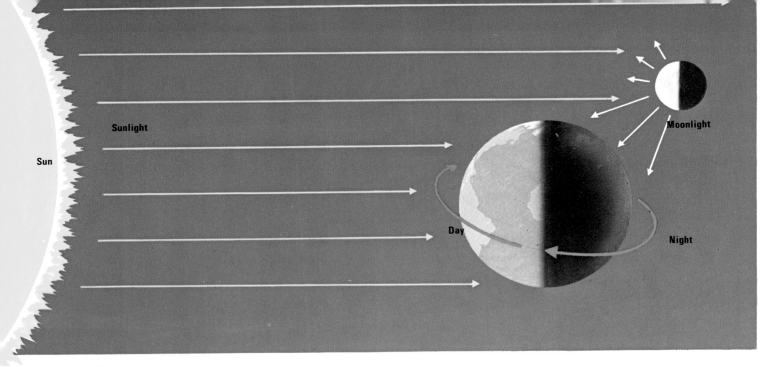

Sunlight
Sun
Moonlight
Day
Night

Light

Light is a form of energy to which our eyes are sensitive. It enables us to see things. The sun and stars, electric lights, candles, fires, and many other things emit light. These sources of light are very hot. All things are made up of atoms. If a substance is heated strongly, its atoms emit light.

The distance which the light from a source travels depends on how bright the source is. A burning match can only be seen up to a few metres away. The light from the sun travels nearly 150 million kilometres to reach us here on earth.

Darkness

Darkness is when there is no light. In a room with no windows or openings to the sunlight and with no other form of light, everything seems black or dark. We cannot see anything in darkness.

When it is daytime here, it is night-time or dark on the other side of the earth. The earth rotates once every 24 hours as it journeys around the sun. The part of the earth facing the sun is lit and this is called day. Night comes as this part of the earth rotates away from the sun's light.

Above
The moon does not produce its own light but acts as a giant mirror, reflecting light from the sun to the earth. As it revolves, we see varying amounts of its surface lit up by the sun at different times each month.

Below right
The electric light bulb contains thin tungsten wire which emits the light when a current is passed through it. Sodium light has a sealed bulb of sodium vapour which emits light when energized by a current. Neon is widely used for display lighting.

Below
A variety of lamps used by people to create artificial light. They range from the tiny flame of a Roman lamp burning vegetable oil, to the colourful glow of the gas-discharge in the neon lights of a modern city, which are powered by electricity.

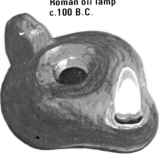

Roman oil lamp
c.100 B.C.

18th C wax candle

19th C gas lamp

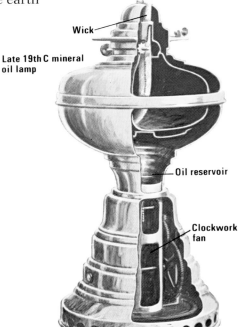

Wick

Late 19th C mineral
oil lamp

Oil reservoir

Clockwork
fan

Nature produces a lot of our light. The main natural sources are the sun, the stars, and the moon. Lightning flashes are also a source of light. The sun is our nearest star. It is a huge ball of spinning gases that flare and spurt flames out into space.

Apart from the sun, other stars can be seen on a clear night. Like the sun, they are balls of blazing hot gases giving off heat and light. However, they are very much further away than the sun. So we only see them as tiny pinpoints of light twinkling in the sky.

On a clear night, the full moon can provide enough light for us to see quite well. The moon is not a star and therefore makes no light of its own; it only reflects the light of the sun on to the earth. So, although the moon is called a natural light source, the actual source of moonlight is the sun.

A light source made by people is called an artificial source. At first people burnt wax or oil and, later, gas, to produce light. Today, electric light bulbs and fluorescent lights are most commonly used. Artificial light is essential to our way of life.

There are two main types of artificial light sources. In one, solid or liquid material is heated. An electric light filament, heated by electricity, glows very brightly, producing a whitish light. The filament is a coil of thin metal, usually tungsten. The metal magnesium can burn in air, producing an almost blinding white light. The colour of the light emitted by the material

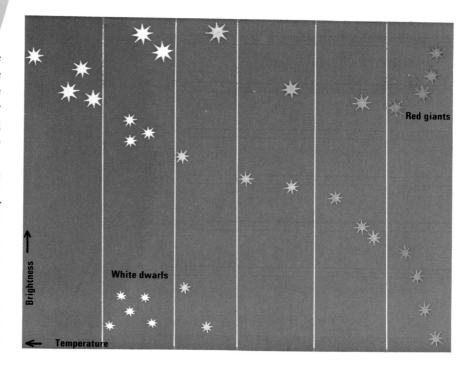

depends on its temperature. The hottest materials glow bluish-white. As their temperature drops, the glow becomes more yellow, then red, and finally disappears. It is still very hot, however.

The other type of artificial source produces light by heating a gas so that its atoms and molecules glow. This occurs in some street lights, such as sodium vapour and mercury vapour lamps.

Above

The colour of the light emitted by stars depends on their temperature. Blue stars and white stars are extremely hot. Yellow and orange stars are cooler. The sun emits yellow light. Red stars are the coolest. The brightness of the star does not depend on temperature. Some red stars, called red giants, are much brighter than the white stars known as white dwarfs.

Sodium vapour street lamp

Argon-filled light bulb

SUNLIGHT

The sun, our nearest star, is about 150 million kilometres from the earth. It is a tremendously hot glowing ball of gases held together by gravity. The temperature of its surface is 6,000°C. At its centre however, the temperature is about 14,000,000°C. The sun is the main source of the earth's heat and light. This energy is produced by complicated reactions occurring in the centre of the sun. These reactions are called thermonuclear reactions (see page 194). They change hydrogen into helium, producing an enormous amount of energy.

During this process the sun loses four million tonnes of hydrogen per second. It is believed that these nuclear reactions will continue for hundreds of millions of years. When the supply of hydrogen is used up, however, the sun will begin to cool down. At present the sun produces so much heat energy that if it were surrounded by ice one kilometre thick, it would melt the ice in about 90 minutes.

The heat produced in the centre moves out to the surface of the sun. The surface is so hot that it glows bright yellow and emits a tremendous quantity of light. This light and heat energy travels through space in all directions.

Infrared and ultraviolet radiation

Some of this energy is infrared radiation. It cannot be seen, only sensed: anything

Left
Without the sun's light plants will not grow. If a log that has lain on grass for a time is moved, the grass lying directly under the log will be pale green or almost white. This is because the grass under the log has not received the light energy to make food and grow.

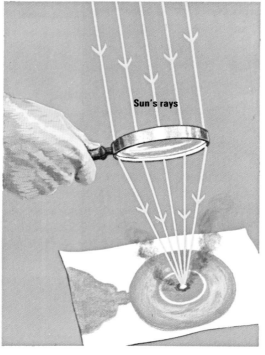

Sun's rays

Left
The heat from the sun can be used to start a fire. A magnifying glass will focus the sun's rays to a point where the strong heat can cause paper, thin twigs, etc. to burn.

Below
A greenhouse provides warmth for growing plants. Infrared radiation from the sun can pass through glass and heat up the air inside. The heat cannot easily pass back out through the glass. So the air inside the greenhouse stays warmer than the outside air. Some greenhouses have internal heating.

absorbing these rays becomes warmer. Another form of energy from the sun is ultraviolet radiation. Unlike light and infrared rays, very little ultraviolet is able to reach the earth's surface. The fraction that does has a good effect on our health. Some chemical reactions can only take place in the presence of ultraviolet radiation. The heat and light from the sun is essential to life. Infrared rays keep the earth and atmosphere at a temperature at which we can live. Light rays enable us to see and are essential for plant growth. Without the sun's energy we should live in extreme cold and almost total darkness. We would not survive for long because plant and other forms of life upon which we feed would die without warmth and sunlight.

Photosynthesis

The process by which most plants are able to absorb the energy of sunlight is called photosynthesis. The green colour of plants is caused by a dye called chlorophyll. This substance absorbs and converts sunlight into chemical energy. Plants take in carbon dioxide and water from their surroundings. They use the chemical energy produced by the chlorophyll to convert the water and carbon dioxide into organic plant material. During this process, the plant gives off oxygen which is essential to humans and all animal life.

There is enough heat, light, air, and water on most of the earth's surface for people to survive quite easily. The same conditions do not exist on the other planets in the solar system. None have an atmosphere containing oxygen or any detectable water. The planets nearer to the sun than the earth are extremely hot, while those further away are much colder. It is therefore impossible for life as we know it to survive on these other planets.

Below
Ultraviolet radiation on the skin produces vitamin D which we need for bone growth. Suntan is also produced by ultraviolet rays. Too much radiation, however, can cause sunburn or have more serious effects.

Below
A swimming pool heated by the sun. Hot water systems heated by the sun have been used for many years in warm countries. Most of these consist of blackened sheets of metal with tubes carrying water running through them. The metal is covered with a sheet of glass. The black metal absorbs the sun's heat and passes it on to the water in the pipes.

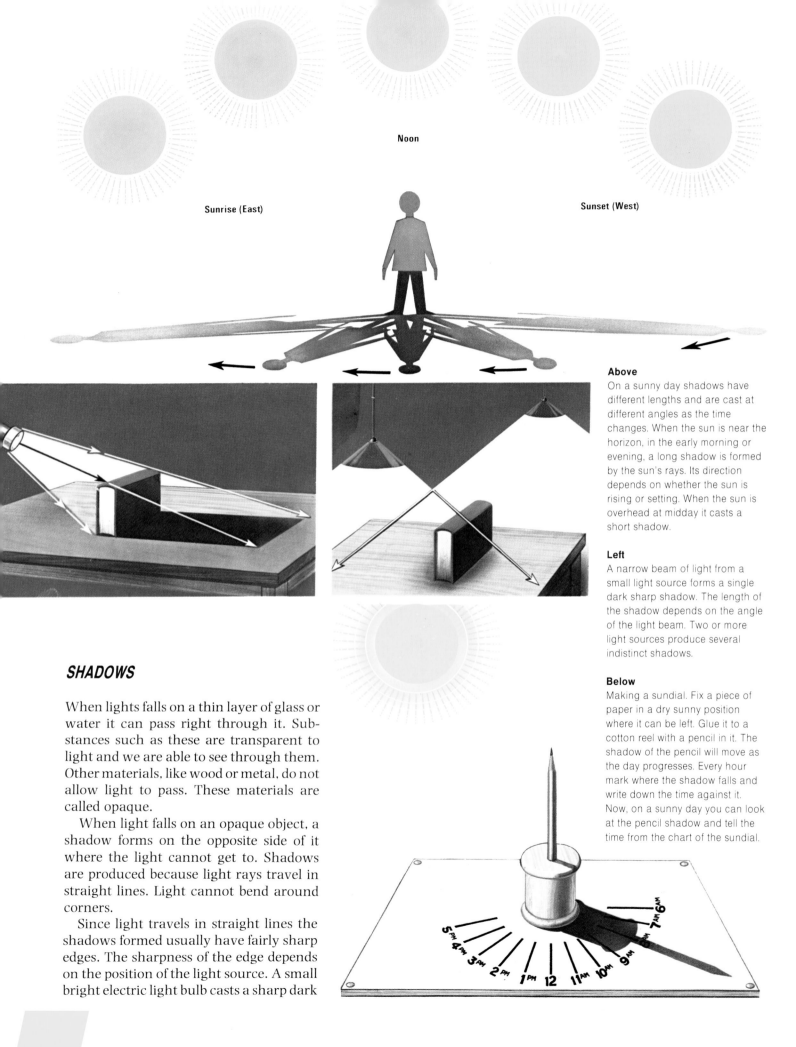

Noon

Sunrise (East)

Sunset (West)

Above

On a sunny day shadows have different lengths and are cast at different angles as the time changes. When the sun is near the horizon, in the early morning or evening, a long shadow is formed by the sun's rays. Its direction depends on whether the sun is rising or setting. When the sun is overhead at midday it casts a short shadow.

Left

A narrow beam of light from a small light source forms a single dark sharp shadow. The length of the shadow depends on the angle of the light beam. Two or more light sources produce several indistinct shadows.

Below

Making a sundial. Fix a piece of paper in a dry sunny position where it can be left. Glue it to a cotton reel with a pencil in it. The shadow of the pencil will move as the day progresses. Every hour mark where the shadow falls and write down the time against it. Now, on a sunny day you can look at the pencil shadow and tell the time from the chart of the sundial.

SHADOWS

When lights falls on a thin layer of glass or water it can pass right through it. Substances such as these are transparent to light and we are able to see through them. Other materials, like wood or metal, do not allow light to pass. These materials are called opaque.

When light falls on an opaque object, a shadow forms on the opposite side of it where the light cannot get to. Shadows are produced because light rays travel in straight lines. Light cannot bend around corners.

Since light travels in straight lines the shadows formed usually have fairly sharp edges. The sharpness of the edge depends on the position of the light source. A small bright electric light bulb casts a sharp dark

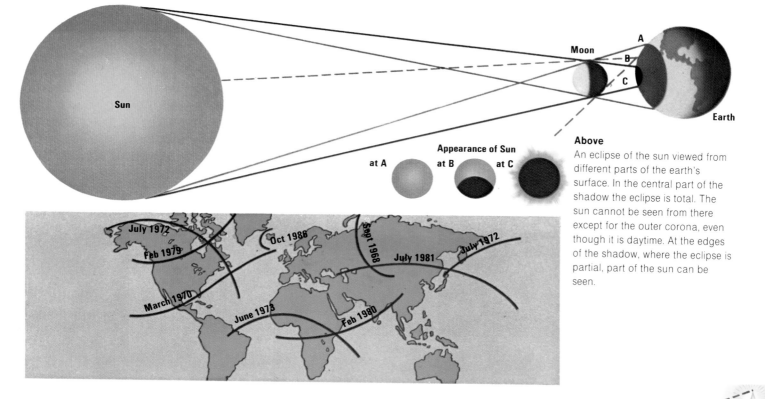

Above
An eclipse of the sun viewed from different parts of the earth's surface. In the central part of the shadow the eclipse is total. The sun cannot be seen from there except for the outer corona, even though it is daytime. At the edges of the shadow, where the eclipse is partial, part of the sun can be seen.

shadow behind an object because the light beam is coming from one direction. If there are a number of electric bulbs, the light comes from several directions and the shadows are very indistinct.

The length of a shadow depends on the angle at which light falls on an object. On a sunny day shadows have different lengths at different times of the day because of the changing position of the sun. The sun rises to its highest position at midday then begins to set. The direction of the sun's rays also changes, so shadows are formed in different directions as the day progresses. This changing direction of shadows is used in the sundial for telling the time.

Solar eclipse

The moon travels round or orbits the earth. Normally, the earth, moon, and sun do not lie in a straight line at any time during the moon's orbit. But a new moon sometimes passes directly between the earth and the sun. Then it casts a huge shadow on part of the earth's surface. This is called a solar eclipse. At the centre of the shadow no light falls on the earth and the eclipse is total. At the edges of the shadow some light can reach earth and the eclipse is partial. During an eclipse it grows cold, for we do not receive any heat from the sun.

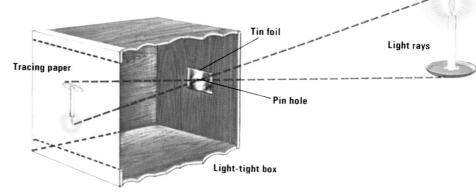

Lunar eclipse

At full moon, the earth may lie directly between the sun and the moon. Then the earth casts its shadow on the moon. This is called a lunar eclipse. The moon becomes invisible at places where the eclipse is total. It is partly hidden when there is a partial eclipse.

You can prove to yourself that light travels in straight lines. Cut a hole out of one side of a box which has a tightly fitting lid. Cover the hole with tin foil and pierce the centre of the foil with a pin. Remove the other side of the box and replace it with a stout piece of tracing paper. Point the tinfoil end of this pin-hole camera towards a candle some distance away. You will see an upside-down image of the candle on the tracing paper.

Above middle
The path of the moon's shadow during solar eclipses occurring between 1968–1989. As the earth rotates on its axis the dark part of the shadow travels in a narrow path across the earth's surface. The shadow's average speed is about 3,500 mph. A total eclipse is only seen for a few minutes from one position.

Above left
A pin-hole camera. The image is produced by rays of light from each point on the source travelling in straight lines through the pin hole and on to the tracing paper. Together these points of light make up the image.

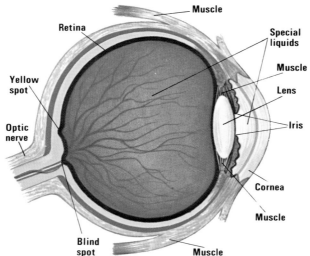

Muscle
Retina
Special liquids
Muscle
Yellow spot
Lens
Optic nerve
Iris
Cornea
Muscle
Blind spot
Muscle

Right

The eye. There is a hard white coating on the outside of the eyeball. The inside wall is black to prevent light being reflected out again or causing false impressions by reflection inside the eye. The yellow spot is most sensitive to light detail. A small part of the retina, called the blind spot, is not sensitive to light at all.

Below

A home ciné projector and a segment of a ciné film. When we watch a film the eye sees the slight changes in detail in each picture as a continuous change, which it interprets as movement. The square holes on the edges of the film guide it through the projector.

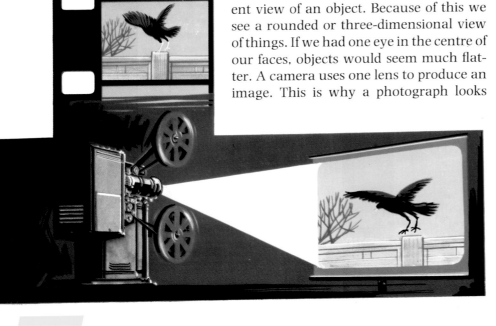

THE EYE

Each of your eyes is shaped like a ball. Most of the ball is safely shielded inside your head. At the front of the eye is a transparent outer layer called the cornea. The coloured part of the eye is called the iris, the middle of which appears black. This is actually a hole, called the pupil. It automatically grows bigger or smaller to let in more or less light.

From the pupil the light passes through a lens. This can alter its shape to focus images from near or far on to the retina. The retina is the back wall on the inside of the eye. It contains millions of light-sensitive cells called rods and cones. These cells convert the light into electrical messages which are carried to the brain by the optic nerve.

Every image that is focused on the retina is upside-down. The brain automatically turns the image the right way up in our minds. Each eye sees a slightly different view of an object. Because of this we see a rounded or three-dimensional view of things. If we had one eye in the centre of our faces, objects would seem much flatter. A camera uses one lens to produce an image. This is why a photograph looks two-dimensional.

With two eyes we are able to judge the relative position of objects accurately. Close one eye and hold your finger upright so that it is in line with a tall thin object such as a ruler, some distance away. Open that eye and close the other one still holding your finger in the same position. You will find the ruler is no longer in line with your finger.

A ciné film consists of a long series of pictures. Each is slightly different from the last and separated by a short space. When you are watching a film in the cinema your eyes cannot form a separate image of each picture. This is because the film is running through the projector too quickly. The normal speed at which films are shown is 24 frames per second. Instead your eyes remember the image of the picture just seen until the next one is shown. Because of the changing positions of the object in successive pictures we get an impression of movement.

Optical illusions

Our brains use the image formed on the retina of the eye to give us a picture of the outside world. Sometimes the brain is misled and interprets the information wrongly. Then we see an optical illusion. Straight lines can be made to appear curved. Two lines of the same length can be seem to be of different lengths. The eye can be misled by what else is surrounding these lines.

We often have a false impression of movement. Suppose two trains are sitting in a station, and then one starts to move. The passengers in the other train often think, incorrectly, that their train is leaving the station. They were expecting to move, and when they see movement assume their train is departing.

Right

This picture can be seen in either of two ways. If you stare at it for long enough you will see first a candlestick. Then suddenly it will look like two faces. You will not see both candlestick and faces at the same time.

Above

The law of perspective. As an object moves into the distance it appears to grow smaller. In the same way parallel lines, like the edges of a road or a railway line, give the illusion of drawing together as they become further away. These things appear to us in perspective.

Far right

Optical illusion of movement. If you stare at the centre of the picture the lines will appear to move in a most disturbing way. You may even see colours moving out from the centre. Now look quickly at a blank wall and you will continue to see movements of the lines for a few seconds.

Right

Optical illusions. In figs 1 and 2 the two red lines appear to be of different lengths because of the angle of the green lines. They are actually exactly the same length. In figs 3 and 4, the red lines appear curved. In fact they are straight.

Below right

What does this look like to you? Is it a duck with a long bill, or a rabbit with its ears back?

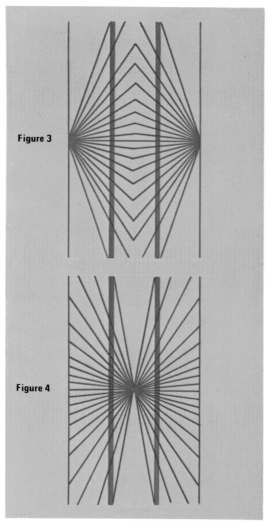

Figure 3

Figure 4

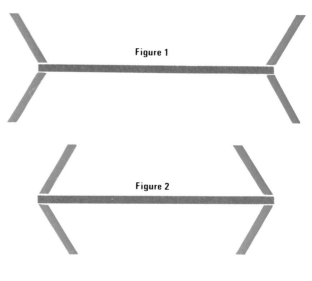

Figure 1

Figure 2

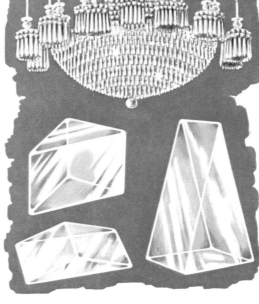

THE SPECTRUM

Look at a glass chandelier which is lit, or at a jewel, such as a diamond, which is cut in a special way. You can see many colours even though the light shining on the glass or jewel appears to be white. This is because properly cut glass and jewels, or even a drop of water, can split up white light into many colours. These colours form a rainbow pattern called a spectrum of light.

Sir Isaac Newton

Sir Isaac Newton was a very great scientist who lived in the seventeenth century. He was the first person to show that light could be split up into different colours.

Newton closed all the shutters in his room, to make it dark. Then he made a small hole in one of them. The sun shone through the hole on to a small piece of glass with triangular sides called a prism and then on to a screen. The spectrum on the screen showed coloured bands of red, orange, yellow, green, blue, indigo and violet. Newton realized that the prism had split the white light up into these seven bands of colour.

Ordinary white light, from the sun or an electric bulb, is made up of thousands of colours, all slightly different from each other. The colours tend to fall into the seven bands mentioned above.

There are many everyday examples of spectra, such as the rainbow. This is formed when the sun shines through thousands of water droplets in a rain storm or in the spray from a waterfall. Different kinds of light form different spectra. Look through an odd-shaped lump of glass. See if you can notice the difference between ordinary electric light, fluorescent lighting, and light from a sodium street lamp. You will find that the light from a sodium lamp will not split up

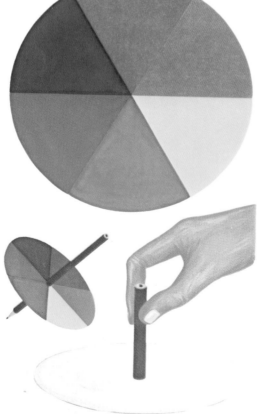

at all, for it is almost pure yellow.

A series of fine lines, close together, can produce a spectrum. You may see colours when you look sideways at a record, look through your hair or eyelashes into a bright light. Thin films too will split white light into colours. The thin layer of oil on water, which is often seen on puddles after rain, looks multi-coloured, as do soap bubbles.

You can test whether white light really is a combination of different coloured lights by producing it from a mixture of several colours. This is not difficult, but needs care. Copy the picture (right) showing a circle, with different colours painted on it. If you spin this circle all the colours seem to merge until the circle looks greyish white.

When the circle is moving quickly, your eyes cannot see each colour separately. Instead you see them all mixed together. Whenever you look at white light you are really seeing all the colours of the rainbow. However, your eye cannot distinguish between them unless the light passes through some material which separates the colours.

Above
Everyday examples of spectra. Soap bubbles and thin oil films on puddles of water produce spectra. If you look at a waterfall, with the sun behind you, you can see a rainbow. This is because the sunlight is split up by the water spray.

Left
Draw a circle very carefully on to white cardboard. Paint on the six colours in the order shown here and make a hole in the centre. Spin the card by placing it on a record turntable or by sticking a pencil through it, making a top. When you spin the card the colours merge and look white.

Above
Scattering experiment. Fill a glass with water and add a few drops of milk. Shine a bright torch beam onto the surface of the cloudy solution and the scattered light should appear bluish. Shine the beam towards you from the other side of the glass and the light should now be reddish.

SCATTERING AND ABSORPTION OF LIGHT

When sunlight reaches the earth's atmosphere it hits the molecules of air and the dust suspended in the air. These scatter or deflect the light in many directions.

The scattering of light explains the colour of the sky. White light is a mixture of colours all having different wavelengths (see page 162). Not all wavelengths are scattered by the same amount. Blue and violet light are deflected more than the other colours. During the day the sky is blue because more blue light is deflected towards the earth. In the morning and evening the sun is low in the sky and light from the sun has to travel through more atmosphere to reach us. So the sunlight is scattered more and some of the blue and violet light is deflected away from the earth. Red and orange light have longer wavelengths and are not deflected as much. Therefore the sky appears reddish at sunrise and sunset.

When light falls on a substance, some of it may be reflected and some may pass through it. The rest is absorbed by the material. The amounts depend on the type of substance. An opaque material, such as wood, passes or transmits no light. It can only reflect some if it has a shiny surface. Most of the light is absorbed. A transparent substance, such as water or glass, transmits most of it.

Light, like any other form of energy, is absorbed by the atoms and molecules of the material that it strikes. Molecules are made up of groups of two or more atoms. Atoms are able to absorb light usually of only specific colours. Light is made up of very many different colours. Each of these numerous colours has its own wavelength.

When white light falls on a material the atoms absorb some of the colours that make up white light. The remaining colours are reflected or transmitted. The reflected colours, seen by the eye, give the object its colour.

Fluorescence and phosphorescence

When an atom absorbs light, its energy increases. We say that the atom becomes excited. An excited atom is unstable and must get rid of this extra energy. It does this by giving off or emitting light of the same or a longer wavelength. Some atoms absorb light and emit it immediately. These atoms are said to be fluorescing and the substance is fluorescent. If there is a

Right
A substance can be made to emit light by heating it. The emitted light will form an emission spectrum by passing it through a prism in a spectrograph or spectroscope. The spectrum consists of coloured lines corresponding to the wavelengths of light emitted.

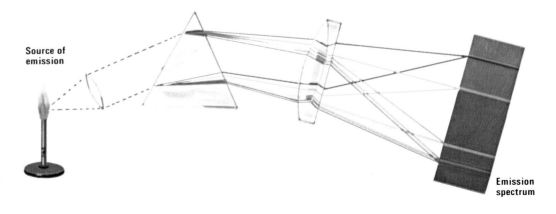

Source of emission

Emission spectrum

brief delay between absorption and emission the substance is said to be phosphorescent and is a phosphor. Phosphors are used on TV screens.

Spectroscopy

The study of this absorption and emission of light is called spectroscopy. Spectroscopy is used in scientific research, medi-

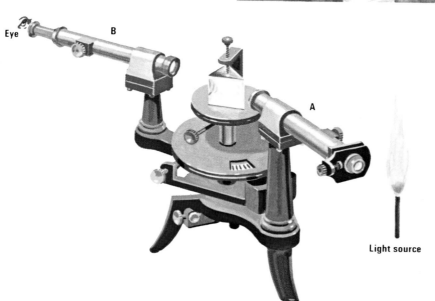

Eye   B   A   Light source

cine, industry, and astronomy. It is a way of analysing and identifying materials. It gives valuable information on the structure of atoms and molecules.

A spectrograph is used to study emission and absorption. This instrument splits up light, by means of a prism, into its different colours or wavelengths. The light then falls on to a photographic plate and an emission spectrum, or absorption spectrum, is recorded.

Transparent absorbing medium

Source emitting continuous spectrum

Absorption spectrum

Right
You can practise mixing coloured lights in a darkened room, using coloured paper and torches. Let the beams cross on a piece of white paper.

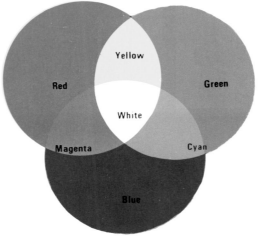

Right
The colours you would see on the paper if green, red and blue light are mixed in the right proportions. Where all three meet the result is white. Where only two primary colours cross, a colour is formed which is complementary to the third primary colour.

Right
Results you can produce by mixing cyan, magenta and yellow light. Yellow and magenta give red. Yellow is a mixture of red and green. Magenta is a mixture of blue and red. When yellow and magenta are mixed you are really mixing red, green, blue and red. The first three make white and the fourth, red, is left to give the result, red. Can you see why magenta and cyan mixed give a blue colour and cyan and yellow mixed give green?

COLOURS

Sunlight, or light from an electric light bulb, is called white light. White light is actually a mixture of many different colours. We are unable to see these colours as the eye cannot split up white light. However, light can be split up into its component colours by water droplets or bits of glass; the rainbow shows the groups of colours – red, orange, yellow, green, blue, and violet – of which light is made. These same colours can be mixed together, in the right proportions, to produce white light.

Primary colours

It is not necessary for all these six colours to be used in forming white light. Only three colours are needed. These colours are called primary colours. Red, green, and blue light are one set of primary colours. In the right proportions they can be mixed to give white light. If these proportions are changed, light of a different colour is obtained. Any colour can be obtained from certain proportions of these three coloured lights. The primary colours for mixing paints are not the same as those for mixing lights: a different process is involved (see page 86).

You have possibly seen lights mixed in the theatre. Two coloured spotlights can produce a third quite differently coloured circle of light where the beams cross on the stage. You could try experimenting at home using three torches producing different colours. For the best results, the experiment should be done in a dark room. Also the beam of light from the torches should be quite narrow. To obtain the different coloured beams, fasten coloured cellophane over each torch with an elastic band. Sweet wrappings are ideal for this. You may have to try several shades of each colour in order to get a good result.

Mixing two of the three primary colours can give interesting results. Red and blue light mixed give a colour called magenta (pinkish-purple). Blue and green produce cyan (greenish-blue). Most surprisingly, red and green light mixed together produce yellow light.

Complementary colours

Any two colours that produce white light when they are mixed are said to be complementary colours. Yellow light (a mixture of red and green light) is the complementary colour to blue light. Together they give white light. In the same way magenta is the complementary colour to green and cyan is complementary to red.

A mixture of the correct proportions of red, green, and blue light gives white light. When yellow, magenta, and cyan lights are mixed they can also give white light. Thus these three colours can be considered as a set of three primary colours. Yellow and magenta together produce red light, yellow and cyan produce green light, and magenta and cyan form blue light. If you find paper or cellophane of these three colours with which to cover torches, you can prove this for yourself.

White light can therefore be thought of as being made up of three primary colours. Light of a colour other than white is produced by mixing the right amounts of primary colours. This is the basis of several processes, including colour vision and colour television (see page 179).

Red filter

Above
Colour filters, used in colour photography, consist of a circular sheet of dyed transparent material called gelatin held in a special metal or plastic ring. Coloured glass can also be used. They are usually fitted to the camera in front of the lens.

Red filter

Yellow filter

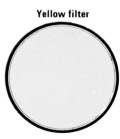

Green filter

Left
Colour filters are used to modify the colour of light before it falls on to the film. A yellow filter allows green and red light to pass through, but stops blue light. A red (or green) filter passes red (or green) light. Objects of colours which have not been transmitted appear darker than normal as less light has fallen on the film.

Above
Coloured objects absorb certain colours from light and reflect the rest. The eye sees the reflected light only, which is therefore the colour the object appears to be.

Right
When light falls on the surface of a blackboard every colour in the light is absorbed and none is reflected. The white chalk marks reflect every colour. The combination of these colours makes the reflected light from the chalk appear white.

Above
The picture drawn in red and green appears normal when viewed in white light. In red light both the white paper and the red marks on it reflect red light. The red marks therefore merge into the background and disappear. As there is no green light to reflect, the green marks appear black.

COLOURED OBJECTS

Mixing coloured lights gives results which are quite different from those obtained by mixing paints. Mixing blue and yellow lights gives white light. A mixture of blue and yellow paint is green. Two different processes of colour formation are involved.

Light

The colour of objects depends on what colours of light they reflect. When light falls on materials, they absorb some of the colours and reflect the rest. Light from the sun or an electric light bulb is a mixture of red, orange, yellow, green, blue, and violet. However it can also be considered as a mixture of the three colours red, green and blue (see page 84). These three are a set of primary colours.

If white light falls on an object and it absorbs green and blue, but reflects red light, then it is a red object. All coloured objects absorb every colour of light except the one which is reflected. This is the colour which your eye sees.

This is true for all colours, not just red, green and blue. Yellow light can be made by mixing green and red light together. A yellow object absorbs only the blue part of white light, and reflects both the red and

the green which appears as yellow.

A black object looks dark because it absorbs all the light falling on it, and reflects no colour at all. White things absorb no colours and reflect every colour falling on them. When white objects are illuminated by white light, they reflect white light. If the light shining on an object is not white, the colour of the object will change. You may have noticed this when you look at people at night, under yellow sodium street lighting. In white light, blue materials absorb red and green. In yellow sodium light they become black, because sodium light contains no blue light to be reflected.

Coloured paints, inks, or dyes

Mixing paint is not like mixing light. For painting, the primary colours are red, blue, and yellow. Mixing these three colours in the right amounts produces blackish-brown paint. Other mixtures are used to produce different colours. You cannot, however, make white paint by mixing other colours.

Coloured inks or dyes are used when

Mixing lights (additive)

Mixing paints (subtractive)

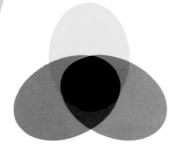

cloth is dyed, or a coloured magazine picture is printed. Layers of primary colours are put on so that the mixing is just right to get the necessary colour tones in the pattern or picture.

Colour film

Colour film consists of three layers of emulsion (see page 106). The image of a red object is recorded on one layer sensitive only to red light. A green object is on a layer sensitive only to green light, and a blue object on the third blue-sensitive layer. A yellow object appears on both red and green-sensitive layers. The colours on the negative are complementary to the actual colours. The red object appears blue-green, the green object appears red-blue, and the blue object yellow. In the same way yellow objects appear blue, purple objects green, black objects white and vice versa. A complementary colour, such as yellow, mixed with its primary colour, blue, produces white light. In the final photo, produced by another process, complementary colours are changed back into their primary colours.

Above right
The different colours obtained when coloured lights (top) and coloured paints (bottom) are mixed.

Left
A colour negative is in complementary colours to the finished photo. The guardsman's jacket is peacock blue (blue and green mixed). He is standing on purple (blue and red mixed) grass; the sky is yellow (red and green mixed). His hat and trousers are white. The final photograph is seen on the right.

Left
In colour printing, the three primary colours – yellow, cyan (blue) and magenta (red) – are printed on paper as tiny coloured dots of ink. The dots merge together in the eye to form a coloured picture. A fourth colour, black, is also used to make the black parts of the picture darker. Each colour is printed separately, so the paper has to go through the printing machine four times.

Right

First law of reflection. The angle of incidence at which light from the candle hits the mirror, is equal to the angle of reflection. If the light arrives at right angles to the mirror, it will be reflected in the same direction. So the angles of incidence and reflection will both be equal to zero.

REFLECTION

When light is bounced off a surface, it is said to be reflected. When you look in a mirror you see a picture of yourself – your reflection. The picture of an object seen in a mirror is called its image. An image is only seen if the mirror is flat. Rough or uneven surfaces can only form a distorted image.

In addition to being flat, a good reflecting surface must be shiny. A piece of flat rubber does not form a reflected image. Rubber is an example of a matt or non-shiny surface.

Metal is a good reflector of light, but it is difficult to make it perfectly flat. Nevertheless, very early mirrors were made of pure metal or bronze. These must have given distorted images and were easily dented. It was a long time before better mirrors were produced.

A modern mirror is made of a small sheet of glass which can be made perfectly flat. The light is reflected off a thin layer of shiny metal, such as silver or aluminium, on the back of the glass. To prevent the metal from being scratched it is protected by a coating of paint.

Angles of incidence and reflection

The laws of reflection show where the image of an object, in front of a mirror, will be formed. The first law states that the angle at which the light from an object hits a mirror (called the angle of incidence)

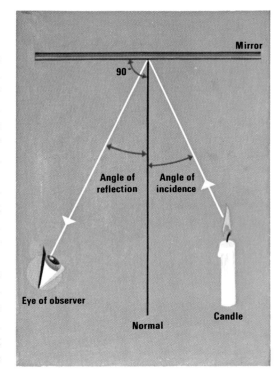

is equal to the angle at which light leaves the mirror (called the angle of reflection). These angles are measured from a line at right angles to the mirror called the normal. The second law is that the incident ray, the normal, and the reflected ray lie in the same plane. This means that they can all be drawn on a flat piece of cardboard.

You can check the laws of reflection by using a small flat mirror. Hold an object, such as a pencil, to one side of the mirror. Move your head until you see the image of the pencil. You can see it when light from the pencil makes an angle with the mirror equal to the angle at which your eye is looking at the mirror.

The shape of an object, and that of its image, are the same in a flat mirror. The image is no bigger, smaller, fatter, or thinner than the object. It is, however, laterally inverted. This means that the left-hand side of the object appears on the right-hand side of the image and vice versa. A reflection of your left hand in a mirror looks like your right hand because your two hands are mirror images of each other. No one sees themselves as they really are when they look in a mirror.

Flat or plane mirrors are used in many optical instruments. In the microscope it directs light on to the object. In the sextant, an instrument used by navigators, a plane mirror is used to determine the exact angle of the sun above the horizon.

Below

Mirror-writing is laterally inverted. Look at the image of some writing in a second mirror. The writing will be inverted a second time and will be turned back to normal.

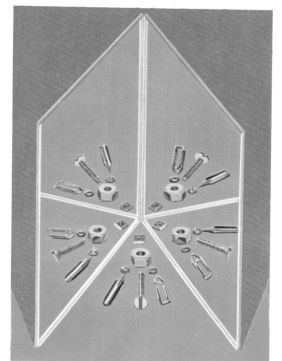

Far left
You can see yourself as you look to other people by looking in two mirrors of a dressing table, set at right angles to each other. The image in the second mirror is the one other people see. By making the angle between the mirrors small, you can see several image of yourself.

Left
Make a pattern of small objects on a piece of paper. Stand two mirrors, edges touching, on the paper, with the pattern lying between the mirrors. Looking down into the mirrors you will see the pattern repeated several times. The smaller the angle between the mirrors, the more images are seen.

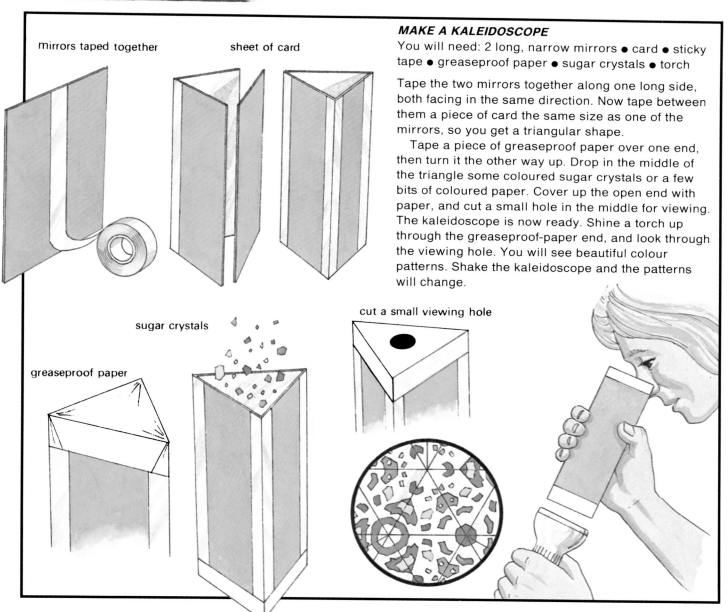

mirrors taped together

sheet of card

MAKE A KALEIDOSCOPE

You will need: 2 long, narrow mirrors ● card ● sticky tape ● greaseproof paper ● sugar crystals ● torch

Tape the two mirrors together along one long side, both facing in the same direction. Now tape between them a piece of card the same size as one of the mirrors, so you get a triangular shape.

Tape a piece of greaseproof paper over one end, then turn it the other way up. Drop in the middle of the triangle some coloured sugar crystals or a few bits of coloured paper. Cover up the open end with paper, and cut a small hole in the middle for viewing. The kaleidoscope is now ready. Shine a torch up through the greaseproof-paper end, and look through the viewing hole. You will see beautiful colour patterns. Shake the kaleidoscope and the patterns will change.

sugar crystals

greaseproof paper

cut a small viewing hole

89

Far right
Total internal reflection in a prism. Depending on the shape of the prism and the direction of the incident beam, the reflected beam can be turned through 90° (as in the periscope), turned through 180°, returning in the same direction, or turned upside down.

Left
The calm surface of a lake will produce a perfect reflection of the surrounding buildings and trees. When the wind ruffles the surface, the light is reflected in all directions and the sharp image disappears.

Left
If a torch beam is pointed towards a shiny flat surface, the reflected beam remains fairly narrow. If the surface is not flat, the light is reflected in all directions. However, the laws of reflection are still obeyed.

Flat surface

Rough surface

Right
You can see your reflection in a car or train window. It looks quite clear if it is dark outside.

REFLECTING SURFACES

A silvered mirror is not the only surface that reflects light. If you can swim, you may have looked upwards at the surface of the water when you were diving. The surface looks very bright from underneath because the sky is above it. It is also shiny, like a mirror, and you can see reflections of things in the water.

You can also see reflections if you look at the surface of water from above. The sharpness of the image depends on how calm the water is. At the seaside the water is constantly moving, but you may see the blurred shadow of a seagull or an aircraft as it flies over.

Many materials can be made smooth enough to reflect light well, but the reflections are most commonly seen in metals, glass, and liquids, like water. Nearly everyone has noticed their own reflections in a car or train window. The image is much better if it is dark outside, so

Below
Pepper's ghost. This theatrical effect can be used to produce a ghost-like image which seems to materialize in the centre of the stage. In fact, it is only a reflection on a sheet of glass across the stage, of a person or object standing in the wings against a black background. In this case the ghost is a lighted candle. Shine a torch on it, and from the front the candle will appear to be standing inside the bottle of water – still burning. Switch off the torch and the candle disappears.

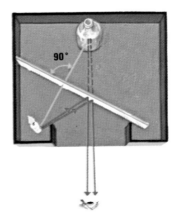

90°

that no confusing light is passing in through the glass. Reflections in shop windows often prevent us seeing the objects on show clearly. Some shops and showrooms have specially curved glass in their windows. This reflects sunlight or street lighting in such a way that it does not confuse the observers' view of the display.

Every substance reflects some light, but unless its surface is smooth the reflections are scattered in all directions. Rooms are bright in the daytime even if the sun does not shine into them. This is because the sky and everything else reflects light in all directions. When the sun is covered in cloud, sunlight enters the cloud and is reflected or scattered off the particles of water vapour at odd angles. Some of this light enters buildings through windows and open doors. In a room, the ceiling and walls reflect light too. This means that no hard shadows can be formed and the light is much softer than it is on bright sunny days.

Total internal reflection

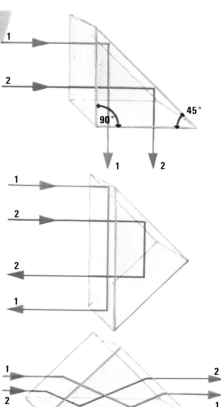

When light enters a transparent substance such as glass or water, most of it passes straight through but some of it can be reflected at the second surface. If the angle of incidence of the ray at this surface is greater than a critical angle no light will pass straight through; it will all be reflected. This is called total internal reflection.

A prism is a piece of glass with triangular ends. If the angle at which the light ray hits a prism is greater than the critical angle, total internal reflection occurs, and the prism acts as a mirror. Prisms are used as reflectors in binoculars, and in submarine periscopes. With a periscope objects can be seen that are not in a direct line of sight. They allow you to look over the heads of a crowd, or see round a corner.

Some optical illusions involve reflections, such as Pepper's Ghost, a popular theatrical effect (see facing page).

MAKE A PERISCOPE
You will need: 2 cardboard boxes ● 2 mirrors ● sticky tape

Submarine commanders use periscopes to look above the surface of the sea while they are still submerged. The idea behind a periscope is that a mirror high up reflects light down to another mirror at eye level, which in turn reflects the light into your eyes. For this to work the mirrors must be angled exactly at 45 degrees, or half a right-angle.

You can use two small boxes to hold the mirrors, and then tape them together to make the periscope. Make a hole for viewing in one side of each box and then tape a mirror opposite the hole at an angle of 45 degrees. Fit the boxes together so that the holes point in opposite directions. Tape cardboard lids on the top and bottom of your periscope to stop stray light from entering.

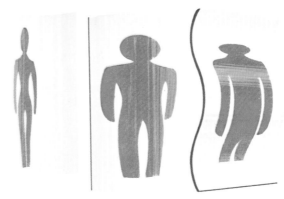

CURVED MIRRORS

A curved mirror is made in a similar way to a flat mirror except that the glass is curved as though it was part of a giant sphere or bubble. A concave mirror curves inwards, into a "cave" shape. A convex mirror bulges outwards. The laws of reflection are the same for curved mirrors as for plane or flat mirrors.

A beam of parallel light consists of light rays travelling in the same direction. If rays of parallel light fall on a concave mirror they are reflected so that they converge to a fixed point, called the focus of the mirror. The focus lies on the principal axis of the mirror. The distance between the focus and the centre of the mirror is called the focal length. Convex mirrors do not bring light to a focus. Instead, the reflected rays are spread out as though they came from a point behind the mirror. This point is called a virtual focus.

A curved mirror can make an object look bigger or smaller. The effect depends on whether the object lies between the focus and the mirror or beyond the focus. The position and size of the image is found by drawing ray diagrams.

Concave mirrors

Shaving mirrors are concave mirrors with a focal length of about one metre. A person standing very close to this mirror is between the focus and the mirror. Rays of light from the person's face produce an image in the mirror which is much larger than the actual face. This is a magnified image. However if the mirror is pointed at an electric light bulb a long way off, the mirror concentrates the light from it. A very small bright image of the bulb can be seen on a piece of paper held at the focus about one metre away from the mirror. This image is upside down or inverted.

Right
Ray diagrams. Convex mirrors spread out the light from a distant object, so it appears to have come from behind the mirror.

Right
An object lying between the focus and a concave mirror is magnified by the mirror. Any ray parallel to the principal axis must pass through the focus. The image is formed where two rays cross.

Right
If the object is a long way from the focus of a concave mirror, a small, inverted (upside-down) image can be seen on a piece of paper held near the mirror.

Right
Convex mirrors collect light from a very wide area round the mirror, producing a small upright image. As the image appears to be formed behind the mirror, it is called a virtual image.

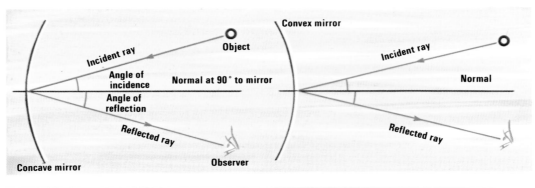

Left
Curved mirrors obey the same laws of reflection as flat mirrors. That is, the angle of incidence is equal to the angle of reflection.

Left
If a concave mirror is held facing the sun, the parallel rays of sunlight are focused, forming a bright spot. On a hot day, the focused light can set paper alight.

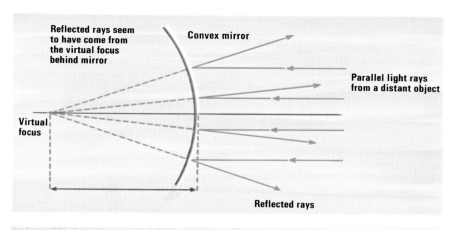

Reflected rays seem to have come from the virtual focus behind mirror

Convex mirror

Parallel light rays from a distant object

Virtual focus

Reflected rays

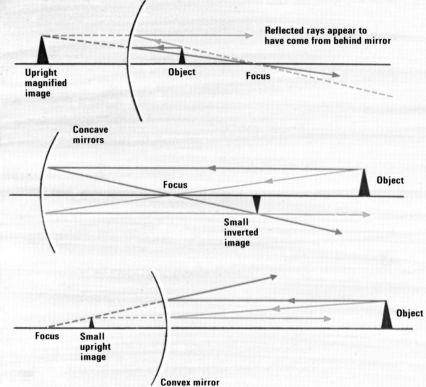

Reflected rays appear to have come from behind mirror

Upright magnified image

Object

Focus

Concave mirrors

Focus

Object

Small inverted image

Focus

Small upright image

Object

Convex mirror

Coloured images of brightly lit scenes out of doors can be shone on to a piece of paper in the same way. The camera obscura works like this.

Very large concave mirrors are used to collect light from distant objects in one spot. This is the way many big astronomical telescopes work. For the best results the mirror is shaped like part of the inside of an eggshell. This parabolic shape can bring light to a perfect focus. Concave mirrors are also used in car headlamps. A parallel beam of light is made by putting the bulb at the focus of the mirror.

Convex mirrors

Convex mirrors behave differently. They can collect light from objects which are widely spread round the mirror, and reflect this light in a narrow beam. Because of this, convex mirrors can be used as driving mirrors. The driver can see a large area of the road behind in a small mirror.

Convex mirrors are used wherever the observer needs to see a large area in the mirror. They are used in buses, where the conductor needs to see a whole deck of the bus from upstairs or downstairs. A supermarket manager uses one to see all the shopping area at one glance and detect shoplifters.

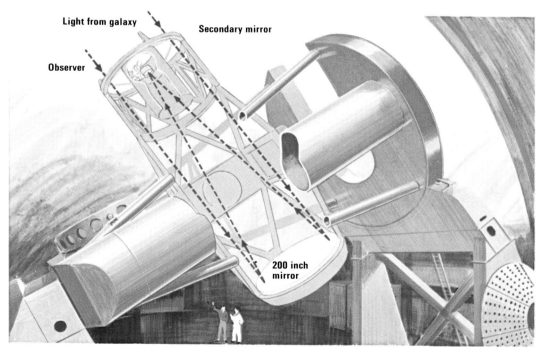

Light from galaxy

Secondary mirror

Observer

200 inch mirror

Left
An astronomical telescope, using a parabolic mirror, collects light from the stars at a small accurate focus. This image can then be photographed.

Above

A narrow beam of light is bent upwards slightly as it passes from air into water. When it emerges from the water into air again it is bent downwards. It is then travelling at the same angle as it was before it entered the water.

Right

A swirling effect is seen as hot sugar solution (containing coffee) is poured into a jam jar of water. Light travels more slowly in the denser sugar solution than in water. The resulting bending of the light rays produces the swirls.

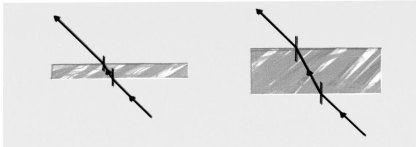

Above

As a ray of light goes from a less dense medium (air) to a more dense medium (glass), it is bent towards the normal. Passing from a more dense to a less dense medium, the light ray is bent away from the normal. The ray of light coming out of the glass is parallel to the ray going in, but it is displaced sideways. The amount it is displaced depends on the thickness of the glass.

Right

A coin in a glass of water will appear much nearer to the surface than it really is, due to refraction of the light ray from the coin to your eye. The eye sees the image as if the ray has travelled straight to it. Real depth divided by apparent depth gives the refractive index of water.

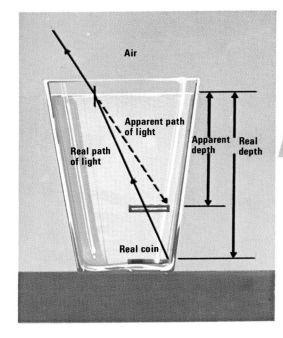

Air

Apparent path of light

Real path of light

Apparent depth

Real depth

Real coin

REFRACTION

Put a pencil in a jam jar of water and look at it carefully. From some angles the pencil will look bent. If you have a pencil torch which produces a narrow beam of light, try shining it into the jar. In a darkened room you can see that the light bends when it passes from air into water. The bending of light, which occurs in both these experiments, is called refraction.

Light travels at different speeds in different transparent materials. Because of this, when light passes from one material to another its direction changes slightly. Refraction causes the shimmering effect just above the ground on a hot day. Light travels through the hot air rising from the ground faster than it travels through the cooler air above, and so a heat haze is produced. You can produce the same effect at home by shining a powerful torch beam at a plain wall just above a candle flame. Dancing patterns and shadows will appear on the wall behind the candle.

Try dissolving about one teaspoonful of sugar in a very small amount of hot water. Pour this solution into water in a jam jar, you will see a swirling effect as the sugar solution sinks to the bottom. This is because light travels more slowly through the sugar solution than through pure water.

Light travels more slowly through denser materials. Glass is denser than air. If light travels from air to glass, it is bent or refracted towards the normal. The normal is an imaginary line perpendicular to the refracting surface. Light passing from glass to air is refracted away from the normal. The light always bends by a definite amount. This amount depends on the angle of incidence (the angle at which the light strikes the surface of the material), and on the material itself.

Refractive index

The refractive index of the material tells us how slowly light will travel through the material and hence how much it will be bent. The refractive index equals the speed of light in air divided by the speed of light in the material. For glass it equals 1.5, for water it is 1.3. The denser the material, the higher the refractive index.

Drop a coin into a jam jar of water and

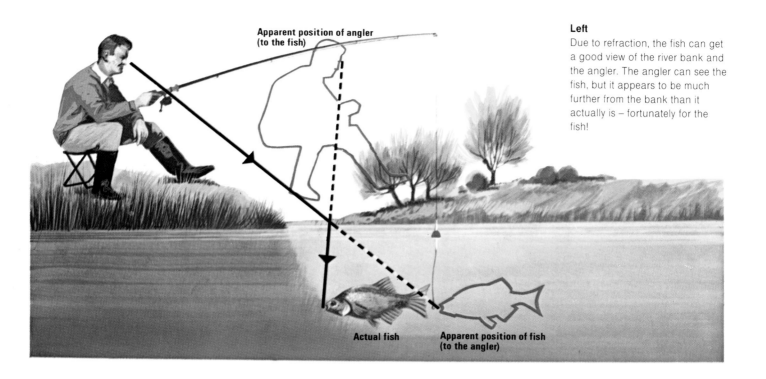

Apparent position of angler (to the fish)

Actual fish

Apparent position of fish (to the angler)

look into it from above. Put a chalk mark on the jar where you think the coin is. You will probably find that the coin is much lower down than you had expected. This too is a result of refraction. Swimming pools and rivers may appear very shallow when you look in, but may really be much deeper.

Prisms or water can split light into the colours of the spectrum (see page 80). This is because the different colours in white light are refracted by the glass or water by different amounts. When white light passes from air into water or glass, violet light is refracted most, and red light least.

In a rainbow, the sunlight is refracted when it goes into the droplets of water. It is reflected inside them and refracted again as it passes out. The colour seen by an observer will depend on the angle at which he or she looks at each droplet.

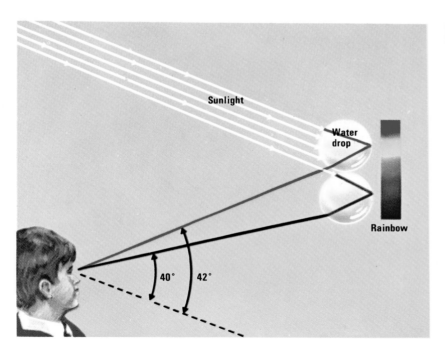

Sunlight

Water drop

Rainbow

40° 42°

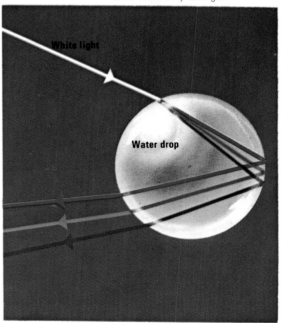

White light

Water drop

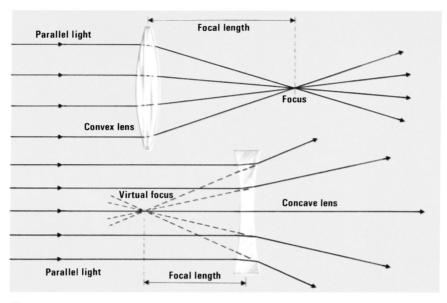

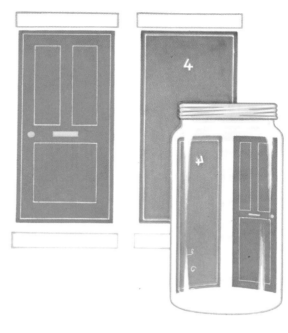

Above

A convex lens makes parallel light falling on it converge to a focus. A concave lens makes parallel light falling on it diverge as though it came from a virtual focus.

Below

Ray diagrams. An object between the focus and a convex lens appears magnified when you look through the lens. If the object is beyond the focus, you cannot see an image by looking through the glass. You can find an inverted image by holding a piece of paper behind it.

Below right

Wherever you put the object, when you look at it through a concave lens you will see a small upright image.

LENSES

A lens is a piece of glass or other transparent solid. It is cut so that it has at least one surface shaped like part of a large sphere.

Lenses are used to spread out (diverge) light, or bring light closer together (converge light). They do this by refraction.

When light passes from air into glass it is bent towards the normal (an imaginary line perpendicular to the glass surface). When the light emerges it is bent away from the normal.

Convex and concave lenses

The path of the light rays through a lens depends on the shape of the lens. The two main kinds of lenses are convex lenses, which bulge out on each side, and concave lenses which cave in towards the centre.

Convex lenses make parallel light rays falling on them converge to a single point called the focus of the lens. Concave lenses make parallel light rays spread out or diverge as though they came from a point called the virtual focus. In each case the distance between the focus and the centre of the lens is called the focal length of the lens.

A convex lens makes a good magnifying glass, if an object is placed between the lens and its focus. From the other side of the lens, the object appears larger, and further from the lens than it really is. If the object is beyond the focus, you will not see an image at all. However you can form a real inverted (upside down) image by holding a piece of paper on the opposite side of the lens to the object, especially if the object is as bright as a light bulb. For a concave lens, it does not matter where the object is. The image is always on the same side of the lens as the object, and is smaller than the object.

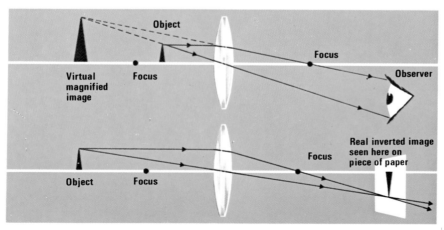

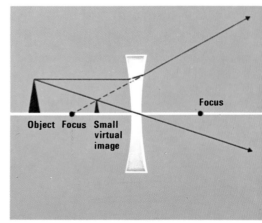

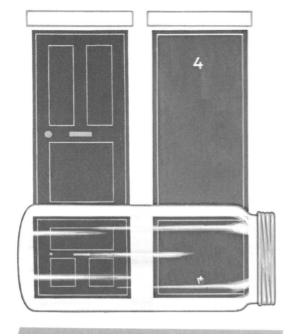

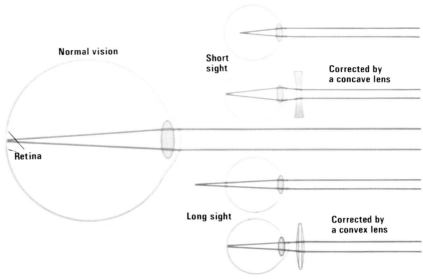

Normal vision

Retina

Short sight

Corrected by a concave lens

Long sight

Corrected by a convex lens

Ray diagrams

To find the position of the image formed by a lens, ray diagrams are drawn. These are similar to the diagrams drawn for curved mirrors (see page 92). A ray of light parallel to the axis of a thin lens must pass through the focus. If the ray goes through the centre of the lens, it does not change direction.

The human eye contains a convex lens which focuses light onto the retina at the back of the eye. Some people's eye-lenses focus the light before it reaches the retina. These people are short-sighted. Others focus light beyond the retina because they are long-sighted. Spectacles contain specially made lenses. These help the eye-lenses to bring light to a focus on the retina, where it forms a sharp image.

Lenses are used in many optical instruments such as cameras, microscopes, projectors, binoculars, and telescopes. For the biggest telescopes, curved mirrors are used. This is because very large lenses are difficult to make, and they produce colour distortion.

All lenses bend light by refraction. The colours, of which white light is composed, are refracted by different amounts in glass. The light emerging from a lens is therefore slightly coloured. This is always a problem with instruments using lenses. It is possible to reduce this coloration by sticking together two lenses, of different shapes and types of glass. This lens combination is called an achromat and is widely used.

Above left

A closed jar full of water makes a simple convex lens. Light from the sun or a torch bulb can be brought to a focus by this lens. If you look at objects through the water they will seem distorted. Their shapes depend on whether the jar is held upright or on its side.

Above

A normal eye-lens focuses light on the retina. If a person is short sighted, light is focused in front of the retina. Concave lenses in spectacles diverge light so that the eye lens can focus it on the retina. If a person is long sighted, light is focused beyond the retina. Convex lenses in spectacles help the eye to focus the light on the retina.

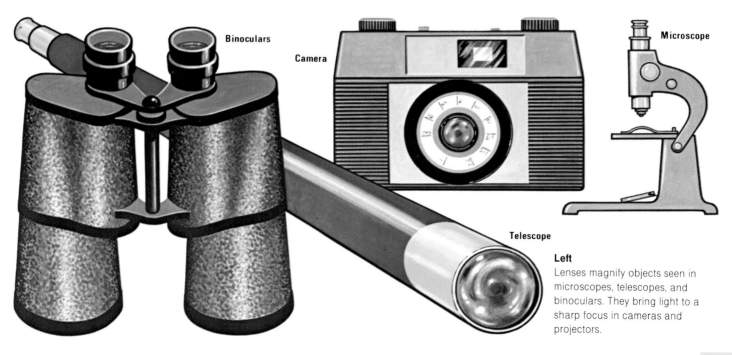

Binoculars

Camera

Microscope

Telescope

Left

Lenses magnify objects seen in microscopes, telescopes, and binoculars. They bring light to a sharp focus in cameras and projectors.

Above
A plane mirror produces a laterally inverted image; that is, the right hand side of the image appears opposite the left hand side of the object, and vice versa. Mirrors have been used for centuries, both for practical purposes and for decoration.

Right:
Some historical optical instruments. A model of the first microscope, devised by Leeuwenhoek (left). A copy of the microscope devised by Hooke before he published his famous book on microscopy in 1665 (centre). A model of a lamp and condenser system designed by Hooke (right).

Leeuwenhoek's microscope

Hooke's microscope

OPTICAL INSTRUMENTS

In order to see a small object clearly, we bring it closer to the eye. This gives a wider angle of view of the object and increases its apparent size. However, somebody with normal vision can bring the object no nearer than about 25 cm from the eye. Closer than that, the object looks blurred.

To increase the size of a tiny or distant object, without straining the eye, a microscope or telescope must be used. These are optical instruments which use lenses or mirrors to help us see small or distant objects more clearly.

The mirror is the oldest optical instrument. Mirrors have been used for over 2,000 years. A mirror changes the direction of a beam of light by reflecting the light from a shiny metal surface.

Magnification

The lens is the main device used in optical instruments. It changes the direction of a light beam by bending or refracting the

Right
A single-lens reflex camera. One lens system is used both for viewing and focusing. The photographer views the subject through the viewfinder. This is linked optically to the lens system by a pentaprism and a mirror. The mirror is hinged so that when the shutter is opened to expose the film, the mirror lifts up.

Far right
A compound lens. The parts of the lens are set in a precision-made mounting which will rotate but will not let in the light.

Right
A simple refracting telescope with a converging objective lens and diverging complex lens for the eyepiece.

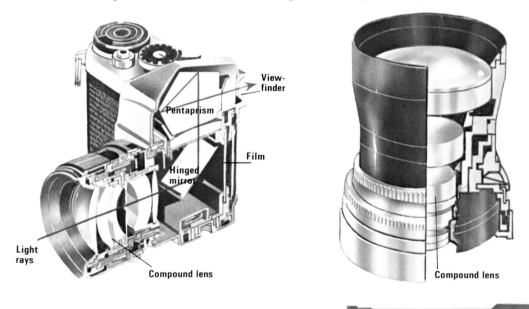

View-finder

Pentaprism

Film

Hinged mirror

Light rays

Compound lens

Compound lens

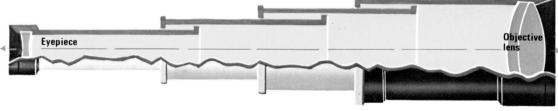

Eyepiece

Objective lens

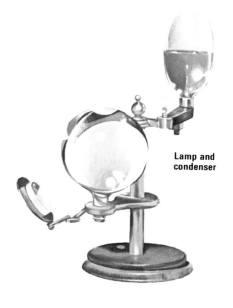

Lamp and condenser

Right
To make a miscroscope, cut an oval-shaped piece of card like a monocle. Cut a hole, cover it with tin foil and make a pinhole in it. Smear a little grease around the pinhole and cover it with a water droplet. Place the card over your eye. Shine a strong light on a small object such as a hair. Hold you microscope close to it until you see a clear magnified image.

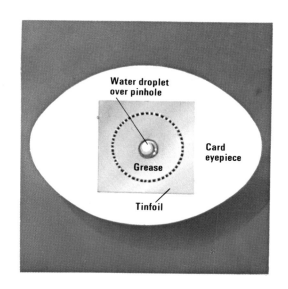

Water droplet over pinhole

Card eyepiece

Grease

Tinfoil

rays as they pass through it. When lenses are in certain positions they can produce a larger or magnified image of the object. The magnification of an optical instrument is equal to the image size divided by the object size. A magnifying glass, consisting of a single convex lens, forms an image several times larger than the object.

The magnification of an instrument can be greatly increased by using more than one lens. Both the simple telescope (page 102) and the microscope (page 100) use two convex lenses separated by a set distance, enabling them to form a greatly enlarged image of the object. Other lenses are used in the instrument to improve the quality of the image.

The camera is a different type of optical instrument. It produces a permanent image of an object or scene by focusing light from the object on to a photographic film. One or more lenses are used for this and the lens system can be extremely complicated.

Polarized light

Some optical instruments contain an important substance called a polarizer. Light normally vibrates in all directions perpendicular to the direction of travel. It is said to be unpolarized. Polarized light contains vibrations in only one direction. A polarizer transmits polarized light. This cuts down glare from scattered or reflected light. Polarizers are used in sunglasses, filters for cameras, and many other optical instruments.

Right
Prisms are used in some optical instruments, such as the periscope. In this, the prisms act as mirrors. They reflect the light through 90° by means of total internal reflection. There is also a system of lenses in a nautical periscope, to magnify and focus the image.

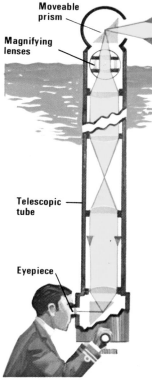

Moveable prism

Magnifying lenses

Telescopic tube

Eyepiece

Left
Polarizing sunglasses cut down glare from scattered or reflected light. The lenses are made from a substance that transmits light which vibrates in only one direction. Unpolarized light normally contains vibrations in all directions.

MICROSCOPES

Some objects are so small that they cannot be seen clearly by eye. A microscope is used to form an enlarged picture or image of the object. The magnification of a microscope is the size of the image divided by that of the object. If the magnification is × 100, the image is 100 times larger than the object.

An optical microscope uses glass lenses to produce the enlarged image. The simplest type is a magnifying glass. This is a converging or convex lens which bulges out in the centre. It is held a short distance above the object and moved towards the eye until the image can be clearly seen. The image is now in focus.

A microscope used in a scientific laboratory is more complicated. It contains a number of different lenses. Only two are used in the actual magnification. The tiny object or specimen is placed on a thin glass plate and strongly lit from below. The convex lens just above the object is called the objective. It produces a magnified image in the same way as the simple magnifying glass. This image is formed between the objective and the second convex lens, called the eyepiece. The eyepiece magnifies the first image even more. The total magnification of the instrument is the magnification of the objective multiplied by that of the eyepiece. The final image can be over 1,000 times the size of the object. Tiny details of

Above
A magnifying glass. It is useful for looking at small objects such as stamps, insects, and small print in books.

Right
A compound microscope with a multiple nosepiece. Three different objective lenses can be interchanged by swinging the nosepiece round. This provides different magnifications. The cutaway objective lens system shown on the right gives a magnification of × 100. The cutaway Huygenian eyepiece shown above it is composed of two lenses. Eyepieces usually have a magnification of about × 5 or × 10. The total magnification of a compound microscope is found by multiplying together the magnifications of the eyepiece and the objective.

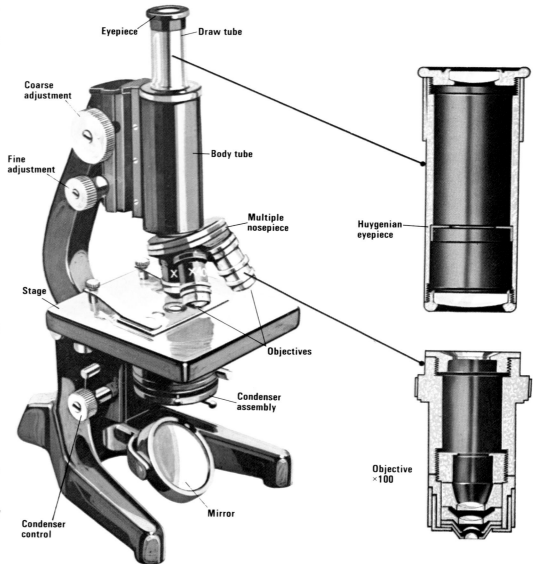

objects such as parts of plants, creatures in pond water, or hairs can be seen.

Limit of magnification

It is not possible to go on increasing the magnification of an instrument simply by improving its optical system. This is because there is a limit to the magnification set by the laws of physics. To view an object under a light microscope it must be illuminated by a beam of light. The magnification limit is determined by the wavelength of the light (see page 162). Since the wavelength is a fixed quantity, the maximum magnification of a light microscope or telescope is also fixed. So, to view very tiny objects, an electron microscope is used (see page 166). This uses a beam of tiny particles called electrons, instead of a beam of light.

Abbe condenser

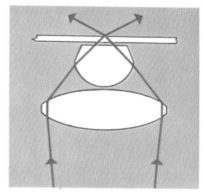

Mirror

Right
The condenser contains lenses held within a frame which can be moved up and down beneath the microscope stage. The Abbe condenser (top) has only two lenses but the one at the bottom has more and is called an achromatic condenser. The mirror (centre) has a concave side, but the flat side is used with artificial light.

Achromatic condenser

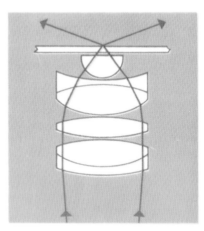

Below
A flea illuminated for viewing. Proper illumination through a microscope requires a lamp to be 20 cm away and light to be reflected into the microscope. The image is then centred and the iris is opened so the field of view fills with light.

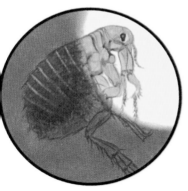

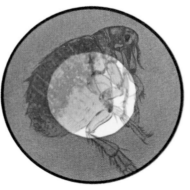

Galileo

REFRACTING TELESCOPES

Telescopes are optical instruments used for observing distant objects. It is believed that the first telescope was made by Hans Lippershey in Holland, in 1608. He was a spectacle maker. Whilst examining a pair of lenses, one behind the other, he accidentally discovered that objects appeared closer. By 1610, an Italian named Galileo had made a much improved telescope, called a Galilean telescope. It had a magnification of 33 times. Many improvements by other scientists and astronomers gradually followed.

Telescopes that use lenses to collect light are called refracting telescopes. The light is bent by refraction through the lenses.

Galileo used his telescope for making astronomical observations. He was able to discover the moons of the planet Jupiter.

not really matter in astronomy and these telescopes were used for many investigations of planets and stars.

Astronomical telescopes

Refracting telescopes are often called astronomical telescopes. The largest one in existence is the Yerkes telescope in Wisconsin, USA. It is over 18 metres long and the objective lens has a diameter of 1 metre (40 inches).

The early refracting telescopes had the disadvantage that their images had coloured fringes around them. This is because a lens focuses light of different colours at slightly different positions, so it breaks up the different colours that make up white light into coloured fringes. This is called chromatic aberration. It is possible to make lenses that do not have this defect. They are used in all modern refracting telescopes, and are called achromatic lenses.

Terrestrial telescopes

Telescopes with two convex lenses are unsuitable for land viewing because they give an inverted image. If a third convex lens is placed in the tube of the telescope, the final image is upright. It can then be used for land viewing and is known as a terrestrial telescope.

Galileo's telescope was used for astronomical work. It can also be a terrestrial telescope because it gives an upright image.

Lippershey, who invented the telescope, is also said to have invented the first binocular telescope in 1608. Unfortunately the idea of using an instrument with both eyes caused little interest.

In 1823 the binocular telescope was re-invented by another Dutchman called J. Voigtlaender. Opera glasses and inexpensive field glasses consist of two telescopes, of the Galilean type. Their magnification is only small. More powerful binoculars use convex lenses for both object lenses and eyepieces. Prisms turn the image the right way up.

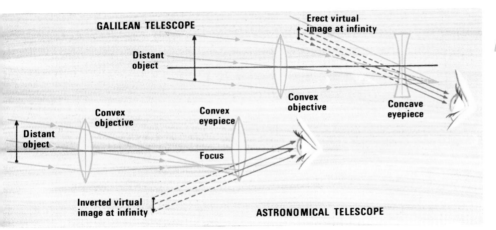

GALILEAN TELESCOPE — Distant object — Convex objective — Convex eyepiece — Focus — Erect virtual image at infinity — Convex objective — Concave eyepiece — Distant object — Inverted virtual image at infinity — ASTRONOMICAL TELESCOPE

Kepler

He also observed that there are hills and valleys on the moon. Galileo's telescope had two lenses. There was a convex lens at the front called the object lens or objective. The other lens is called the eye lens or eyepiece. This was a concave lens in Galileo's telescope. With this lens arrangement the image and object are the same way up.

Later telescopes used two convex lenses. The object lens brings the light to a focus between the two lenses. Another convex lens, the eyepiece, magnifies this image to produce a larger image seen by the eye.

The image formed by this type of telescope is upside down or inverted. This does

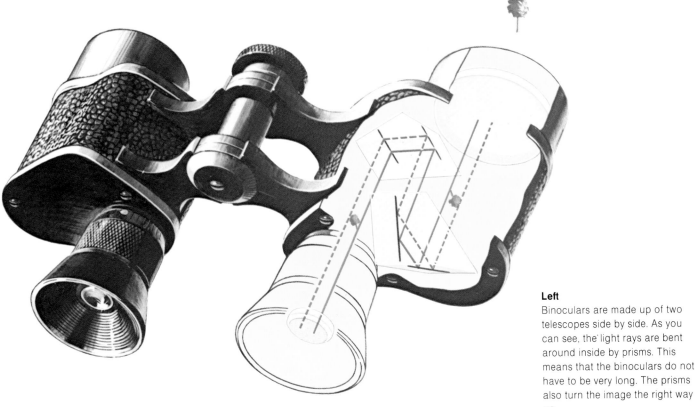

Left
Binoculars are made up of two telescopes side by side. As you can see, the light rays are bent around inside by prisms. This means that the binoculars do not have to be very long. The prisms also turn the image the right way up.

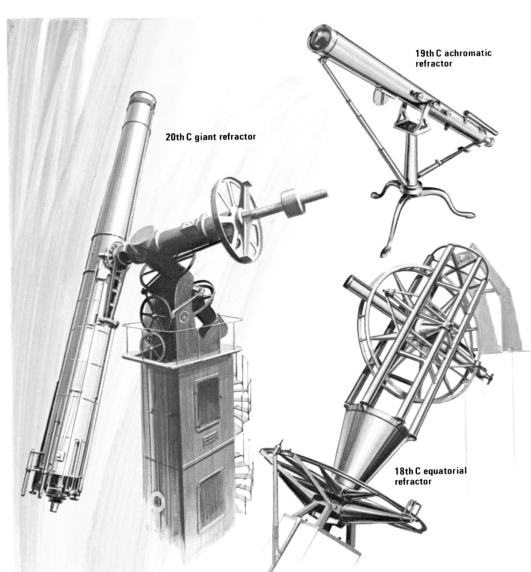

19th C achromatic refractor

20th C giant refractor

18th C equatorial refractor

Left
An eighteenth century equatorial refractor with a 4.2 inch objective, made for the Shuckburgh observatory. A nineteenth century achromatic refractor with a 3.25 inch objective composed of two lenses. A giant refractor of the twentieth century with a 26 inch object lens. This telescope is at the Naval Observatory in Washington USA.

REFLECTING TELESCOPES

The early refracting telescopes did not give clear, sharp images. This was because it was difficult to make good lenses. In 1668, Sir Isaac Newton invented a reflecting telescope. This telescope had no object lens at all. The light came down an open tube to fall on to a curved mirror at the bottom. The mirror reflected the light back up the tube on to a second flat mirror placed at an angle. This directed the rays to the side of the tube on to the magnifying convex lens of the eyepiece. Newton's telescope produced clearer images free from chromatic aberration.

The world's largest telescopes are of the reflecting type because mirrors can give very sharp images free from colour fringes. Also, it is much easier to make large mirrors than large lenses.

Most of the objects studied by astronomers are extremely distant and faint. They can be seen only in telescopes which collect a lot of light. Large modern reflecting telescopes gather enormous amounts of light and reveal fine detail. Large numbers of very faint, very distant stars can be seen.

Cameras are often fitted to these telescopes. With long exposures, they can gather a tremendous amount of extra information about stars and galaxies. No telescope yet built is able to show a star as anything more than a dot of light. Telescopes, however, can still tell us much about the stars. They can show the different star colours. Double and quadruple stars (groups of two or four stars close together) can be seen.

Photographing galaxies

Galaxies or star systems have thousands of millions of stars in them. Outside our own galaxy there are over 1,000 million other separate galaxies. Only three can be seen with the naked eye.

Many galaxies have been photographed using telescopes. Astronomers can only learn a limited amount about the stars with visual telescopes. Other instruments have been developed which can tell us much more about the make-up of the stars. One of these instruments is the spectroscope (see page 83).

A large reflecting telescope is found in nearly every major observatory. Throughout the world there are over 300 observatories. They are built far from the bright lights of cities, often in areas which are usually fine and clear.

One of the largest reflecting telescopes in the world is at Mount Palomar Observatory, California, USA. There, the climate and atmosphere enable the telescope to be used, on average, 300 days every year. The concave mirror is made of glass, coated with a thin layer of aluminium to give it high reflecting power. It is 200 inches in diameter and the telescope can be used in Newtonian or Cassegrain form.

Right
In Newton's telescope a large concave mirror is used. This has a parabolic shape. It brings parallel beams of light to a point. A small plane mirror is used to reflect the light out of the telescope through an eyepiece. Usually photographs are taken with an attached camera.

Far right
A later instrument is the Cassegrainian telescope. The light is first collected with the large concave mirror. It is then reflected back through a hole by a small convex mirror.

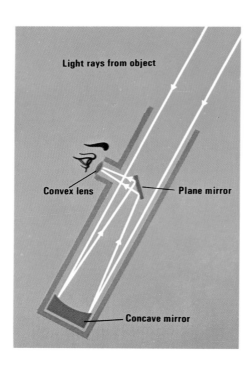

Light rays from object

Convex lens — Plane mirror

Concave mirror

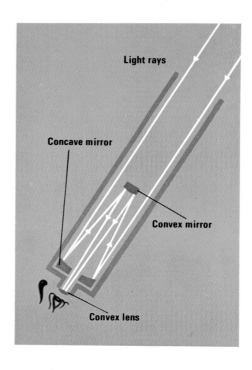

Light rays

Concave mirror

Convex mirror

Convex lens

One of the largest telescopes is on Mount Palomar in California. It is housed in this observatory. The dome weighs 1,000 tonnes. It has a shutter through which the telescope points at the sky. The dome can be revolved so that the telescope can point in different directions.

Above

Tycho Brahe (1546–1601) was a Danish astronomer. He set up magnificently equipped observatories at Uraniborg and Stjerneborg near Copenhagen. His most famous work was his accurate observations of the planets. This provided information used by Kepler when he worked out the laws of motion of the planets.

Right

This is the Hale telescope inside the dome at Mount Palomar. The concave mirror is 200 inches in diameter. It is mounted on the bottom end of the steel framework tube. The astronomer sits in a small cage at the top end to make observations.

Above

Joseph Niépce (1765–1833) produced the first photograph (a very blurred one) in about 1826. He worked for many years with Louis Daguerre (1787–1851) improving his methods of processing film. Daguerre continued after Niépce's death. Fox Talbot (1800–1877) worked on a different process and was producing small negatives in 1835.

Above right

Film development using a lightproof tank. In total darkness the film is fed into the spiral groove of the reel by turning the top. The reel is put inside the tank. The chemicals are poured in and out, first developer, then water, and then fixer. After washing in water for about 45 minutes, the film is taken out and dried.

Right

An enlarger. This instrument contains a glass convex lens acting as a magnifying glass (see page 100). The negative is placed above this lens and illuminated by a flash of light from above. An enlarged image of the negative is formed on the photographic paper placed beneath it.

Far right

The negative and final photo of a subject taken with black-and-white film.

PHOTOGRAPHY

A camera focuses light from a scene or subject on to photographic film. This contains chemicals which change colour when light falls on them, that is they are light-sensitive. Light makes certain silver compounds turn black (after they are treated with the right chemicals). These compounds, in particular silver bromide, are used in the manufacture of photographic film.

There are many types of film and they all have at least one light-sensitive layer. This layer is called the emulsion. In black-and-white film, a thin layer of emulsion is coated on to a plastic or glass base. It contains tiny silver bromide crystals in a jelly-like substance called gelatin.

When the camera's shutter is opened light from the subject is focused by the lens on to the emulsion. The light from different parts of the subject activates the silver bromide crystals by varying amounts; the stronger the light, the greater the reaction. An image of the subject is formed in the emulsion, but until the film is developed it cannot be seen. It is called a latent image.

Developing a film

To make this image visible, the film has to be treated with certain chemicals. This is done in a dark room to prevent any more light falling on the emulsion. The film is placed for a certain length of time, at about 20°C, in a dish or tank containing developer. The developer turns the light-activated crystals to grey or black metallic silver. The shade of grey or black depends

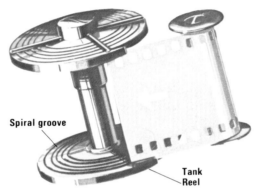

Spiral groove

Tank Reel

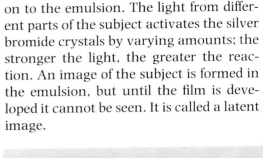

Screw top

Chemicals can be poured in through a special hole in the lid; no light reaches the film

Lightproof tank

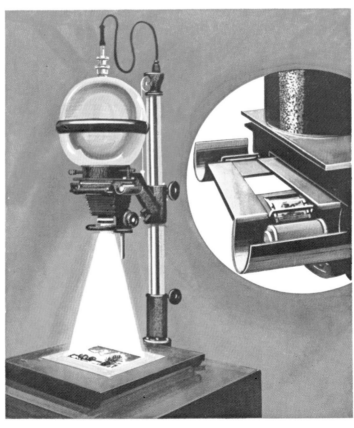

Negative print

Positive print

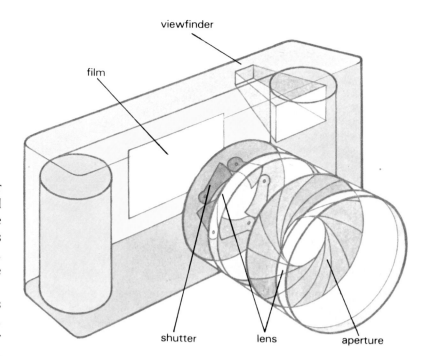

film / viewfinder / shutter / lens / aperture

on how much light fell on a particular area of the film. In this image light and dark are reversed. Dark shadows on the original subject appear clear (the film is transparent) while bright spots are black. The individual pictures on the film are therefore called negatives of the subject.

After washing the film in water, it is immersed in another chemical called fixer. This dissolves away the unactivated silver bromide and makes the image stay in position. The film is then washed and dried.

Making a photographic print

To obtain a photograph from the negative, it is placed against a special photographic paper. This paper contains a layer of light-sensitive crystals. The paper and negative are exposed to a brief flash of light. The dark areas of the negative let only a little light through on to the paper. The clear parts allow much more light through.

The photographic paper is then developed and fixed in the same way as the film. The image produced on the paper is white in areas that are dark in the negative, and vice versa. It is therefore identical to the subject that was originally photographed.

Films are now much smaller than they used to be. If the negative is placed in contact with the paper, a rather small photograph, the same size as the negative, is obtained. An enlarger is used to produce a larger photograph, or to enlarge one part of a photograph.

A Polaroid camera uses a special type of film. This Polaroid film is developed by a process inside the camera. Black-and-white photographs are obtained about 10 seconds after the picture is taken.

Colour photographs are made using film with three layers of emulsion. Film can also be made sensitive to X-rays (see page 164).

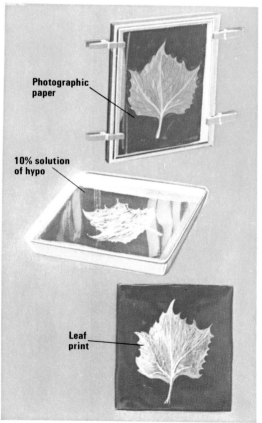

Photographic paper

10% solution of hypo

Leaf print

Above

An infrared photo, taken from the air, of some trees without leaves. These appear blue whereas healthy trees are purplish red. Film can be made sensitive to invisible infrared radiation. All warm things give off or reflect different amounts of infrared. The amount determines the colour. Grass and leaves reflect it strongly, so faraway objects show up easily on these photographs.

Left

You can make a type of photograph without using a camera. Get a piece of slow photographic printing paper. Place something flat, like a leaf, on the sensitive side of the paper and press it between a board and sheet of glass. Leave it in the sun until the paper turns dark violet. Take out the paper and you will have a pale print of the leaf. The thick veins will show up white because they let the least amount of light through. You can fix the print using hypo solution.

LASERS

The laser is a device that produces a very thin bright beam of light. The word laser stands for 'Light Amplification by Stimulated Emission of Radiation'. The name shows that a laser persuades, or stimulates, its atoms to amplify, or make stronger, a flash of light.

The first laser

The first laser was made in 1960 by an American, Theodore Maiman. He used a small rod of crystalline ruby with a powerful flash tube wrapped around it. At each end of the ruby rod was a mirror. One of the mirrors had a small hole in the centre. To work the laser, the flash tube was turned on, bathing the ruby in light. The atoms in the ruby absorbed the light. After a short time, however, the atoms could no longer hold the light and they released it as a pulse of light. All the atoms released light waves which were in step. The pulse escaped through the hole in one of the mirrors to form a narrow beam.

When all the light waves in a beam are in step, it is called a coherent beam. Such a beam does not spread out like ordinary light. So it can travel very long distances and be directed very accurately. The beam can also be very powerful. Ruby lasers are still used, but new types have been invented that use gases, such as carbon

dioxide and helium, or liquids instead of ruby. Different lasers produce beams of different power. A high-power laser can cut through the hardest substances, such as diamonds. Lasers are used in the home, factory, and hospital. A compact disc player contains a low-power laser. The laser beam reads the music on the disc, in place of the stylus on an ordinary record player. Small pits in the disc reflect the laser beam into a light-sensitive detector. This produces the music from the pattern of light reflected from the disc. Lasers are used in a similar way in video disc players.

Surgeons use lasers to carry out delicate eye operations, engineers use them to measure distances very accurately. A laser has been used to measure the distance to the moon. They are used in fibre optic communications systems, in which light beams are sent along thin fibres of glass to carry telephone conversations.

Holograms

One important application of lasers is to produce holograms. A hologram is a three-dimensional image produced using laser light. If you move your head slightly when looking at a hologram, you see the scene in the hologram from a slightly different angle. To produce a hologram, laser light is shone on the object being photographed. The light is reflected off the

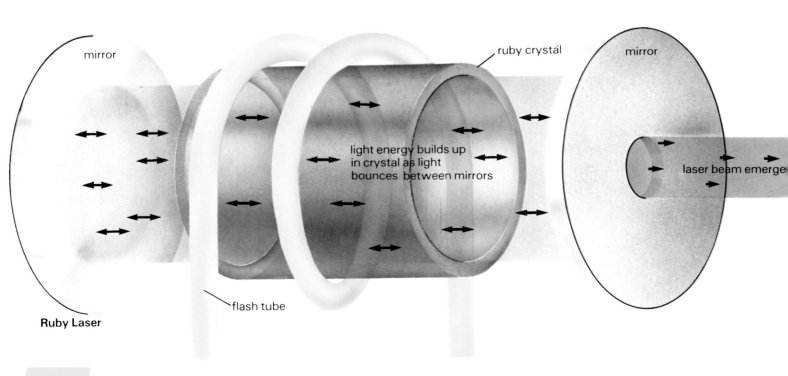

mirror

ruby crystal

mirror

light energy builds up in crystal as light bounces between mirrors

laser beam emerge

flash tube

Ruby Laser

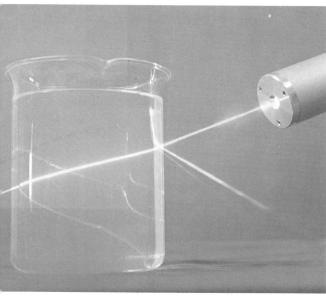

object on to a photographic plate. At the same time, light from the laser is shone straight on to the photographic plate. The two beams of light reaching the plate produce a pattern, called an interference pattern. Later, if light is shone on to the plate, the pattern becomes the three-dimensional picture.

Holograms are printed on credit cards because they are hard to forge. In the future, they may be used on identity cards. Doctors may use them to see how bones are knitting, or to plan operations more easily.

Above

The elastic band will make a twanging sound if pulled and then let go. This is caused by the elastic hitting against the air molecules as it vibrates rapidly back and forth.

Right

If an electric bell is put inside a jar and all the air is pumped out, no sound will be heard. The hammer can be seen to vibrate rapidly making the bell ring, but because there is no air the sound will not travel.

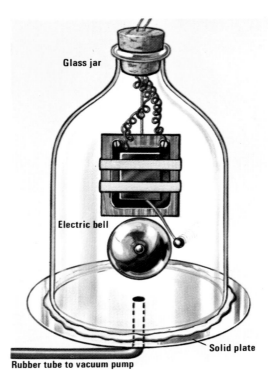

Glass jar

Electric bell

Solid plate

Rubber tube to vacuum pump

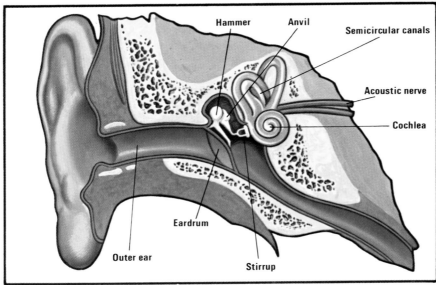

Hammer Anvil

Semicircular canals

Acoustic nerve

Cochlea

Eardrum

Outer ear

Stirrup

Above

The ear has three parts, the outer, middle and inner ear. In the middle ear, vibrations of the ear drum move three tiny bones. These are named from their shapes, the hammer, anvil, and stirrup. They carry sound to the cochlea in the inner ear.

Right

A drum is a percussion instrument. It consists of a piece of skin, parchment, plastic, or nylon stretched tightly over a wooden or metal frame. The bass drum is the largest orchestral and military drum. The diameter is much greater than the depth. Usually it is played with a felt-headed stick.

Bass drum

Toy drum

Sound

Sound is always made by some kind of movement. For example, hitting your hand against a table or plucking a guitar string produces sound. There are many different kinds of sounds, and they can be pleasant or unpleasant. Music has rhythm and is usually pleasant to hear. You might like pop music, but others may think it is noisy. Noise is any sound that is unpleasant to a person. It is not usually as rhythmic as music.

When something vibrates it produces a sound. Vibrations are movements to and fro. The energy or strength of the vibrations is passed on to the tiny molecules in the surrounding air and makes them move. The stronger the vibrations, the louder the sounds. To make the molecules move requires energy. The further a sound travels the more molecules are moved. The energy of the vibrations is therefore slowly used up and the sound becomes quieter. This is called attenuation of sound.

Sound waves

The vibrations moving through the air are called sound waves. You cannot see them, but they would look similar to the movement of corn in the wind. The corn stalks are blown over slightly. As they vibrate to and fro, wave movements are seen to travel across the field although each corn stalk moves only a short distance.

Sound waves move the molecules of air against each other. Each molecule bumps its neighbour, which in turn bumps its neighbour. The molecules crowd together and then move back again. This crowding together causes a slight increase in pressure. As the molecules move apart the pressure drops. A sound wave therefore produces a change in pressure as it travels through the air. If there were no air, as in outer space, sound would not travel and nothing could be heard.

It is only when the sound wave falls on the ear that a sound is heard. The flap of the outer ear is a funnel to collect the sound waves. These pass along a short tube to the ear drum. The sound waves make the drum vibrate, causing tiny bones in contact with it to vibrate. These carry the sound to the inner ear. Here the vibrations are converted, by a shell-shaped organ called the cochlea, into electrical messages. These are carried by nerves to the brain.

Producing musical notes

There are many way of producing a musical note. Percussion instruments are played by striking a surface in a particular manner. The surface of a bell is struck by a heavy clapper. The oldest bell in the world, found near Babylon, is over 3,000 years old. The largest is the Tsar Kolokol (King of Bells) in the Kremlin, Moscow. Cast in 1734 it weighs 220 tons and stands on the ground where it fell whilst being hung. The earliest English bell, 1296, is at Claughton, Lancashire. The largest is Great Paul, weighing 17 tons and hanging in St. Paul's Cathedral, London. Big Ben (London) and Great Tom (Oxford) are two other famous English bells. The most famous bell in the US is the Liberty Bell (Philadelphia).

Above
Alarm clocks can be mechanical (wind up) or electrical. This one has bells on top, but usually they are inside. The hammer between the bells starts to vibrate against the bells at the set time.

Left
Different types of bell. When the lever on a bicycle bell is pressed a metal propeller revolves inside the bell, hitting the sides and making them ring. A hand bell is rung by swinging it so that the hammer inside hits the metal. In an electric bell an electric current makes the hammer vibrate. Two famous bells are the Babylonian bell, which is the oldest bell in the world, and the Liberty Bell, rung on the signing of the Declaration of Independence, 1776, in America.

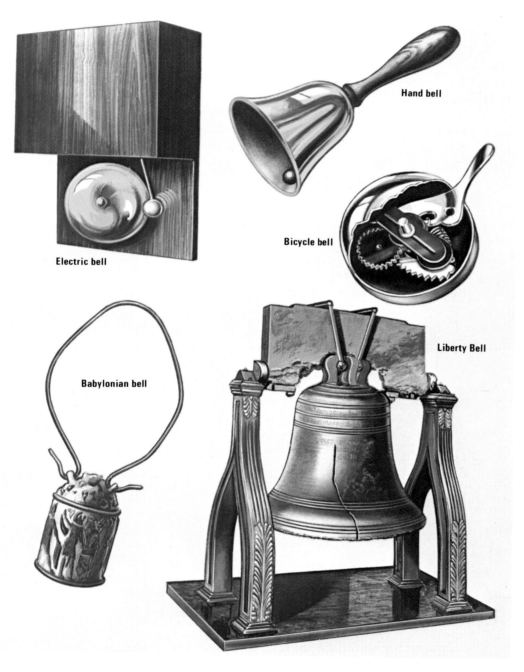

Hand bell

Electric bell

Bicycle bell

Babylonian bell

Liberty Bell

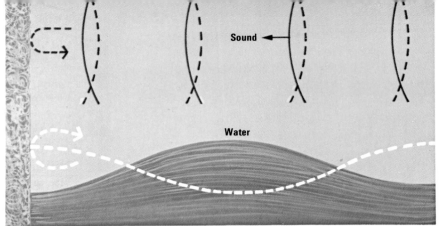

obstacles or prey are.

Echoes are useful to fishermen for detecting shoals of fish. Geologists use them to find minerals beneath the earth's surface.

Acoustics is the study of sound as it travels. It is especially concerned with the way sound travels in cinemas, concert halls, classrooms, and any place where sounds must be clearly heard by an audience.

Reverberation

In a large room with wide hard unbroken walls, the sound echoes off the walls. The audience hears a jumble of noises making it impossible for even the slowest, clearest speaker to be understood. This is called reverberation. It can be reduced by padding the walls, hanging curtains, and using padded seats. These absorb some of the sound and the echoes become less loud. There are fewer echoes in a full hall because people also absorb the sound.

The shape of a hall is specially designed so that, if possible, every sound can be heard clearly by everyone there. Some of the sound is heard directly; the rest is

Above
The sound wave of an echo bounces back by reflection, much like water waves bouncing from a wall.

ECHOES AND ACOUSTICS

An echo occurs when sound waves hit a barrier like a cliff, hill, or high wall. The waves bounce off and the sound is heard again. This is called a reflected sound. The time between the sound and its echo is the time taken by the sound wave to hit the barrier and return to the listener. The sound wave loses energy as it travels so the echo is fainter than the original sound.

Whales, porpoises, bats, and some other living creatures can navigate and also locate their prey by using echoes. They emit a stream of sounds in all directions. The path of returning echoes shows where

Right
A cutaway view of an oil deposit in the earth. An underground explosion directs sounds downwards. Oil reflects a certain pattern of echoes, which are recorded by a sensitive instrument called a seismograph. The geologist can therefore locate the oil and find the best place to sink a well.

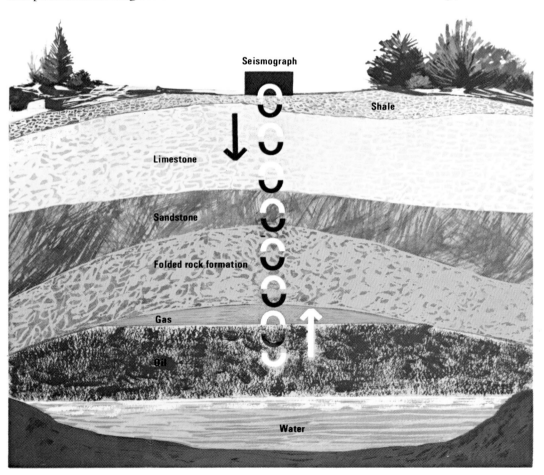

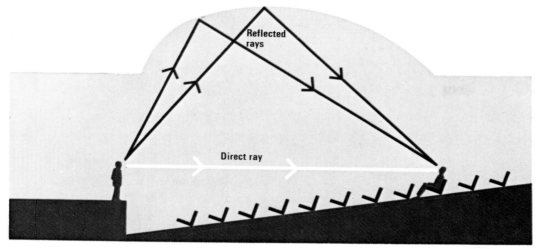

Left
Acoustics of a domed hall. The clearest speech is heard when there is a time lag of 1/20th of a second between the reflected rays and the direct rays. The reflected rays then travel 20 metres more than the direct rays. For music, the time lag should be $\frac{1}{15}$th of a second, with a path difference of 27 metres.

reflected off the walls and ceiling. The distances travelled by these two sets of waves are carefully worked out to make the sound clear.

Sound must travel through a medium, such as air. The molecules of the medium carry the vibrations from the source of sound to the listener's ears. Liquids and solids transmit sound even better than air.

Sound waves travel at a speed that depends on the medium. They travel faster in a denser medium such as water or glass, than in air. The speed of sound in air can be measured by placing an explosive charge 1 km from some measuring instruments and then exploding it. The flash of light is recorded by one instrument. A few seconds later a second instrument records the noise of the explosion. Sound does not travel nearly as fast as light. The time between the flash and the noise is found to be three seconds. This is the time taken for sound to travel 1 km through air.

In a thunderstorm, lightning is always seen before the clap of thunder is heard. This is because light travels so much faster than sound. Count the number of seconds between the lightning flash and the first sound of thunder and divide the answer by three. This gives the distance, in kilometres, of the lightning.

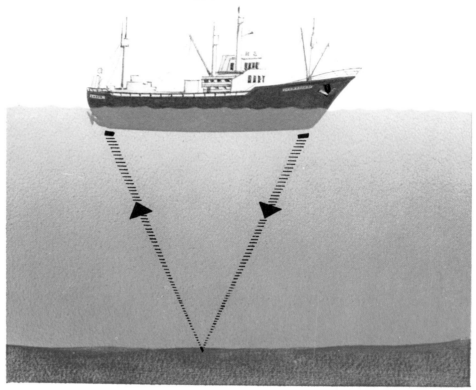

Above
The ocean depth can be found by measuring the time between sending out a sound signal and receiving the echo reflected from the ocean bed. Half this time, multiplied by the speed of sound in sea water, gives the depth. Many readings can be taken in a short time.

Left
The Whispering Gallery of St Paul's Cathedral, London. If someone whispers up against the wall in one part of the gallery, the sound is reflected around the wall and can be heard on the other side of the gallery.

SOUNDS FUN!

RING TIN-TIN

You will need: 2 tin cans ● twine ● hammer ● nail ● a friend

When you speak to a friend, a pattern of sound waves leaves your mouth. These waves are vibrations, or movements back and forth, of the air. When they reach you friend's ears, they make his or her eardrums vibrate. And your friend hears what you said. If you speak quietly, your voice won't carry very far. So you'll need a phone.

Here is one you can make from a pair of tin cans and some thick twine. Use tins that had a lid, and that were not opened with a tin opener, otherwise they will have jagged edges. Using a hammer and nail, make a hole in the bottom of each tin. Thread the twine through the holes and tie a knot each end to prevent the twine pulling out.

Your phone is now ready. Give one tin to a friend and walk away from each other until the twine is stretched tight. Motion your friend to speak quietly into his or her tin, while you put yours to your ear. You should be able to hear what he or she is saying quite clearly. The stretched twine carries the vibrations of your friend's voice from his or her tin to yours. Solid things like twine conduct, or pass on, sound waves better than the air does. This is why you voice carries further when you use your phone.

don't use tins with jagged edges

thick twine

SOUNDS BETTER

You will need: a watch ● a wooden table

How good is your hearing? Can you hear a watch ticking when it's a metre or more away? Almost certainly you can't if you listen in the ordinary way, with your ears separated from the watch by air. Air doesn't conduct (pass on) sound waves very well.

Now, place the watch on one end of a table, and hold your ear to the other end. You will then be able to hear the watch ticking very clearly. This shows that wood is a very much better conductor of sound than air.

Metals are better still. If you want to send messages around the house, you can do so by tapping on the water pipes.

MAKE A GUITAR

You will need: shoebox ● elastic bands ● tacks ● wood

An old cardboard shoebox and a few elastic bands are all you need to make a working guitar! Cut a hole in the lid of the box. Choose some bands of different thicknesses and tack them to the box as shown. Slot a wedge of wood in under the bands. Now play away.The vibrations of the bands set the air inside the box vibrating. The strings and the air are then in resonance. This makes the sounds louder and richer than those of the bands alone.

The pitch of a note is how high or low it sounds. Pitch depends on the number of vibrations made by a band each second. The more vibrations per second of a string, the higher the pitch.

You will find that plucking a thin band produces a higher sound than plucking a thick band. Tightening a band makes it thinner and so increases its pitch. Pluck the tight string and notice the pitch. Place a finger firmly in the middle of the band, pluck it, and again notice the pitch. As the plucked string gets shorter, the pitch gets higher.

If you pluck very hard on your guitar bands they will make louder notes than if you pluck gently. You may be able to sing a note in the same pitch as a train whistle but you cannot sing as loudly. The loudness of a sound depends on the amount of energy that goes into making the sound. So, by plucking hard on the guitar you put in more energy and obtain louder notes.

SPEEDY WAVES

Sound waves travel quite slowly in air – at a speed of about 1,200 kph (760 mph). In a metal such as steel they travel at an astonishing 24,000 kph (15,000 mph)! Water is also a good sound conductor. That is why ships and submarines use sound waves to communicate underwater.

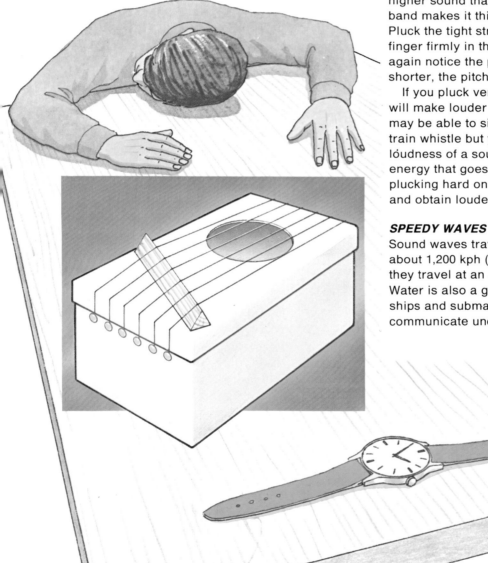

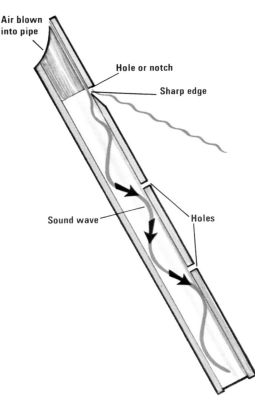

Air blown into pipe

Hole or notch

Sharp edge

Sound wave

Holes

Right

A pipe contains a sharp edge against which the air is blown. The edge causes air to move to either side of it. Sound waves are created in the air outside the pipe and in the air column inside the pipe. These waves produce the musical note.

Below

A diagram of a wave. Where the lines cross, the molecules are at rest; this is called a node (N). Where the lines are widest apart the molecules are vibrating most and have their greatest energy; this is called an antinode (A). The wavelength of a wave is the distance between nodes or between antinodes.

Bottom right

Waves in open and closed pipes. The fundamental note has the longest wavelength and thus the lowest pitch or frequency. The frequency of the overtones are all whole number multiples of the frequency of the fundamental.

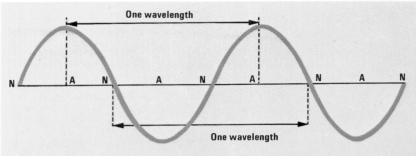

One wavelength

N A N A N A N A N

One wavelength

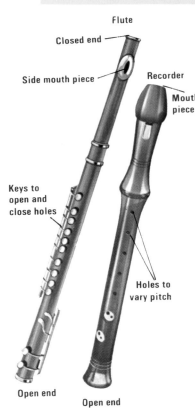

Flute

Closed end

Side mouth piece

Recorder

Mouth piece

Keys to open and close holes

Holes to vary pitch

Open end

Open end

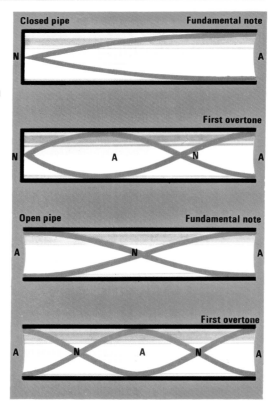

Closed pipe — Fundamental note

First overtone

Open pipe — Fundamental note

First overtone

PIPES

Wind instruments that are called pipes are the trombone, trumpet, bugle, tuba, flute, piccolo, clarinet and saxophone. When you blow into one, the column of air inside vibrates, producing a note.

Air can be made to vibrate as it is blown into the pipe by making it move past a sharp edge. This edge causes eddies or waves in the air column. If you could see them, they would look like the waves on a flag flapping in the wind.

The frequency (number of vibrations each second) of the vibrations depends on the length of the air column inside the pipe.

The shorter the air column, the higher the frequency, or pitch, of the note produced. By opening or closing holes at different places on the tube, the length of the vibrating air column is altered which changes the pitch.

Pipes are called open pipes if both ends are open and closed pipes if one end is closed off. An open pipe and a closed pipe of the same length have different tones. In an open pipe the frequency, and therefore the pitch, is twice that of a closed pipe of the same size. This is because the waves have a different shape in the two pipes. At an open end the molecules of air have their largest vibrations. At a closed end they do not vibrate at all.

The waves inside the pipes can have different wavelengths – as long as there is a node (no vibrations) at a closed end and an antinode (greatest number of vibrations) at an open end. As the wavelength gets shorter, the frequency or pitch of the note gets higher. This means that when you blow down a pipe, you produce a main note, called the fundamental, and other fainter notes of higher pitch. These are called overtones. The overtones give an instrument its characteristic sound.

The organ is the largest of all musical instruments. It covers the widest frequency range, and has the greatest variety of tone. Air is blown into the many pipes, either by hand bellows or now mainly by motor-driven fans. The long, wide organ pipes make low-pitched sounds and the short narrow pipes make high-pitched sounds.

Far bottom left
The recorder, first made in the sixteenth century, can be up to four metres long. It is played by blowing down the mouthpiece; different notes are produced by opening and closing holes down its length. The flute is a side-blown wind instrument, closed at one end. The holes are opened or closed mainly by keys operated by the fingers. It produces a very pure clear note.

Right
The organ. One picture shows an Ancient Roman organ, dating back to the fourth century. The other picture shows a modern organ, built in 1959, at Valparaiso University, USA.

MAKE A PIPE

You can make a simple pipe from bamboo and soft wood. Cut a notch in the hollow bamboo. Carve a short cylinder of wood and shave off one side to make it flat. Then push it into the bamboo pipe in front of the notch. It should fit tightly. Cut a curved block from the end of the bamboo and cylinder to make a mouthpiece. Carve another long cylinder of soft wood which will fit loosely into the open end of the pipe. Glue this cylinder to a pencil.

Blow into the mouthpiece of the pipe near the notch and you will hear a whistle. The air is hitting the edge of the notch and causing the column of air in the pipe to vibrate. By pushing the cylinder on the pencil in and out of the pipe while you blow, you can produce different notes. This is because you are changing the length of the column of air inside the pipe.

MAKE A BOTTLE ORGAN

Fill eight bottles of the same type with different amounts of water. Blow across each bottle in turn. The more water in the bottle the higher the note it produces. With the right amount of water in each bottle you can play a musical scale. You can use a vacuum cleaner hose to blow air across their tops.

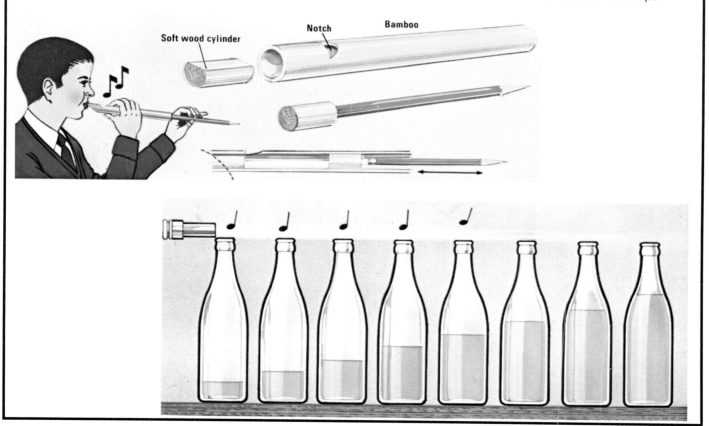

Soft wood cylinder   Notch   Bamboo

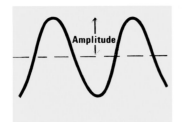

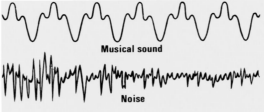

Musical sound

Noise

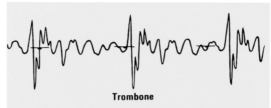

Trombone

Violin

Saxophone

Clarinet

MUSICAL SOUNDS

Any sound that we consider pleasant to hear is said to be musical. Music is the sound made by an orchestra, a musical instrument, a singer or a choir.

The ancient Greeks were the first people to study music scientifically. They put together a series of musical sounds in ascending (higher) and descending (lower) pitch to make a scale.

Musical instruments

Musical instruments can be put into four main sections: strings, percussion, wind, and electronic instruments. The different designs and shapes of the instruments and the different materials from which they are made causes them to have different sounds. A violin made of thick, good-quality wood will make different sounds from a similar looking violin of thinner or poor quality wood.

Two other important factors are an instrument's size and the musician's skill.

In good music, only the desired vibrations are heard. If the vibration has the right pitch and amplitude (loudness), a musician should be able to recognise which note is being played, for example the note "A" of the musical scale.

Notes and scales

Each musical note has a definite pitch or frequency that is the same for every instrument. It is called the fundamental frequency. The note A on a piano has the same fundamental frequency as that note played on a guitar or a flute. It is produced by 440 vibrations of the string or air column in one second.

No musical instrument produces a perfectly pure note of one frequency. Instead it produces a number of fainter overtones at the same time as the fundamental frequency (see page 116). These overtones can have two, three, four, five, six times the frequency of the fundamental. Different instruments produce different amounts of some or all of these overtones. This is why each instrument has a definite and recognizable sound.

Above

Musical sounds have wave patterns that are evenly spaced or regular. They also have the same loudness or amplitude pattern. The amplitude is the greatest distance above and below the line passing through the centre of the wave pattern. It gives a measure of the energy of the vibrations. Unpleasant sounds have an irregular pattern.

Right

The waveforms of the notes of different instruments. The waveforms are found by adding the amplitudes of the fundamental and the various overtones. The fainter the overtones, the smaller the amplitudes. Each instrument has a different waveform because of the different overtones present.

Right

A musical scale of one octave. This is the scale of C, which has no sharps or flats (black notes). The last note in the scale, C′, is one octave higher than the first note. The 12 semitones making up one octave include the seven white notes and five black notes between C and B.

Right

If you sing the notes, starting at number 1 or C and continue to note 8 or C′, the sound is the familiar "doh-ray-me-fah-soh-lah-te-doh".

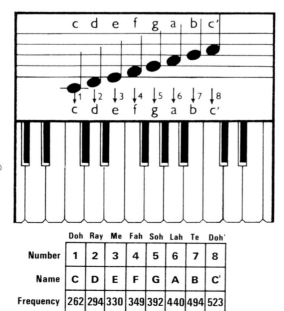

	Doh	Ray	Me	Fah	Soh	Lah	Te	Doh′
Number	1	2	3	4	5	6	7	8
Name	C	D	E	F	G	A	B	C′
Frequency	262	294	330	349	392	440	494	523

Musical scales are made up of groups of twelve notes, called semitones. The notes are arranged on a scale which rises from low to high pitch. Each group of notes is called an octave. Each note in an octave has a frequency that is 1.0595 times higher than the frequency of the note immediately below it. If you multiply 1.0595 by itself 12 times you get the answer 2. This means that a note one octave above another one has twice its frequency. The frequency of upper C is 523.2 vibrations per second, twice that of middle C (261.6).

Lord Rayleigh was one of Britain's greatest scientists. He worked out a new method for measuring the strength and loudness (amplitude) of sound vibrations. He wrote the *Theory of Sound* which describes the movement of sound-producing objects, and how they cause the surrounding air to vibrate.

Left
Music is made all over the world on a bewildering variety of instruments. Here is a collection of Indian musical instruments. The tambura is a long-necked lute whose strings are plucked to make a droning sound. The vina and the sitar are also lutes, while the sitar is played with a bow and the strings stopped with the fingers which move along them to make the notes slide.

Below
Some African musical instruments. The rattle is found all over the continent. The hourglass drum can be squeezed while playing to change the pitch of the note. Ivory horns may be blown at the side instead of the end, while the xylophones range in size from big ones that rest over pits in the ground to small ones that hang round the player's neck.

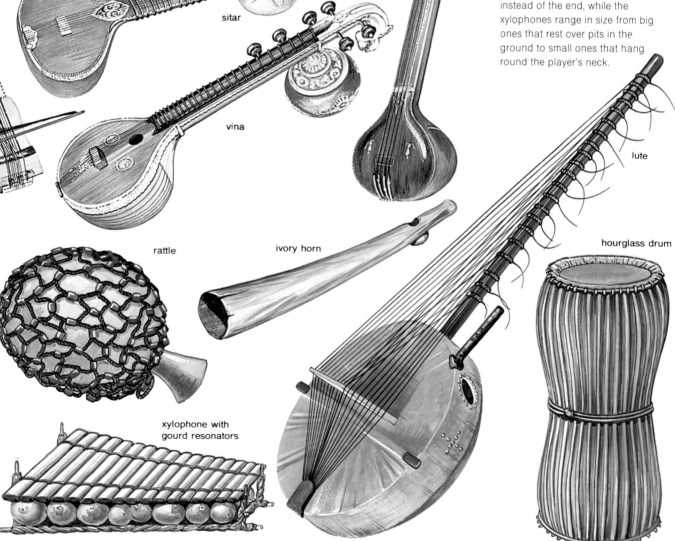

tabla

shehnai

tambura

sitar

sarangi

vina

lute

rattle

ivory horn

hourglass drum

xylophone with gourd resonators

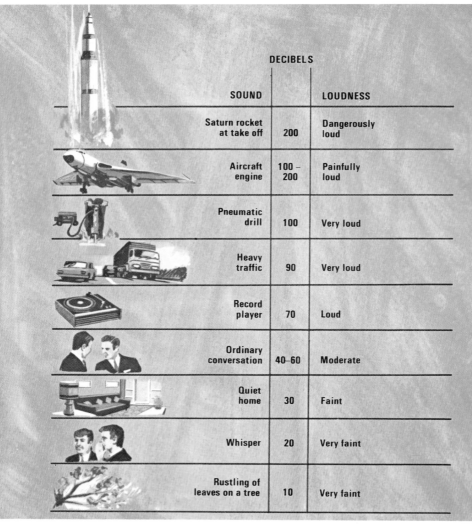

SOUND	DECIBELS	LOUDNESS
Saturn rocket at take off	200	Dangerously loud
Aircraft engine	100 – 200	Painfully loud
Pneumatic drill	100	Very loud
Heavy traffic	90	Very loud
Record player	70	Loud
Ordinary conversation	40–60	Moderate
Quiet home	30	Faint
Whisper	20	Very faint
Rustling of leaves on a tree	10	Very faint

NOISE

Any sound that a person finds unpleasant can be called noise. A noise to one person, however, might be thought a nice sound by somebody else. In scientific terms noise is sound made by an irregular pattern of waves.

There are many things which could make our world unpleasantly, even dangerously, noisy. These include jet aircraft taking off, road drills, and heavy traffic. Too great a noise can damage the ears. Laws forbid the making of noise above a certain level.

You may have noticed that a car horn or fire engine siren seems to have a higher pitch as the vehicle rushes towards you, than when it is moving away from you. This is most noticeable as the vehicle reaches you. At that moment the pitch of the horn or siren suddenly drops to a much lower note.

Sound waves move outward from the horn. The waves moving in the same direction as the vehicle travel towards you at the speed of sound plus the speed of the vehicle. So as the car comes towards you, more than the normal number of sound waves reach you each second. The frequency of the waves is higher than it would be if the vehicle were not moving. The pitch of the note is also higher.

When the car has passed you the sound waves reach you at the normal speed of sound minus the speed of the car. Fewer sound waves reach you per second. So the frequency is lower than when the vehicle is stationary. The pitch of the note is lower. This is why the pitch suddenly drops as the vehicle passes you.

Above
A scale of noises. The loudness of a noise is found by measuring the energy of a sound wave. Loudness is usually measured in decibels. A sound of zero decibels is just too faint for the human ear to hear. Lorries are not allowed to make a noise above 90 decibels. Sounds above 140 decibels are dangerous to the unprotected ear.

Right
The sound wave of a musical note and a noise. Fig. A shows the waveform of a piano note. The waves have a regular pattern and the note makes a pleasing sound. Fig. B shows the waves made when a piano pedal is pressed down. There is no regular pattern and the sound, being unpleasant, is called a noise.

Right
The Doppler effect. As the fire engine rushes away from you, ringing its siren, fewer sound waves reach you than when it approached you. The pitch of the siren's note drops suddenly as it passes you.

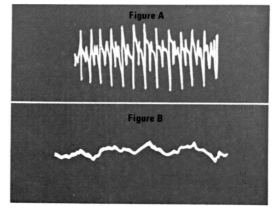

Figure A

Figure B

Low pitch

High pitch

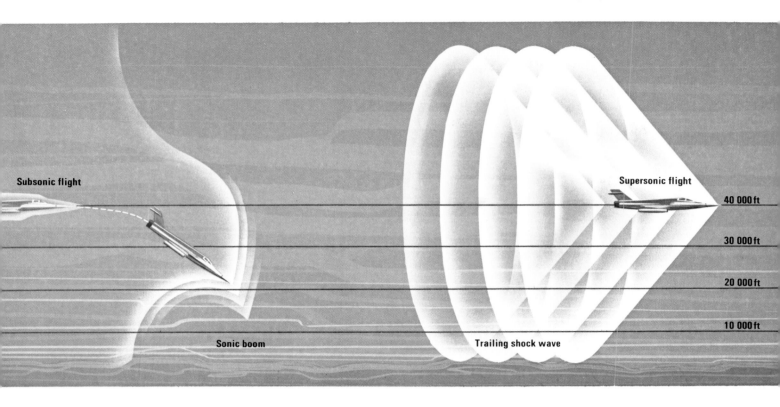

Subsonic flight

Sonic boom

Supersonic flight

40 000 ft

30 000 ft

20 000 ft

10 000 ft

Trailing shock wave

Doppler effect

This seeming change in pitch of a moving sound source is called the Doppler effect. It is named after Christian Johann Doppler who worked out the reason for it in 1842. The Doppler effect also occurs with light waves.

If a source of light, such as a star, is moving towards or away from an observer, the normal frequency of the light waves is increased or decreased. This effect is very useful in astronomy for calculating the velocities of stars.

One very recent noise is the sonic boom produced by supersonic aircraft. As an aircraft flies, it pushes air in front of it in waves. These are like the waves you see moving forward and outward from the bow of a moving ship. As the aircraft flies faster it pushes the waves of air against each other. This forms a wall or barrier of compressed air in front of the aircraft.

At about 1,200 km per hour (750 mph) an aircraft reaches the speed of sound. At this moment the powerful air pressure wave at the nose of the aircraft is disturbed and turns into a sound wave. A noise like a tremendous clap of thunder is heard directly below the aircraft. This is called the sonic boom.

Above
Sonic boom. Flying below the speed of sound, the aircraft compresses the air in front of it. At 1,200 km per hour (the speed of sound) the nose pressure waves become sound waves. This produces a shock wave in the air that causes the sonic boom.

Left
Supersonic aircraft. There are many aircraft that can fly faster than the speed of sound. Most of these are military aircraft. The world's fastest jet aircraft is the *Lockheed* SR-71. This American plane has reached a speed of 3,520 km per hour (2,200 mph). *Concorde* was developed jointly by Britain and France and is the only supersonic passenger plane. It travels at more than twice the speed of sound, reaching London from New York in about three hours.

ULTRASOUND

Ultrasound is sound vibrations which are too high in pitch and frequency for us to hear. Humans can hear sounds with a frequency below about 20,000 Hz (vibrations per second). Some animals, such as dolphins and bats, can hear sounds of greater frequency and pitch. There is evidence that dolphins and other whales communicate by using ultrasound. Bats use ultrasound to catch flying insects and avoid obstacles. Some night moths use ultrasound in the same way.

Piezoelectric crystal

Although we cannot hear ultrasound, we can produce and detect ultrasound by using a piezoelectric crystal. This is a crystal that produces an electric signal when it is gently squeezed. As a sound wave passes over a piezoelectric crystal, the crystal is squeezed by the pressure of the sound wave and produces a pulse of electricity. In this way, the crystals can detect ultrasound. The same crystals can produce ultrasound because they vibrate at a high frequency when a suitable electric voltage is applied to the sides of the crystal.

Ultrasound is very similar to ordinary sound. In particular, it can be reflected and produce echoes like ordinary sound. However, ultrasound has an additional feature. Because of its high frequency, it

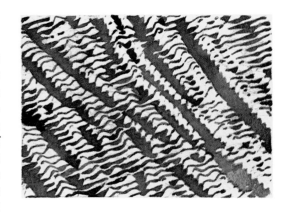

can produce narrow beams of sound. The beams can travel in straight lines without bending around obstacles. This makes ultrasound very useful.

The SONAR system

One of the earliest uses of ultrasound was to detect enemy submarines. High-frequency sounds were beamed into the water from a transmitter, or transducer, on the bottom of a ship's hull. The direction and time of any returning echoes were used to work out the position of a submarine. This system is called SONAR, or Sound Navigation and Ranging. Today, SONAR is used by fishermen to locate shoals of fish and to help in navigation.

In industry, ultrasound is used to measure the thickness of metal sheets and to detect faults in metal objects. A short burst of sound is passed into the metal sheet. The sound does not pass out of the other

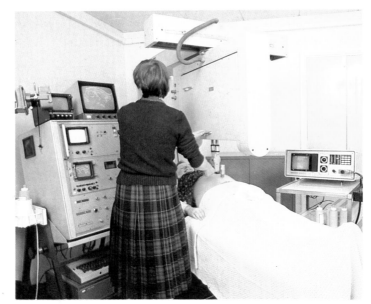

side of the sheet but bounces back as an echo. The thicker the sheet, the longer the time between the sound and the echo. If there is a fault, such as a crack in the metal, the echo is changed and the crack can be detected. Ultrasound is also used to clean greasy objects, to count objects on conveyor belts, to open doors as they are approached, and in security systems.

In hospitals, ultrasound scans are used to examine pregnant women to see if their baby is growing normally. A small ultra-sound generator is moved over the woman's body. Ultrasound passes through the tissues and is reflected as it passes through different kinds of tissue. The reflected sounds are picked up by a detector and converted into a picture on a television-like screen. Some systems produce moving pictures so that the doctor and mother can see the baby move. Ultrasound scans are completely safe for mother and baby, unlike X-rays which have a slight risk.

Below
The Horseshoe bat has folds around the mouth through which it sends out pulses of ultrasound. The bat uses these pulses to locate its prey and to avoid obstacles.

Below
During an ultrasound scan, a probe emits a pulse of ultrasound. This is reflected from both the baby and the womb holding it. The echoes are converted into a picture on a computer screen.

1 Probe emits ultrasound pulse.

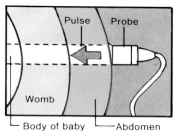

Pulse
Probe
Womb
Body of baby — Abdomen

2 Echo returns from womb.

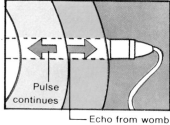

Pulse continues
Echo from womb

3 Echo returns from baby.

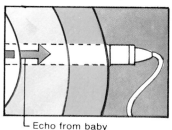

Echo from baby

4 Computer plots picture on screen.

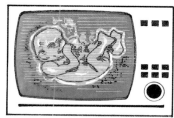

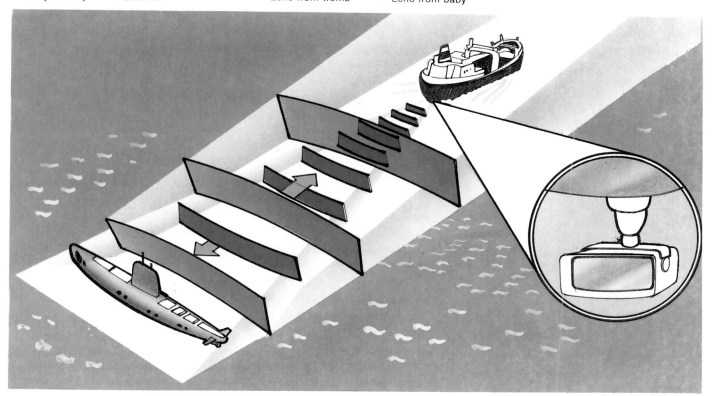

Electricity and Magnetism

STATIC ELECTRICITY

Some 600 years before the birth of Christ, a Greek philosopher called Thales discovered that amber (in Greek *elektron*), a fossil resin, could attract small pieces of fluff or feather, after being rubbed with fur. His discovery laid the basis for the whole science of electricity. The British scientist, William Gilbert (1544–1603), first suggested that the word electricity (from the Greek *elektron*) should be used to describe this force.

If you comb your hair with a plastic comb you will find that the comb can attract small pieces of paper. This is the effect Thales saw in his experiment. What creates this force of attraction? Until the end of the nineteenth century no one knew the answer. Now we know part of the answer, but not all.

Electric charges

The central nucleus of an atom consists of protons and neutrons. Protons have a positive electric charge and neutrons have no electric charge and move round the central nucleus. Each atom contains the same number of electrons as protons. The charge on the electron is exactly equal but

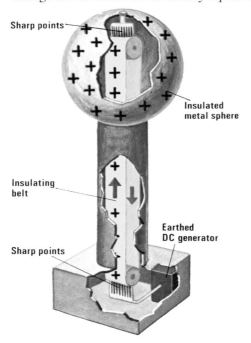

Sharp points

Insulated metal sphere

Insulating belt

Earthed DC generator

Sharp points

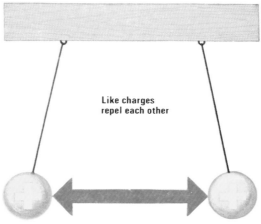

Unlike charges attract each other

Like charges repel each other

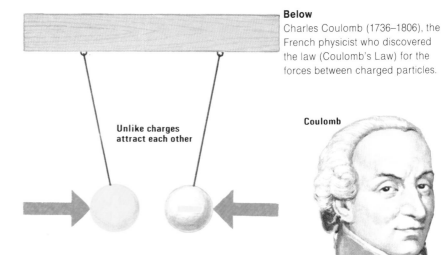

Coulomb

Left
Coulomb's Law. Unlike charges attract each other, like charges repel each other. The size of the force, in both cases, depends on the size of the charges. It also depends on the square of the distance between the charges. This means that if the distance is halved, the force is four times bigger.

opposite to the charge on the proton. So an atom has no charge and we say it is electrically neutral.

When you pull a comb through your hair, some of the electrons from the atoms of your comb are left behind on your hair. So the protons in these atoms do not have sufficient electrons to balance them. The result is that the comb is positively charged. The comb is then able to attract the electrons in the atoms of the paper. This creates the force between comb and paper.

The kind of electricity produced by the comb is called static electricity. The basic rule for static electricity is that unlike (different) charges attract, and like (the same) charges repel one another. A positive charge and a negative charge will attract each other. But two positive or two negative charges will always repel one another.

We can measure the attraction and repulsion of electric charges. We know about electricity in atoms. But we still do not know exactly what an electric charge is or what the difference is between negative and positive charge.

Left
A Van de Graff generator is used to produce a higher electric charge in science laboratories. The air molecules are broken up at the lower points. A positive charge is carried up on the moving belt. This charge is then conveyed to the insulated metal sphere by the upper set of points.

INVISIBLE INFLUENCE

You will need: comb ● bits of paper ● balloons

Can you bend water? It might sound impossible, but it isn't. You can do it by using your hair.

Comb your hair vigorously for a few seconds and move the comb near to a thin stream of water running from a tap. You will see the water bend because it is attracted by the comb. The comb can also be made to attract other things, such as tiny pieces of paper.

You can give other materials a static electrical charge by rubbing them against wool or fur. Balloons are charged when they are rubbed against your sweater. In this state they can stick to the walls or ceiling.

Charged balloons do not always attract. Tie some string to two balloons. Rub them both against your sweater, and then hold them up by the strings. You will see the balloons push apart, or repel one another. This is because they both have the same electric charge.

You will need: old LP ● glass ● cloth ● silver foil

Charge a long-playing disc (LP) with static electricity by rubbing it vigorously with a woollen cloth. Place it on a glass. The glass will act as an insulator and stop the static electricity on the disc leaking away. Throw a few crumpled pieces of silver foil on to the disc (the little silver balls used to decorate cakes will work just as well).

The balls will start dancing about all over the disc. This happens because they become electrically charged themselves as they touch the disc. And because they have the same electric charge, they repel one another. This is what sets them moving.

You can control the balls leaping about. Try holding a plastic pen and a comb near the balls. What happens? Charge up the pen and comb by rubbing them on your hair or sweater. How do the balls react now?

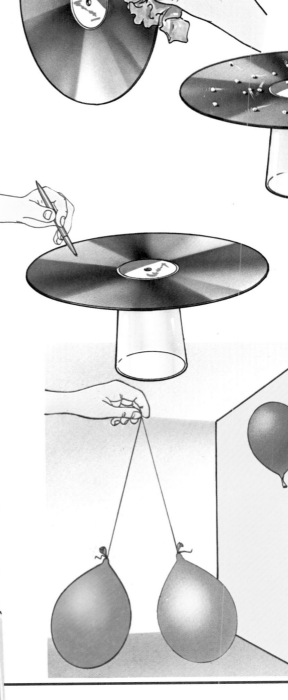

If you comb your hair in a dark room and then hold the comb close to your thumb you will see a small spark. This is because the energy stored in the charge is making the air atoms between the comb and your thumb emit light. In 1708, a British scientist called William Wall suggested that a lightning flash in the sky was a similar process on a grand scale.

Benjamin Franklin's experiment

Fifty years later an American inventor, Benjamin Franklin, carried out an experiment to try to prove that a lightning discharge was, in fact, caused by electricity. In a thunderstorm he flew a kite to which he attached a metal wire. The wire was connected to a silk thread, the other end of which was held by Franklin. A metal key was attached to the thread just above Franklin's head. Franklin flew the kite into a thundercloud and then held a finger close to the key. A spark jumped across the gap. Each time Franklin flew the kite into the thundercloud he made the key spark. This proved that thunderclouds were charged with electricity and that some of the charge was being conducted down the silken thread to the key. The build-up of charge on the key caused a spark to jump the gap to his finger.

It was a brilliant experiment but a very foolhardy one. The next person to try it was killed by the discharge. Franklin was very lucky to escape with his life. However, the risk he took turned out to have been well worth it. Having shown that lightning is caused by an electric discharge, Franklin went on to invent a way of protecting tall buildings from being struck by lightning. The invention was a simple step from the kite experiment. He attached a metal rod to the highest point of a building and connected the rod by a wire to the earth. Thus if lightning struck the building the charge was led safely down the wire to earth.

Damage by lightning has been greatly reduced by the use of lightning conductors. Even so, throughout the world, on average some twenty people a day are killed by lightning.

Above
Benjamin Franklin's experiment with a kite. He could have electrocuted himself by allowing the thundercloud to discharge through the cord of his kite. A later experimenter was killed because the charge in the cloud built up to such an extent that the current passing through him to earth was large enough to be fatal. A current of only 15 thousandths of an ampere is sufficient to kill a person.

Cloud-to-cloud lightning

Cloud-to-ground lightning

Left
In storm clouds the cold upper part of the cloud contains positively charged particles. The middle region contains negative particles. The rain areas at the base of the cloud are sometimes positively charged. When lightning flashes from the negative part of one cloud to the positive part of another cloud it is called cloud-to-cloud lightning. When it flashes to earth it is called cloud-to-earth lightning.

Lightning can pass from one cloud to another or from a cloud to the ground. In both types a single flash usually consists of between five and ten closely spaced strokes following the same channel. The interval between the strokes is only a few hundredths of a second and to a human eye they appear as one flash. The current carried by each discharge heats the air causing it to expand. The repeated expansions and contractions caused by the five to ten strokes generate massive sound waves. This is the thunder. As light travels more quickly than sound there is a delay between seeing the flash and hearing the thunder. The speed of sound is 330 m per second. So for every second's delay between seeing the flash and hearing the sound the thunder has travelled 330 metres.

Below
St Elmo's fire is a bluish glow sometimes seen on the wings of aircraft during an electrical storm. Storm clouds carry a heavy electrical charge at their bases. The static charge acquired by pointed objects on aircraft discharges into the oppositely charged cloud with a visible light. It used to occur on the masts of wooden ships and is named after St Elmo, the patron saint of Mediterranean sailors.

Lightning conductor

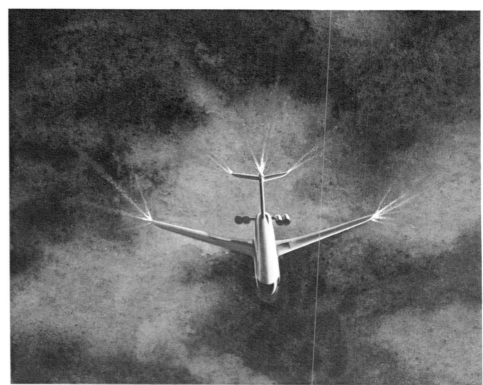

Above
The metal lightning conductor at the top of the church tower conducts the electricity of the discharge down the metal conductor safely to earth. The lightning conductor was invented by Benjamin Franklin.

Right
Electrical transmission lines are sometimes struck by lightning, as they have sharp points sticking up from the ground. When lightning strikes a pylon, large voltages build up across the insulators. This can cause them to break down. The line may then have to be repaired.

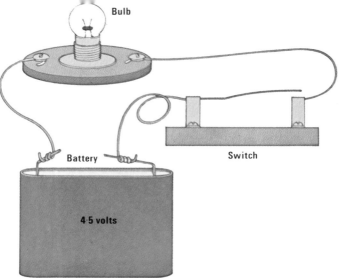

Bulb

Battery

4·5 volts

Switch

Left
A simple circuit consisting of a torch bulb, a battery, three pieces of wire and a switch. When the springy metal strip of the switch is pressed down the electrons flow round the circuit and the light bulb lights up.

Above
André Marie Ampère (1775–1836) was a French scientist and mathematician. The unit of electric current, the ampere or amp, is named after him.

Right
A simple switch made from two drawing pins and a paper clip.

Below
The atomic nucleus consists of tiny particles called protons and neutrons. The proton is positively charged and the neutron has no charge. There are negatively charged electrons around the nucleus. Each atom has as many protons as electrons. So their charges balance each other out. In the hydrogen atom the nucleus consists of one proton. Neutrons occur in all nuclei except hydrogen.

Hydrogen nucleus

Carbon nucleus

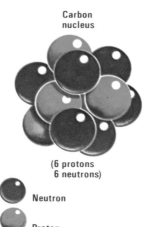

(6 protons 6 neutrons)

Neutron

Proton

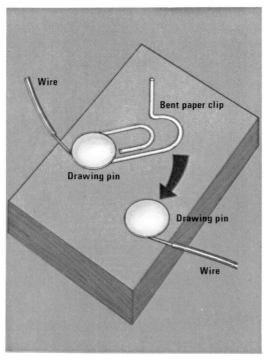

Wire

Bent paper clip

Drawing pin

Drawing pin

Wire

ELECTRIC CURRENTS

If you connect a torch bulb to a battery through a switch you have a simple electric circuit. When the switch is open there is no flow of electricity. When you complete the circuit by closing the switch, electricity flows through the wires from the battery and the bulb lights. What is it that flows through the wire when the switch is closed? An electric current consists of a flow of electrons and it is this flow of electrons that the switch interrupts.

Below
The first 18 elements showing the shells of the electrons. In the centre of each is a positively charged nucleus. The charge on the nucleus is equal to the number of electrons circulating around it.

The chemical properties of each element depend on the number of electrons in the outer shells of its atoms. If the electrons become detached, as they do in metals, the substance can conduct electricity.

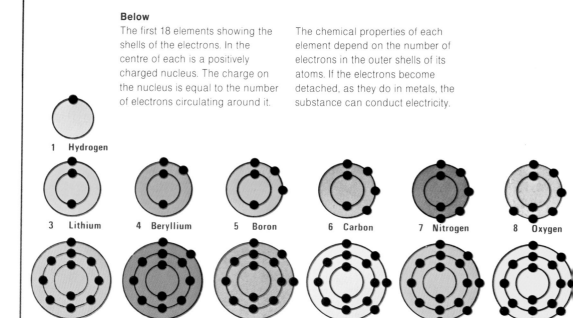

1 Hydrogen

3 Lithium 4 Beryllium 5 Boron 6 Carbon 7 Nitrogen 8 Oxygen

11 Sodium 12 Magnesium 13 Aluminium 14 Silicon 15 Phosphorus 16 Sulphur

Atoms and electrons

An electron is a very tiny negatively charged particle. To make the torch bulb stay alight for one second takes a flow of about one million million million electrons. These electrons occur in atoms. Atoms consist of a central nucleus. The electrons move round the nucleus, at different distances from it, in groups called shells. The simplest atom is hydrogen, consisting of one electron circling round the nucleus. The atoms of the different elements all have different numbers of electrons.

Each shell of an atom can contain a certain number of electrons. In the atoms of most elements, the outer shell is not full. Atoms combine with each other to form molecules. They tend to do this so that the combining atoms each end up with a full outer shell. Atoms with only a few electrons in their outer shell may do this by losing their outer electrons. These outer electrons detach themselves from the nucleus and wander at random around the atoms. Elements which can combine in this way are called metals. They conduct electricity because these detached electrons are free to move.

The function of the battery in the simple circuit described is to push the free electrons in the metal wire so that they all move in the same direction. When a current flows through a wire, it consists of these detached outer electrons all flowing in the same direction. When the switch is turned off and the battery is disconnected the electrons cease to have this push and they return to random motion.

When the torch switch is pushed down, the electrons flow through the wire and pass through the very thin wire in the bulb. This wire is called a filament. The wire is so thin that the collisions between electrons and atoms are much more frequent. This increases the temperature of the filament and makes the atoms emit light (see page 73). The filament emits red light and then, when it gets hotter, white light.

Electrons not only flow through wires, they also flow through nerves in the body. For example, when you see something, an electrical impulse travels from your eye to your brain. These impulses consist of a flow of electrons passing down the optic nerve from the retina of the eye to the optic centre of the brain. Muscles, too, are controlled by a flow of electric pulses from the brain passing down nerves to the muscles.

Thomson

Above
Sir Joseph John Thomson (1856–1940), the Cambridge scientist who discovered the electron in 1897. This enabled us to understand electric current.

Bragg

Above
Sir William Henry Bragg (1862–1942) was a British scientist who was awarded the Nobel prize for physics in 1915. He helped to discover the structure of atoms and crystals, and developed the X-ray spectrometer.

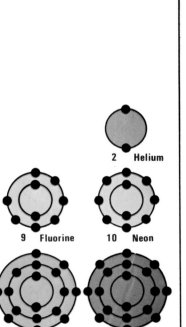

2 Helium

9 Fluorine

10 Neon

17 Chlorine

18 Argon

Inside a Wire

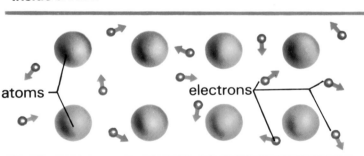

atoms — electrons

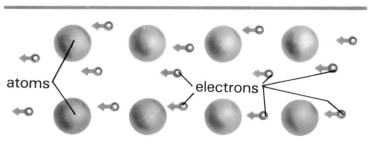

atoms — electrons

Left
In a metal wire the outer electrons move at random about the atoms. When a current flows these electrons all move in the same direction.

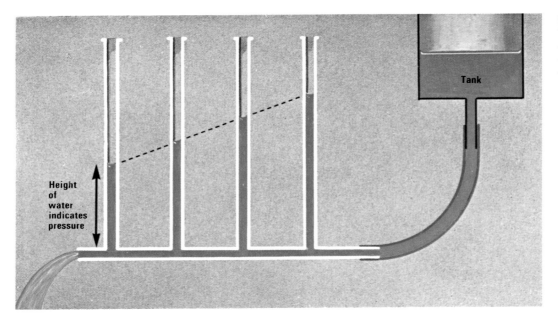

Left
The flow of electricity through a wire is similar in some respects to the flow of water through a tube. Water flows from a tank through a horizontal tube. Because of friction between the water and the walls of the tube, the pressure along the tube is reduced. You can see this if you have vertical tubes sticking out of the tube. The height of the water in the tube shows the pressure in the tube. In the same way, the voltage falls along a wire, due to the resistance. The current is like the quantity of water flowing, the potential difference is like the pressure.

Tank

Height of water indicates pressure

VOLTAGE AND RESISTANCE

Electrons do not flow as a fluid down the wire as water flows in a tube. However, in some ways an electric current resembles the flow of water in a tube. In both cases power is necessary to maintain the flow – the weight of the water or a pump in the case of a tube, and a battery or mains supply in the case of an electric current.

Imagine a steady flow of water passing through a narrow horizontal tube. If vertical tubes are fixed to the horizontal tube they can act as pressure gauges. The height of water in the vertical tubes indicates the pressure. If you were to carry out this experiment you would see the pressure in the tube fall between the inlet end and the outlet. The flow of water depends on the difference of pressure between the two ends of the tube.

Ohm's law

The difference of electrical pressure, which forces the electric current through a wire, is called the potential difference (pd). The current of electricity depends on the potential difference between the ends of the wire. This relation was first discovered by Georg Ohm and is known as Ohm's law. This states that the current increases and decreases in proportion to potential difference.

The size of the potential difference is measured in volts, a unit named after the Italian scientist called Volta. The pressure falls along the tube of water because of the friction between the water and the sides of the tube. Similarly with an electric current, consisting of a flow of electrons, there is resistance to the electron flow. This is caused by the electrons bumping into atoms or into each other. The resistance of a wire or conductor is equal to the potential difference divided by the current in amperes. This is another way of putting Ohm's law; and the unit of resistance is called the Ohm.

Ohm's law is used in calculating the resistance of the fuses in our homes. A fuse protects an electrical appliance if the insulation breaks down and the current flows where it should not be flowing. Suppose, for example, you knock over a table lamp that is switched on and the glass bulb breaks. It is possible for the two wires attached to the end of the filament to touch each other. This is called a short circuit. There will now be a very high current flowing through the flex, as the current is no longer limited by the high resistance of the thin filament wire. If this were allowed to continue for any length of time the flex would become very hot and it

Ohm

Above
George Simon Ohm (1789–1854), a German scientist who discovered that the current is proportional to potential difference (Ohm's law). The unit of resistance, the ohm, is named after him.

Volta

Above
Count Alessandro Volta (1745–1827). The Italian scientist who first worked out the idea of electric currents and made the first battery.

could start a fire in the house.

In order to avoid this danger, nearly every device now has a fuse in the plug. This consists of a piece of thin wire which melts and breaks the circuit if the current is greater than it should be for safety. The high resistance of the fuse restricts the amount of current that can flow. It is important to use fuses of the correct resistance for each electrical appliance.

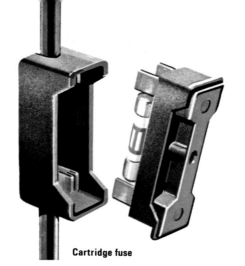

Left and below
Some fuses' are built into cartridges, while some are bare wire. In houses the fuses are usually all together in a fuse box. Each plug has its own fuse too.

Cartridge fuse

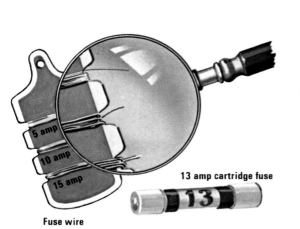

5 amp
10 amp
15 amp

Fuse wire

13 amp cartridge fuse

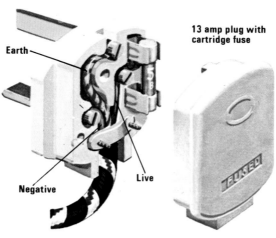

Earth

Negative

Live

13 amp plug with cartridge fuse

Wired fuse

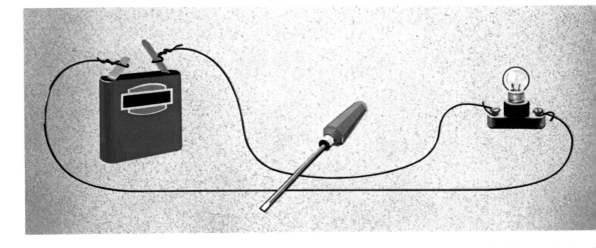

Right
A simple demonstration of a short circuit. Wire up a small bulb to a battery with bare wire. Place a metal conductor, such as a screwdriver, across both wires and see the bulb go out. The screwdriver has caused a short circuit. The current flows through it rather than through the bulb as the thick screwdriver has a lower resistance than the thin bulb filament.

Right
A variable resistor is called a rheostat. You can make one from a piece of pencil lead. Attach wires to each end so that one wire can slide along the lead. As you increase the length of lead in the circuit you increase the resistance and the bulb will grow dimmer.

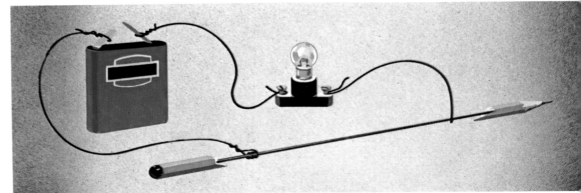

131

CONDUCTORS AND INSULATORS

In metals, like copper, the atoms combine with each other to form crystals in which the outer atomic electrons are free to move about. When these free electrons move in one direction an electric current flows (see page 129). In non-metals, like sulphur, there are usually no free electrons and so no current flows. These substances are called insulators. Most compounds are insulators and some, like rubber, are particularly good insulators. We use conductors to carry electricity to where it is needed and we use insulators to prevent it from leaking into a place in which we do not want it. Wires are usually covered with rubber or plastic to make them safe to handle.

One of the main uses of insulators is to protect our bodies from electric current. This is because our bodies can conduct electricity, especially when they are wet. If, by mistake, you touch live mains wires you will get a very nasty shock. If you hands are wet the shock can kill you. Never touch electrical appliances when you have wet hands – if there is a fault in the insulation it can be very dangerous. Never take electrical appliances into the bathroom and never touch light switches or plugs when your hands are wet.

The thickness of the insulator needed to protect a wire depends not on the current flowing through it but on the voltage driving the electrons through the wire. If the voltage is high, for example in the wires leading to the plugs of a petrol engine, the insulation has to be thick. The voltage in this case is several thousand volts. The insulation used on wires connected to a torch battery can be very thin as the voltage is only about $1\frac{1}{2}$ volts.

Semiconductors

As well as conductors and insulators, there are substances called semiconductors. In these substances, some of the electrons can, under certain conditions, break free from the atoms. Examples of semiconductors are silicon, germanium, and selenium. One way to make them conduct electricity is to heat them. A more effective way is to add certain impurities.

If arsenic is added to germanium, free

Metal lightning conductor

Left
The lightning conductor provides a harmless path for the lightning discharge to reach earth. It travels down the metal lightning conductor instead of down the side of the building which might catch fire.

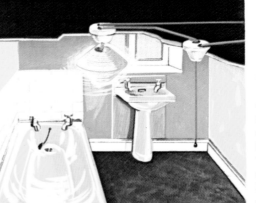

Below left
In bathrooms, and sometimes in kitchens, ceiling switches are used. They consist of a switch, operated by a piece of string, attached to the ceiling. With these switches there is no danger of electrocution even when the light is switched on or off with wet hands. The current-carrying wires are embedded in the ceiling. The string is an insulator.

Below
Mains cable may be made of copper, which is a very good conductor, or aluminium, which is cheaper. The cables are usually insulated with the plastic PVC. Those that come from the power station carry a high voltage and have to have special insulation for carrying the current.

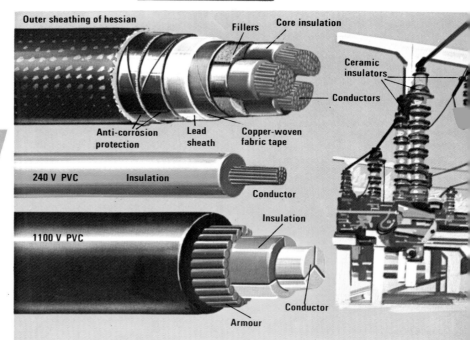

Outer sheathing of hessian · Fillers · Core insulation · Ceramic insulators · Conductors · Anti-corrosion protection · Lead sheath · Copper-woven fabric tape · 240 V PVC · Insulation · Conductor · Insulation · 1100 V PVC · Conductor · Armour

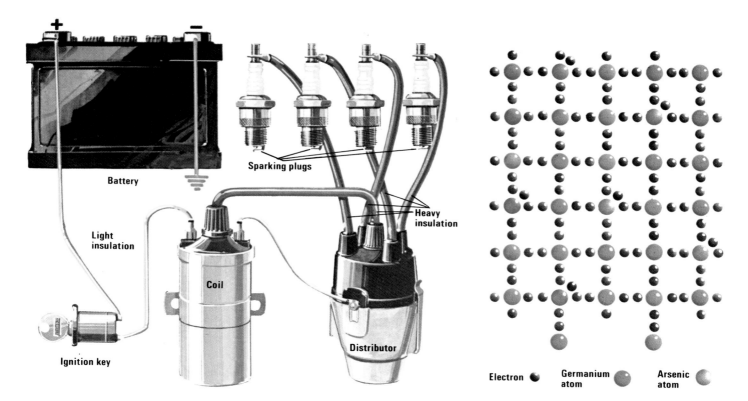

Battery

Sparking plugs

Light insulation

Heavy insulation

Coil

Distributor

Ignition key

Electron ●   Germanium atom   Arsenic atom

Above

In a car engine the battery voltage (12 volts) is fed to the coil. These wires have only a thin rubber or plastic insulation. The coil changes this low voltage into a high voltage to give the spark. So the wire from the coil to the distributor and the wires from the distributor to the plugs have to have a thick rubber or plastic insulation.

Above right

A germanium crystal with a small proportion of arsenic has one spare electron for each arsenic atom. This electron can detach itself from the nucleus and move through the crystal enabling a current to flow. This type of semiconductor is used in transistors.

electrons occur in the crystal. This is because the outer shell of these elements' atoms can contain eight electrons. The germanium atom has four electrons in its outer shell and arsenic has five outer electrons. So when the atoms combine, there is one electron over. This electron can be used as a conduction electron. When a voltage is applied the electron moves away from its atom and flows like the electrons in a metal. This type of conduction is called *n*-type.

If another element called indium is added to the germanium there is a different type of conduction. Indium has only three outer electrons and therefore when it combines with germanium there is a missing electron. This missing electron or hole, as it is called, can also act as a

conductor. This is called *p*-type (positive) conduction. Various types of semiconducting material are used in making transistors (see page 169).

Superconductors

There are also superconductors – materials that offer no resistance to the flow of electricity. Materials need to be cooled to very low temperatures before they exhibit this strange behaviour. Mercury, tin and lead become superconducting if they are cooled to $-268.9°C$, the temperature of liquid helium. Recently new ceramic materials have been discovered that become superconductors at $-180°C$, above the temperature of liquid nitrogen.

Right

Electrical appliances and tools for making electrical repairs have insulated rubber or plastic handles. But you must still take precautions against electric shocks. Always switch off before attempting to repair anything. Never touch anything electric when you have wet hands, as water is a conductor.

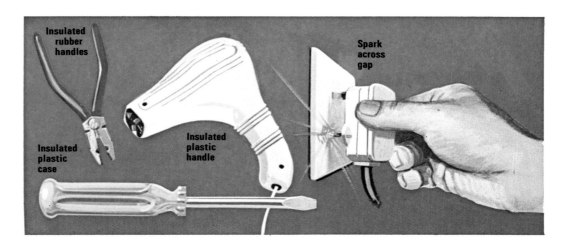

Insulated rubber handles

Spark across gap

Insulated plastic case

Insulated plastic handle

Right

An iron is heated by an element consisting of a conducting wire wound on to an insulating sheet. A thermostat cuts off the current when the iron reaches a certain temperature. One type of thermostat, called a bimetallic strip, consists of a strip of two metals. When heated, these metals expand at different rates and so the strip bends. At the required temperature, the strip has bent enough to open a switch. This stops the current flowing so that the element cools down.

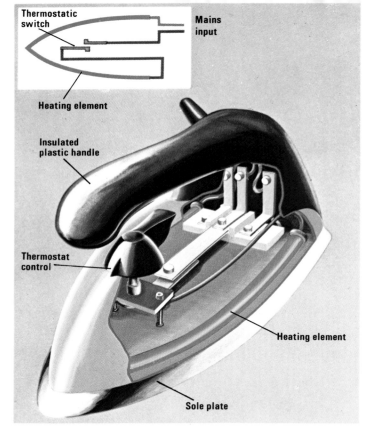

Thermostatic switch

Mains input

Heating element

Insulated plastic handle

Thermostat control

Heating element

Sole plate

Far right

Thermocouple. Two wires of different metal such as iron and copper are connected together to form a loop. A sensitive ammeter, which measures current, is connected to one wire. One of the junctions is heated by a candle, the other is cooled in ice. The greatest current is shown on the ammeter when the temperature difference is biggest. Take away either the flame or the ice and the current is reduced. The current is too low to light a torch bulb but it is very useful for measuring temperature.

Right

Thermocouples can be used to measure the strength of the sun's rays. Two glass hemispheres are arranged so that the top one faces the sun and the bottom one faces the ground. Each glass hemisphere is on a blackened disc. Between the two blackened discs a series of thermocouples are arranged so that one set of junctions is heated by the rays direct from the sun, whereas the bottom junctions are heated by the reflected rays. The difference in temperature between the two sets of junctions creates a current which can be recorded. The record shows the variations in the strength of the sun during the day.

Right

The reverse of the thermocouple effect occurs when a current is passed through wires of two different semiconductors. One junction is then cooled and the other warmed.

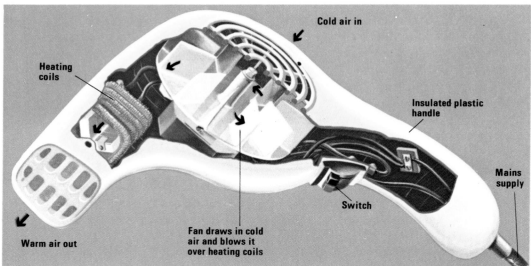

Cold air in

Heating coils

Insulated plastic handle

Switch

Mains supply

Warm air out

Fan draws in cold air and blows it over heating coils

Above

An electric hair drier. When you switch it on, the heating coils behind the nozzle start to glow. At the same time an electric motor starts the fan rotating. This sucks a stream of air in through the side vent and out through the nozzle. This air stream is heated as it passes over the coils.

Right

A home made electric heater. Instructions for making this are in the panel opposite.

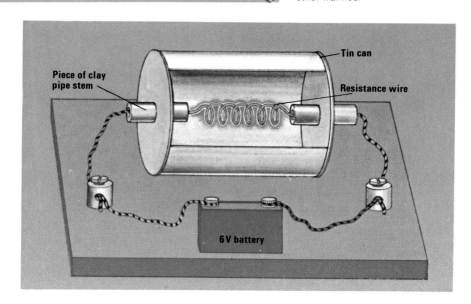

Piece of clay pipe stem

Tin can

Resistance wire

6 V battery

HEATING COILS

Electric current has to overcome resistance as it flows through a wire. At normal temperatures, every conductor has a resistance, although some have only a very small resistance. Electricity produces heat as it forces its way through a resistor. The greater the resistance, the greater the heat produced. Sometimes the conductor becomes warm, sometimes red hot, as in an electric fire, and sometimes even white hot as in the case of an electric light bulb.

Thick copper wires have a very small resistance. Thin wires made of special

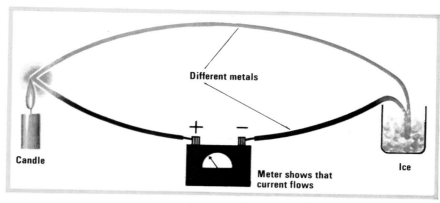

Different metals

Candle

Meter shows that
current flows

Ice

mixtures of metals called alloys have large resistances. Long pieces of thin wire are used to make heat. The wire is wound into a coil so that it takes up less space. Heating coils are used in electric fires, irons, toasters, kettles and immersion heaters.

In an electric iron the coil becomes hot but not red hot, otherwise the iron might burn the clothes. In an electric fire and an electric toaster the heating coil, sometimes called an element, becomes red hot.

Thermocouple

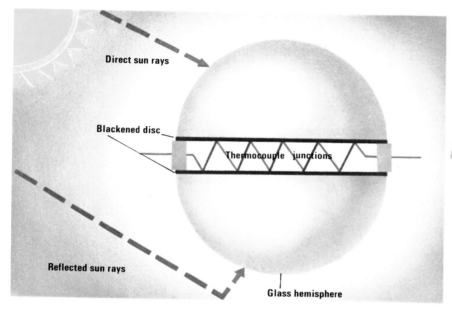

Direct sun rays

Blackened disc

Thermocouple junctions

Reflected sun rays

Glass hemisphere

Electric heating elements are a way of converting electric energy into heat. To create electric energy from heat a thermocouple can be used. A thermocouple consists of two wires of different metals joined at two places so that they form an electrical loop. If the two junctions are at different temperatures a small current will flow through the wire. This current depends on the difference in temperature between the junctions; the higher the difference the higher the current.

This effect also works in reverse. If a current is passed through the loop containing the two metal junctions, one junction will be cooled and the other will be warmed. The effect is too weak with metals to be of much value but it can be made stronger by using two different types of semiconductor.

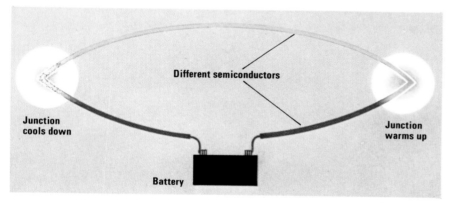

Different semiconductors

Junction
cools down

Junction
warms up

Battery

MAKE A SMALL ELECTRIC FIRE

You will need: a tin can about 10 cm in diameter and 13 cm high ● a broken stem of a clay pipe ● about 30 cm of No 24 SWG nichrome wire ● wooden base containing 2 terminals ● 6V battery ● nails

ASK AN ADULT TO HELP YOU DO THIS. Cut out about a third of the side of the tin can, as shown left. Knock a small hole in each end of the tin. Insert a

piece of clay pipe in each hole to act as an insulator for the wire. Wind the nichrome resistance wire round a knitting needle to make a coil. Withdraw the needle, and put the ends of the wire through the holes of the two bits of clay pipe. Connect these ends to two terminals on a wooden base. Finally, nail the tin can to the base. Connect the terminals to a 6 volt battery and the element will glow red. The heat from the element will be reflected from the inside of the tin.

Inside a Torch Battery

carbon rod

paste of chemicals

zinc case

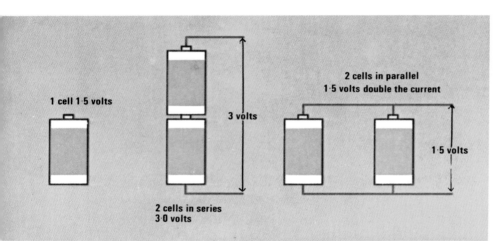

1 cell 1·5 volts

2 cells in series 3·0 volts

3 volts

2 cells in parallel 1·5 volts double the current

1·5 volts

DRY BATTERIES

If you undo a torch you will find inside one or more dry batteries, sometimes called cells. Inside the battery there is a zinc metal case. In the centre of one end of the case there is a brass cap which forms one terminal. Under this cap there is a rod of carbon. The bottom of the zinc case forms the other terminal.

The carbon rod with the brass cap is called the positive terminal and the zinc case is the negative terminal. We say that an electric current flows from the positive terminal round an electric circuit to the negative plate. The carbon rod is surrounded by a chemical, called manganese dioxide, in a muslin bag. Between the manganese dioxide and the zinc case there is a paste made from another chemical called ammonium chloride. A reaction between these chemicals takes place slowly. This produces the potential difference which lights the torch bulb when it is connected to the battery. When the chemicals are used up the battery weakens and has to be replaced.

Below
Batteries can have different voltages. They are built up from single cells connected in series. A 4.5 volt battery is made up of three 1.5 volt cells. A 9 volt battery is made up of six.

Top
The dry battery. This was derived from the Leclanché cell invented by the French chemist Georges Leclanché (1839–82). The Leclanché cell used liquids, which are not very convenient or portable. The modern dry cell uses a paste of ammonium chloride in place of a liquid.

Above
Connecting two cells of the same voltage in series doubles the voltage. Connecting these two cells in parallel doubles the current. To obtain 30 volts from a dry battery requires 20 cells connected in series.

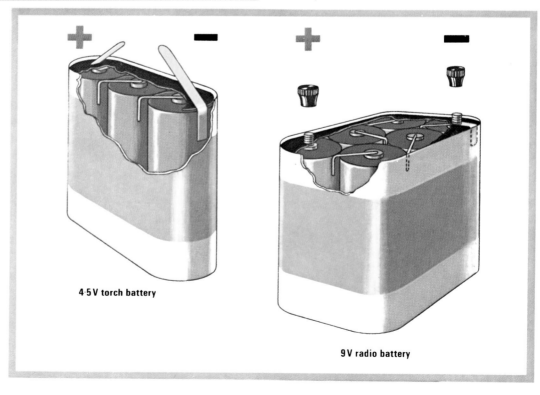

4·5 V torch battery

9 V radio battery

This sort of battery is called a primary cell. The normal dry battery has a fixed potential difference or voltage of about 1.5 volts. A small torch needs only one battery, and does not shine very far. A larger torch has two batteries one on top of the other. This increases the voltage to about 3 volts and the torch gives a stronger light.

Some dry batteries which have a much higher voltage, 10 or 20 volts, are in fact a number of single dry batteries joined together.

There are two ways of joining batteries together. If they are connected end to end so that the brass positive terminal of one touches the negative case of the other, the voltages add together. This is called connecting the batteries in series. If both brass terminals are connected together and both cases are connected together the batteries are connected in parallel. In this case the potential difference is only 1.5V, but the total current available is doubled.

Batteries are used to provide the power for a number of domestic appliances. Portable radios use only one or two batteries in series. Some portable tape players have the batteries driving the motor connected in parallel.

Some devices only take a small amount of power and they can therefore use very small batteries. Toy cars, electric razors, and hearing aids are examples. Sometimes a different type of cell is used in these small devices, called a mercury cell. Some types of mercury cell can be recharged. Electric toothbrushes often contain this type of cell. The toothbrush fits on to a vibrator unit containing the batteries. When not in use the vibrator unit fits into a charging unit.

Below
A large torch uses two batteries in series. The bulb presses on to the brass positive terminal of the top battery. The negative zinc case of the bottom battery connects, through a spring, to a brass strip running up the side of the torch to the switch. This joins the strip to another brass strip to contact with the metal case of the bulb. In some torches the body is metal rather than plastic, and the body acts as one conductor.

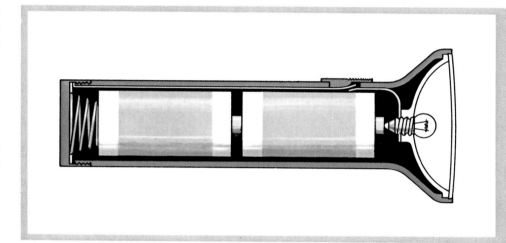

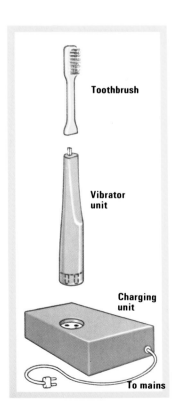

Toothbrush

Vibrator unit

Charging unit

To mains

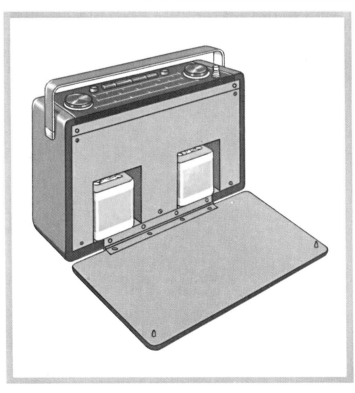

Far left
The cordless electric tooth brush. The tooth brush fits on to a battery-operated vibrator unit. The battery in this unit is rechargeable. When not in use it fits into a charging unit.

Left
Portable radio. The transistors in a radio work at a low voltage and therefore can operate with only one or two small batteries.

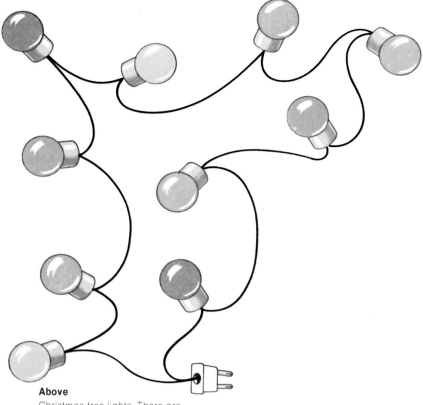

Above
Christmas tree lights. There are ten coloured bulbs each of 24 volts connected in series to the mains. If one bulb fails the circuit is broken and all the lights go out.

Right
A model set of traffic lights. Wire three torch bulbs to a three-way switch made out of four drawing pins and a paperclip. Wire the three bulbs together and connect them to a 4.5 volt battery. Connect the other side of the battery to the paper clip switch. Paint the bulbs red, amber and green. These bulbs are connected in parallel so that they can be switched on separately.

Right
A model street lighting system. Build a row of wooden lamp posts. Fix a bulb on each post. Wire the bulbs in parallel so that if one bulb fails, the rest will stay lit. Connect them to a battery via a paper clip switch.

CIRCUITS

The best way to learn about circuit electricity is to build some simple circuits with batteries. A circuit is simply a route for

MAKING A SWITCH
You will need: a piece of wood • 4 brass drawing pins • a paper clip

Stick two brass drawing pins into the wood. Straighten out a paper clip and attach it to one of the drawing pins. To close the switch simply press the paper clip down on to the other drawing pin.

With wire, connect one drawing pin on the switch to one terminal of the battery. Connect the other drawing pin with wire to a 4.5 volt bulb and then to the other terminal of the battery. When you close the switch, the bulb should light up.

LIGHTING UP
You will need: a 4.5 volt battery • two 4.5 volt bulbs in their holders • two 2.5 volt bulbs • a switch • wire

Now connect into the simple circuit an extra bulb, so that the current passes first through one bulb and then through the other. These bulbs are in series. Press the

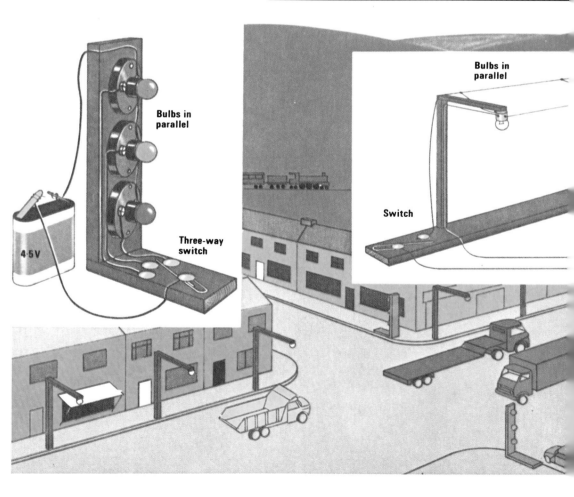

Bulbs in parallel

Three-way switch

4·5V

Bulbs in parallel

Switch

electric current like a motor racing circuit. To control the flow, you need a switch. In the box you will find instructions on how to make one.

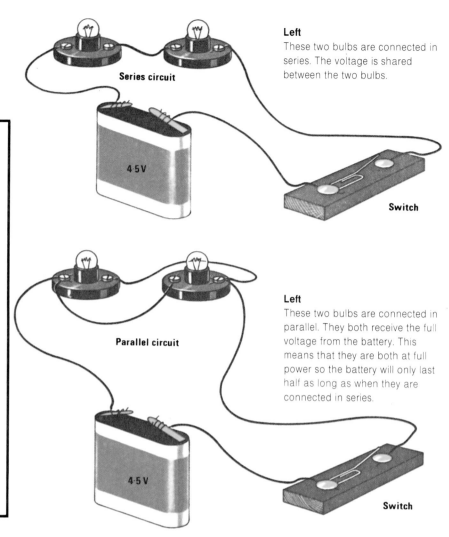

Series circuit

Left
These two bulbs are connected in series. The voltage is shared between the two bulbs.

Parallel circuit

Left
These two bulbs are connected in parallel. They both receive the full voltage from the battery. This means that they are both at full power so the battery will only last half as long as when they are connected in series.

switch and notice how bright the bulbs are; they will not be as bright as when only one bulb is used. This is because the two bulbs are sharing the 4.5 volts betwen them.

Now replace the bulbs in their holders by two 2.5 volt bulbs. Notice that the bulbs are brighter this time. They are each receiving about the correct voltage. Now try the two first bulbs connected in a parallel circuit as shown. Notice that both bulbs are bright this time even though the same battery is being used. In this kind of circuit the battery is doing twice as much work and it will not last long. Both bulbs are receiving the full 4.5 volts from the battery and therefore they are working correctly.

If a room needs more than one bulb, they are connected in parallel. In this way two bulbs can be switched on at the same time and they will both be as bright as all the other lights in the house.

You can put your circuits to the test by making some models and toys out of them.

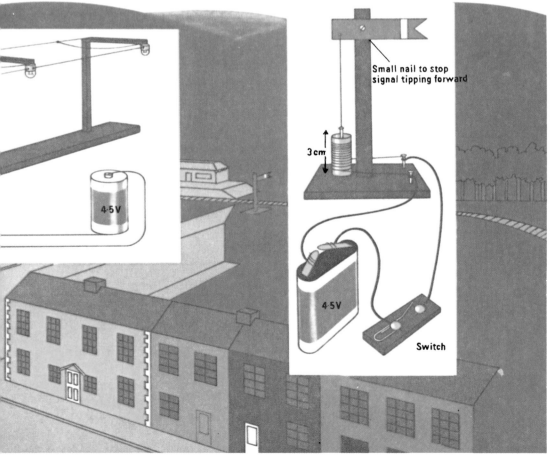

Small nail to stop signal tipping forward

3 cm

4·5 V

Switch

Left
A model railway signal.
Take some insulated copper wire (swg No 36 is best) and wind it round a piece of thin tube, such as a piece of the barrel of a ballpoint pen. Wind the wire round about 1,000 times. Make the winding about 3 cm long. This is the first part of the electromagnet which will work the signal. Make the signal on a wooden base and fix the signal arm so that it can move up and down easily. Glue the winding to the base close to the upright piece. Tie a piece of thread to the back of the arm of the signal and attach a nail to the other end of the thread. Arrange the length of the thread so that the nail goes in and out of the electromagnet as the signal arm goes up and down. Now connect the ends of the winding wire to two nails on the wooden base. Connect the two nails to a switch and a 4.5 volt battery. The model is now ready to operate. When you close the switch the signal will rise. The electromagnet pulls the nail downwards when the current flows, and this lifts the signal.

CELLS AND ELECTROLYSIS

The dry cells used in electric torches are examples of primary cells. In these cells electricity is made by chemical changes. The earliest form of primary cell is called the voltaic cell after its inventor, Count Alessandro Volta. It consists of a copper rod and a zinc rod dipping into a sulphuric acid solution. The solution is called the electrolyte and the rods are called the electrodes. If the copper electrode is connected to the zinc electrode outside the electrolyte then a current will flow.

To understand how this happens we must think of the structures of the atoms and molecules. An atom of zinc contains a nucleus made up of protons and neutrons. The protons have a positive charge and this makes the nucleus positive. Electrons are moving around the nucleus and these all have negative charges. There is the same number of electrons as protons and so the atom is neutral.

If an atom of zinc loses an electron it will have more protons than electrons and the atom will no longer be neutral. It will have a positive charge. Charged atoms are called ions.

When an atom gains an extra electron there are more electrons than protons and the atom has a negative charge. It has become a negative ion. Positive and negative ions produce electricity in batteries.

Opposite bottom left

In the voltaic cell the zinc electrode is negative and is called the cathode. The copper electrode is positive and is called the anode.

Opposite bottom right

In a voltaic cell a chemical reaction causes an electric current. In the same way if an electric current is passed through an electrolyte it can cause a chemical reaction. This is called electrolysis. Here a current is passing through a solution of copper sulphate. The cathode becomes coated with a thin layer of copper. This is an example of electroplating. At the anode, oxygen gas is given off.

PLOP AND GLOW

You will need: 9-volt battery ● 2 carbon rods ● 2 test tubes ● bowl of water ● lighted taper

ASK AN ADULT TO HELP YOU DO THIS. Chemists refer to water as H_2O. This is a chemical formula. It shows that water is made up of the chemical elements hydrogen (H) and oxygen (O), and that there are twice as many hydrogen atoms in water as oxygen atoms.

You can show this to be true by the electrolysis of water. Electrolysis is a way of splitting up substances into their chemical elements by means of electricity. Use a 9-volt battery or similar to supply the electricity. DON'T TRY TO USE THE MAINS

ELECTRICITY – IT IS VERY DANGEROUS.

Connect wires from the two terminals of the battery to the two electrodes (carbon rods). These carry the electric current into and out of the water in the bowl. Over the electrodes place two test tubes full of water.

When the battery is connected, you will notice bubbles of gas rising from the electrodes. The gas collects in the top of the tubes. After a while, you will notice that twice as much gas collects in one tube as in the other. When you have collected quite a lot of gas, test it to find what it is, using a lighted taper. You may need to ask an adult to do this.

Take the first tube out of the water and immediately plunge a lighted taper inside it. There will be quite a loud "plop" as the gas inside burns up. This shows that the gas was hydrogen. Take the second tube out of the water and plunge into it a glowing, but not burning, taper. The taper will immediately burst into flames, showing that the gas was oxygen.

Note which electrode gave which gas in the experiment above. The hydrogen is given off from the cathode, the electrode connected to the negative (−) terminal of the battery. The oxygen is given off from the anode, the electrode connected to the positive (+) terminal.

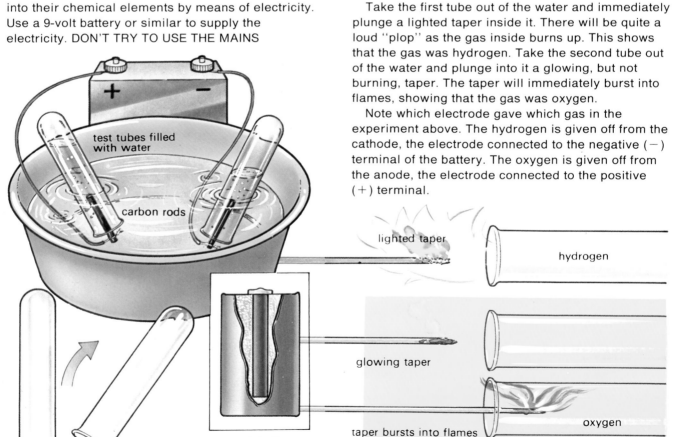

test tubes filled with water

carbon rods

torch battery

lighted taper

glowing taper

taper bursts into flames

hydrogen

oxygen

In the voltaic cell, the zinc rod consists of many zinc atoms. Some of these change into positive zinc ions and go into the sulphuric acid solution. The electrons are left behind on the zinc rod and a negative charge builds up on this rod. At the copper rod a different process takes place. In the solution the sulphuric acid gives positive hydrogen ions. These combine with electrons from the copper rod and turn back into hydrogen atoms. This causes bubbles of hydrogen gas to form on the rod. It also causes the copper rod to build up a positive charge because it is losing electrons. Thus the zinc rod contains more electrons than protons and the copper rod has less electrons than protons. When they are connected by a wire outside the solution, the electrons in the zinc move through the wire to the copper. In other words there is a flow of electric current.

Anodes and cathodes

In the cell the zinc rod dissolves in the sulphuric acid to give zinc ions. Sulphuric acid is a compound sometimes called dihydrogen sulphate. It loses its hydrogen as hydrogen gas. Electricity is produced by a chemical reaction in which zinc and dihydrogen sulphate change to zinc sulphate and hydrogen. The copper is not changed by the production of electricity but it is necessary to have a copper rod to give electrons to the hydrogen ions. In the voltaic cell the copper is the positive electrode or anode and the zinc is the negative electrode or cathode.

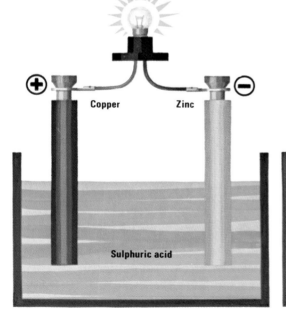

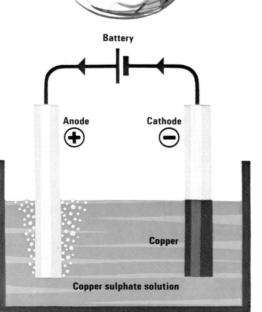

Above

Electrolysis is used for coating metal objects and parts with a thin layer of a different metal. Here are some objects that have been coated in this way. The part to be coated is hung in a bath of electrolyte and made the cathode of a cell. The anode is made of the metal to be deposited. When an electric current is passed, the object is covered with a layer of this metal. This is called electroplating. Usually objects are electroplated with expensive metals, such as gold, silver, copper, and chromium. Car bumpers are made of steel and covered with chromium to make them shiny. It would be too expensive to make the whole bumper out of chromium.

Right

In a car battery the electrodes are lead plates and the electrolyte is dilute sulphuric acid. When the battery is uncharged both these plates are coated with a thin layer of a brown compound called lead sulphate. To charge the battery an electric current is passed into the positive terminal, through the sulphuric acid and out of the negative terminal. This causes a chemical reaction. The lead sulphate on the positive plate turns to another compound called lead peroxide. On the other plate the lead sulphate turns to lead. This makes the sulphuric acid solution stronger.

Far right

When the battery is being discharged the opposite reactions take place. On the negative plate lead turns back to lead sulphate. On the positive plate lead peroxide changes to lead sulphate. The sulphuric acid in the electrolyte gets weaker. Note that when the battery is supplying electricity the current flows in the opposite direction to when it is being charged.

Below

Each pair of plates in an accumulator can give about 2 volts. Most car batteries have 6 pairs of plates, that is they have six cells connected in series. In this way they give 12 volts.

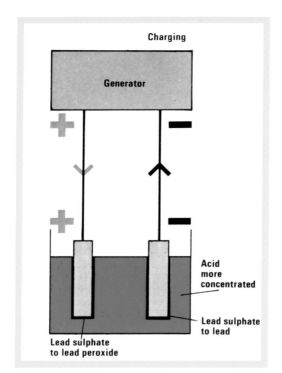

Charging

Generator

Acid more concentrated

Lead sulphate to lead

Lead sulphate to lead peroxide

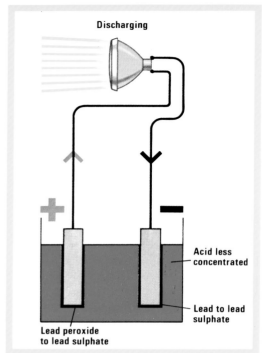

Discharging

Acid less concentrated

Lead to lead sulphate

Lead peroxide to lead sulphate

THE CAR BATTERY

In a normal dry battery the chemicals which produce the electric current are slowly used up. The whole battery has to be thrown away when it no longer works. Cells of this kind are called primary cells. They are expensive and cannot be used to produce large currents. So a cell has been developed which can store electrical energy passed into it. The electricity can then be drawn from the cell in the form of an electric current. Such a cell is called a secondary cell or, sometimes, an accumulator. An example is the car battery.

Accumulators

In an accumulator two lead plates are used as electrodes in a solution of sul-phuric acid. When a current is passed through the lead plates chemical changes take place in the electrodes, the sulphuric acid solution gets stronger and the cell becomes capable of driving an electric current. We call this charging a battery.

When the charging current is stopped, the battery can be connected to an electrical device, such as a light bulb. Current will flow for a time from the anode to the cathode. The chemical change which took place during charging is reversed as electricity is drawn from the accumulator. However the materials in the accumulator are not used up, merely changed. Therefore the whole process can begin again. When the accumulator is providing an electric current it is said to be discharging.

The accumulator does not make electricity in the way that the dry battery does. Electricity has to be put in before any can be taken out. The same amount of electricity can be obtained from an accumulator as was put into it.

In a normal petrol driven car the battery is used to produce the electric spark which starts the engine. It also supplies current for the car headlights and indicators, the heater fan, windscreen wipers, and horn. The battery is charged up by a battery charger or by a dynamo which is turned by the car engine.

Today many people are greatly concerned about the pollution of the air caused by the large number of cars, and

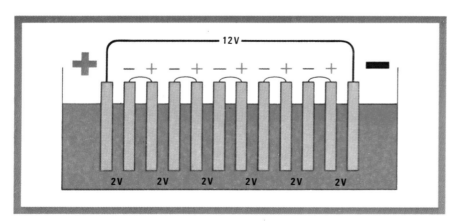

12V

2V 2V 2V 2V 2V 2V

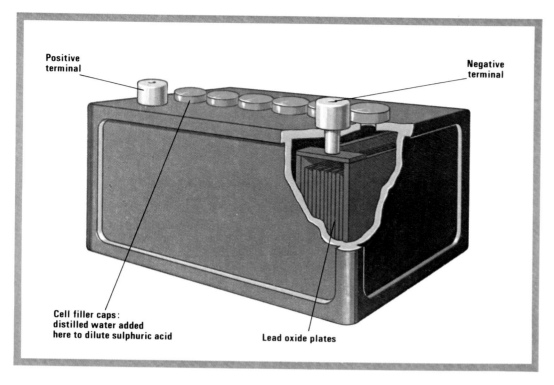

Positive terminal

Negative terminal

Cell filler caps:
distilled water added
here to dilute sulphuric acid

Lead oxide plates

especially lorries on the road. The gases that come out of their exhausts are poisonous.

One well-known vehicle does not poison our air. This is the milk float which is driven by electricity. It has an electric motor instead of a petrol or diesel engine. The power comes from large accumulators which are charged with electricity every night. Because no fuel is burnt there are no poisonous exhausts to pollute the atmosphere. Several car manufacturers are developing battery-driven cars for use by commuters in towns. The problem is to make accumulators that can hold large amounts of electricity and are not too heavy. Better and better accumulators are now being made for use in electrically powered cars.

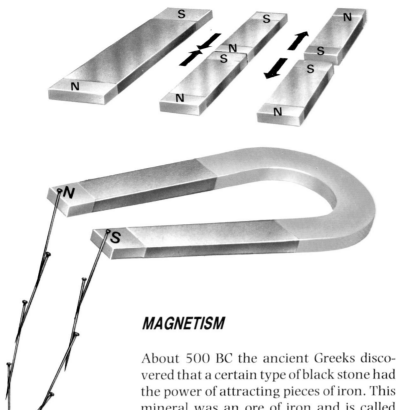

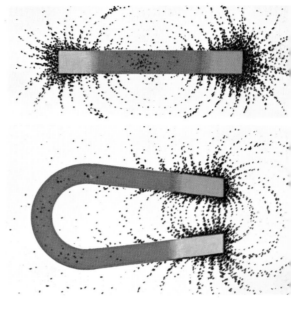

MAGNETISM

About 500 BC the ancient Greeks discovered that a certain type of black stone had the power of attracting pieces of iron. This mineral was an ore of iron and is called magnetite. Anything that has this property of attracting iron is called a magnet and the property itself is magnetism.

Magnetite is a compound of iron and oxygen. The common magnets that you see are made of iron or steel. A magnet can have any shape but is usually in the form of a bar magnet or a horseshoe magnet.

The Greeks used to think that pieces of iron stick to a magnet because it has small hooks on its surface. It is easy to show that this cannot be true. If you push a magnet close to a pin the pin will jump to the magnet. You can also attract objects by magnetism through a piece of paper.

Magnetic fields

Two things do not have to be touching one another to be attracted by magnetism. How do they affect one another? How does the pin know that the magnet is close to it? Obviously there must be some influence of the magnet passing through space. One way in which scientists have tried to explain this influence is by thinking of magnetic fields. The magnet affects the region around it and can influence other magnets or magnetic materials in this region. This region is called a field of force or a magnetic field.

It is possible to show a magnetic field by laying a piece of paper over a magnet and sprinkling iron filings on to it. When you tap the paper the filings arrange themselves into a pattern. The iron filings cluster together in the regions in which the magnet has most effect, that is, in the places where the field is strongest. You can see that there are more filings close to the ends or poles of the magnet. They also tend to arrange themselves in lines running between the poles of the magnet. These are called lines of force and are imaginary lines running from one pole of the magnet to the other. They shows the direction in which the magnet acts when anything is put into its field. The influence of a magnet falls off as one gets further away from it. We say that its field gets weaker.

Compasses

The earliest use of magnets was in compasses, for showing direction. This use depends on the fact that the earth has a magnetic field. It acts like a large bar magnet. Think of the earth spinning on an imaginary axis. One end is the North Pole and the other the South Pole. These are called the geographical poles of the earth. The earth acts like a large bar magnet lying almost along this axis. Any magnet suspended in the field will line up with the lines of force. The needle of a compass is a small magnet and always points north and south. The end of the magnet pointing north is called its north-seeking pole, or north pole. The other is its south pole.

In fact a compass needle does not point to the true North Pole. It points to the magnetic North Pole which is many hundred kilometres from the true North Pole.

Navigators always have to make a correction for this variation of the compass. This is complicated by the fact that the positions of the magnetic poles vary slightly from year to year. In some places the needle of the compass does not read true because of magnetic material such as iron ore in the earth, or a large piece of steel nearby. A compass can be shielded from stray magnetic fields by a piece of soft iron.

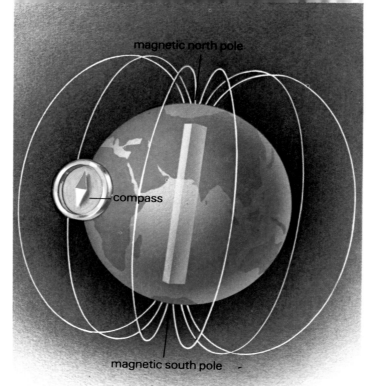

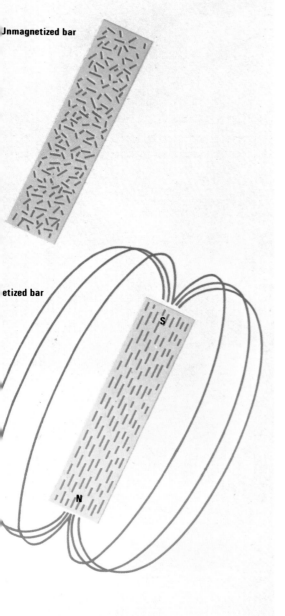

Unmagnetized bar

Magnetized bar

S

N

Above
The earth acts as a large magnet and this is why a compass needle can be used to show north and south. The needle is a small magnet balanced on a pivot and it always comes to rest along the lines of force. In fact, the earth's magnetic field is not symmetrical, as shown. It is distorted by the influence of the sun's magnetism.

Far left
In magnetic materials like iron the atoms themselves are little magnets. Usually they are all pointing in different directions so the metal is not a magnet. In a magnet the atom magnets all point in the same direction. If it is brought close to the unmagnetized metal it causes the atom magnets to line up and thus makes the metal into a magnet. When magnets are heated, they lose their magnetic properties because the heat disarranges the atoms. A magnet can also be demagnetized by hammering it or dropping it.

Left
This is the aurora borealis or northern lights. It is seen at night in Arctic regions and is caused by charged particles from the sun trapped by the earth's magnetic field. In the Antarctic the aurora australis is seen.

MAGNET MAGIC

FLOATING MAGNETS
You will need: 2 bar magnets ● cardboard box ● lolly sticks ● compass

Hang each magnet in turn from a piece of thread. Let them come to rest. You will find that both magnets end up pointing in the same direction. If you check with a compass, you will find they point north-south. Write N or S on the ends of each magnet to mark the north and south poles.

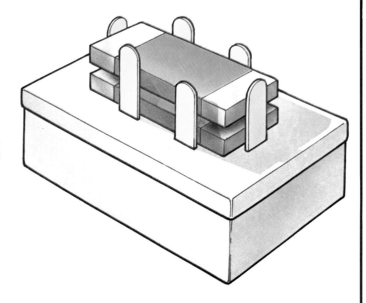

Place one of the magnets on top of a cardboard box. Draw around it with a pencil and stick ice lolly sticks along the line. Place the magnets in the middle so that the two north poles and the two south poles of the magnets are together. Watch how the top magnet floats in the air!

This shows you that two north poles and two south poles repel, or push against each other. If you place the top magnet the other way round, the two magnets will stick together. The north and south poles of magnets attract each other.

MAKING A COMPASS
You will need: card ● magnet ● tape ● needle ● cork ● glass of water ● detergent

You can easily make a simple compass yourself, using a sewing needle as a compass needle. But first you must magnetize it. Only then will it point north–south. Stick the needle on a piece of card with tape to hold it down. Then with one end of a magnet, stroke the needle from the middle towards one end about 50 times. After each stroke, raise the magnet clear of the end of the needle and come back down to the middle in a circular motion. Always stroke the needle in the same direction and with the same end of the magnet.

After 50 or so strokes, the needle will be well magnetized. Now you have to support it so that it can turn whichever way it wants, just like the needle of a proper compass. Stick the needle on or through a thin slice of cork, and then float the cork on a glass of water. Add a little detergent to the water to help it float freely.

When you have made your cork or jar compass, you will notice that the needle always comes to rest pointing in the same direction. One end will point north, the other south.

You can fix other directions with your compass by drawing a compass card, which shows all the compass points. Slip this card under your compass.

MAKING FACES

You will need: card ● copper wire ● tape ● iron filings ● battery

On a piece of card, draw the outline of a face, and then follow the line with a length of copper wire. Tape it in position. Cover the wire with a piece of thin card, and sprinkle some iron filings on top. Connect the ends of the wire to a battery (NOT THE MAINS) and tap the card lightly. The face will suddenly appear.

This happens because when electric current flows in a wire, it creates magnetism. It sets up a magnetic field. The face appears because the iron filings are attracted to the magnetic field around the wire.

The connection between electric current and magnetism is very important. As a result we can make electric motors and electromagnets.

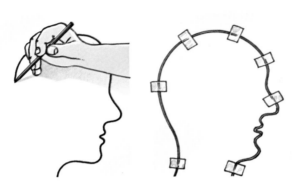

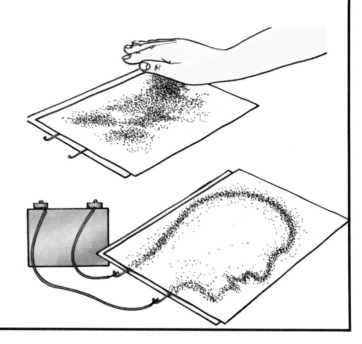

SWITCH-ON POWER

You will need: copper wire ● nail or bolt ● battery ● switch ● paper clips

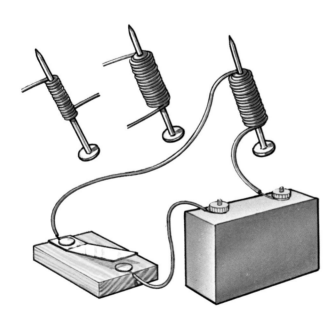

You can make an electric-current magnet using a length of copper wire and a large nail (or bolt). Wind the wire around the nail many times and tape it in place. Join the ends of the wire to the terminals of a battery through a simple switch (see page 138). Switch on. Bring the nail head near some paper clips and drawing pins, and watch them jump to it.

By winding the wire in a coil around the nail, you have made it into a magnet. We call such a magnet an electromagnet.

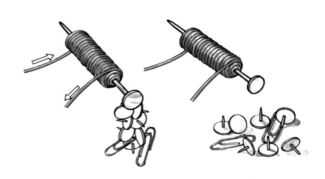

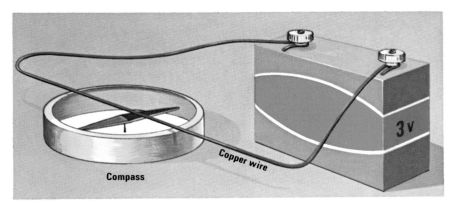

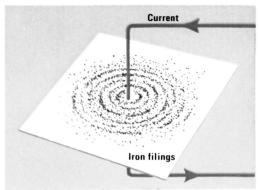

Iron filings

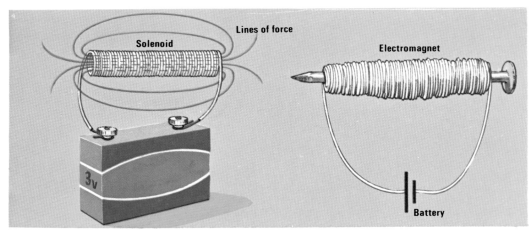

Solenoid

Lines of force

Electromagnet

Battery

Above

This simple experiment shows how a wire produces a magnetic field. When the battery is connected the compass needle moves.

Below

Hans Christian Oersted (1777–1851) was a Danish scientist. He believed that there was a connection between magnetism and electricity. He discovered the magnetic effect of an electric current in 1820.

Oersted

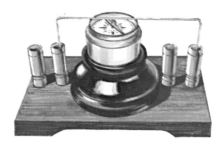

Above

A model of the apparatus used by Hans Oersted to demonstrate the magnetic effect of an electric current on a compass needle.

ELECTROMAGNETISM

In 1820 a Danish scientist, Hans Christian Oersted, made a very important discovery. He noticed that a magnet was affected by an electric current flowing in a wire.

You can easily do an experiment similar to this. Take a 3 volt battery, a length of copper wire, and a small pocket compass. Connect one end of the wire to one terminal of the battery and lay the wire over the compass. Now touch the free end of the wire to the other terminal of the battery. The compass needle will change direction. When you remove the end of the wire it swings back to its original position. Do not keep the battery connected for too long or it will soon go flat.

This experiment shows that a flowing electric current produces a magnetic field. The shape of this field is not the same as that of an ordinary bar or horseshoe magnet but it has the same properties. In fact a current in a wire can be made to act just like an ordinary magnet.

The "Switch-on Power" experiment on page 147 shows how to make an electric current magnet. The coil of wire wound round a core such as a nail is called a solenoid. Pass a current through it and put each end in turn near a compass needle. You will see that one end of the solenoid attracts the north pole of the needle and the other repels it. The solenoid has a north and south pole just as a bar magnet has. Find out what happens when you change the direction of the current by connecting the battery the other way round.

Electromagnets

Magnetism produced by an electric current is called electromagnetism. When you wind turns of wire around a large steel nail and connect it to a battery you produce a strong magnetic field. A magnet of this kind is called an electromagnet.

If you switch off the current you will probably find that the nail still acts as a magnet. It has been magnetized by the effect of the current. Magnets of this kind are called permanent magnets.

Left

If iron filings are used they can show the field of a single wire. This experiment requires a high current and you could not do it with a small battery.

Left

A coil of wire like this is called a solenoid. It acts as a magnet. You can make a good electromagnet by wrapping a coil around an iron core. Note that the more turns of wire you use, the stronger the magnet. The wire used has to be covered with an insulator.

Left

A large electromagnet can be used in a crane for moving scrap iron. To release the load, the driver simply switches off the current to the coils of the electromagnet.

If, instead of steel, you had used a piece of soft iron as a core you would find that the magnetism disappeared when the current was switched off. It is not easy to do this experiment as soft iron is difficult to find. You may be able to make a piece by heating an iron nail to red heat and letting it cool slowly. The soft iron does not keep its magnetism like steel. It is a temporary magnet.

Electromagnets have many uses, such as in electric bells, loudspeakers, electric motors and generators.

The fact that an electric current can create a magnetic field shows us where the magnetism of permanent magnets comes from. In a piece of magnetic material the atoms all act as little magnets (see page 144). An electric current in a wire is a flow of electrons along it. So a magnetic field is formed by movement of electrons. We know that atoms contain moving electrons. Thus we can see that the magnetism of a permanent magnet is caused by the motion of electrons in its atoms.

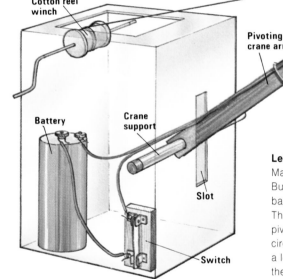

Cotton reel winch

Pivoting crane arm

Electromagnet

Metal picked up

Battery

Crane support

Slot

Switch

Left

Make a model magnetic crane. Build a wooden box to hold a battery and a cotton reel winch. The winch raises and lowers the pivoting crane arm. Make up a circuit with a battery, a switch, and a long loop of wire running along the crane arm. Wind the end of the loop around an iron bolt to make an electromagnet. When the current is switched on, the bolt becomes magnetized and will pick up scraps of metal.

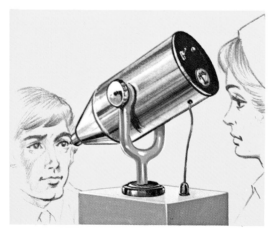

Left

A large electromagnet can be used to remove steel splinters from the eyes.

ELECTROMAGNETIC INDUCTION

After Oersted had shown that an electric current could produce a magnetic field (see page 148), scientists began to wonder whether they could use a magnetic field to produce an electric current. There were many attempts to do this. All were unsuccessful until in the 1830s Michael Faraday began a series of experiments with magnets and coils.

To detect an electric current some kind of instrument has to be used. The earliest form of current detector was the galvanometer. This was a compass surrounded by a flat vertical coil of many turns of wire. A current flowing through the coil produces a magnetic field which affects the compass needle.

The current is induced in the solenoid when the magnet is moved because the magnetic field is changing. A current also flows through a wire if the wire is moved through a magnetic field. Again, the wire is cutting the lines of force.

Faraday also did experiments on the opposite effect. When a wire is placed in a magnetic field and a current passed through it the wire moves. There is a force on it due to the effect of the current and the field. Thus we see that if a wire is moved through a magnetic field, a current flows in it. This principle is used in generating electricity (see page 152). If a wire carrying a current is placed in a a magnetic field, the wire is made to move. This principle is used in electric motors (see page 158).

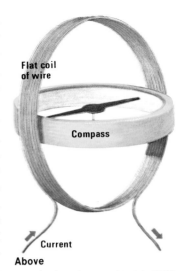

Flat coil of wire

Compass

Current

Above
In a simple galvanometer a current passing through the flat coil produces a magnetic field. This deflects the compass needle and so the current is detected.

Faraday's experiments

One of the experiments performed by Faraday was to take a large wire coil (solenoid) and connect it to a galvanometer. When a bar magnet was placed near the coil of wire the galvanometer was not affected. No electric current was produced by the magnet. However when the magnet was pushed into the solenoid the galvanometer needle moved slightly and then went back to its original position. When the magnet was pulled out of the solenoid the needle "kicked" in the opposite direction. Faraday realized that an electric current was being produced when the magnet was moving. The direction of the electric current depended on the direction in which the magnet was moved. This behaviour is called electromagnetic induction. A moving magnet induces an electric current in the solenoid.

This discovery was of immense importance. Up till then electric currents had been produced by electric cells. Now a method existed for converting the energy of motion (mechanical energy) into electrical energy.

For example, if the magnet was continually pushed and pulled in and out of the solenoid, an electric current flowed first one way and then the other. This produced an alternating current. A mechanical engine was used to move the magnet, making a simple generator.

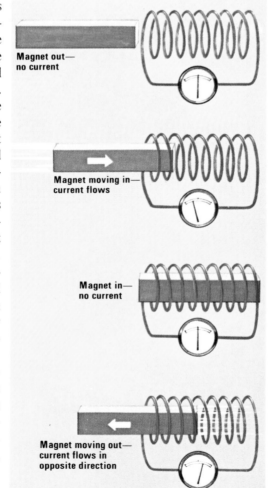

Magnet out— no current

Magnet moving in— current flows

Magnet in— no current

Magnet moving out— current flows in opposite direction

Left
When the magnet moves into the coil the galvanometer needle moves one way. When it is pulled out of the coil the needle moves in the opposite direction. The current only flows when the magnet is moving.

Maxwell

Above
James Clerk Maxwell (1831–1879) was a brilliant Scottish physicist and mathematician. He produced a mathematical theory of electromagnetic fields.

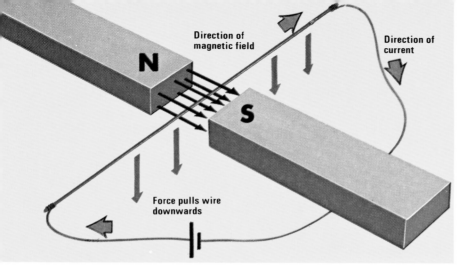

Direction of magnetic field

Direction of current

N

S

Force pulls wire downwards

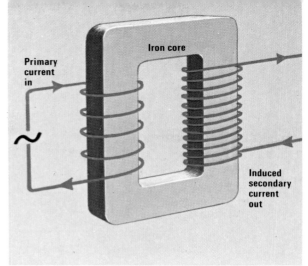

Primary current in

Iron core

~

Induced secondary current out

Above left
Electromagnetic induction occurs when a conductor moves through a magnetic field. The opposite effect is used in electric motors. A current is passed through the wire and this makes the wire move.

Above
Transformers also work by electromagnetic induction. They are used to change an alternating current of one voltage to an alternating current of another voltage. The current to be tranformed is passed through the first coil. As the current increases and decreases it produces a magnetic field which also increases and decreases. This changing magnetic field induces a current in the second coil which has a different number of turns. The difference in the number of turns causes a difference in the voltage.

Left
This is a large transformer used in a power station. The two coils of wire are wound on to the same iron core, one over the other. There are more turns of wire on the first coil than on the second. Because of this the voltage in the second coil is less than in the first. Transformers like this are called step-down transformers because they reduce the voltage. Step-up transformers are also used.

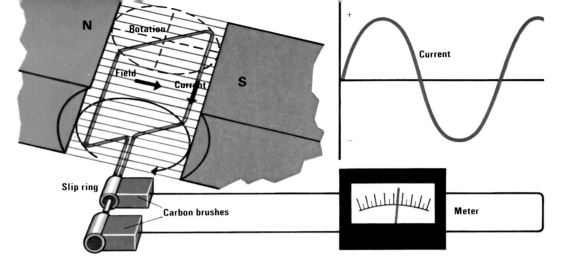

N

Rotation

Field

Current

S

Current

Slip ring

Carbon brushes

Meter

Left

If a coil of wire is rotated in a magnetic field a current is produced in the coil. The direction of the current reverses as the coil rotates. The first half of the revolution produces a current in one direction, the second half in the other direction. This is shown by a graph having the shape of a wave. The current varies from zero to a maximum (or minimum) and back to zero in each half cycle because the strength of the current depends on the number of magnetic lines of force that the coil cuts.

ELECTRIC GENERATORS

There are two main ways of making electricity. The first is to generate it in a cell by chemical reactions. The second is to produce it by the electromagnetic effect using a rotating machine. Rotating machines are called generators. Small generators are sometimes called dynamos.

The principle of the generator was discovered by Michael Faraday. He showed that if a conducting wire is moved across a magnetic field an electric current is generated in the wire.

The most convenient way to arrange this conducting wire is to rotate a coil of it between the poles of a permanent magnet. This is exactly what Faraday did in 1831.

The whole of our present way of life is based on his discovery. Without electricity modern society would come to a standstill. There would be much less lighting and heating. There would be no movement from the millions of electric motors that we use for trains, lifts, factory machines and the hundreds of other electrical appliances we use every day.

Faraday's first generator

Faraday's first generator was a small laboratory-bench model that he rotated by hand. In the modern power station, machines rotate the generators. In a coal, oil, or nuclear power station the generators are rotated by steam turbines (see page 155). The turbines are connected directly to the generators and the set is called a turbo-generator.

In a hydroelectric station the rotation of the generator is produced by a water turbine. These power stations are situated

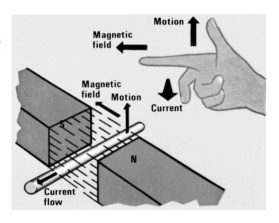

Motion

Magnetic field

Magnetic field Motion

Current

Current flow

Below

Michael Faraday (1791–1867) was a great British scientist. He made many discoveries in electricity and magnetism and studied electrolysis.

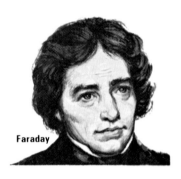

Faraday

Left

Fleming's right hand rule is a way of remembering in which direction the current flows when a conductor moves through a magnetic field. The thumb, forefinger, and second finger are extended at right angles to one another. If the thumb indicates the direction of motion and the forefinger the direction of the magnetic field (north to south), then the second finger indicates the direction of the current.

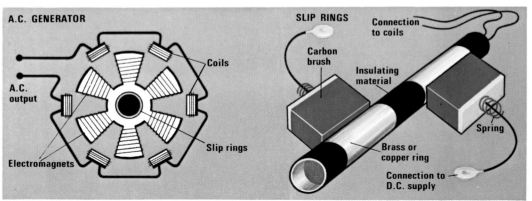

A.C. GENERATOR

A.C. output

Coils

Electromagnets

Slip rings

SLIP RINGS

Connection to coils

Carbon brush

Insulating material

Spring

Brass or copper ring

Connection to D.C. supply

Left

In a power station the generators have rotating electromagnets. The current needed to energize these electromagnets is fed to them by carbon brushes rubbing on slip rings. The advantage of this arrangement is that large currents and voltages can be generated on the coils since no moving contacts are required.

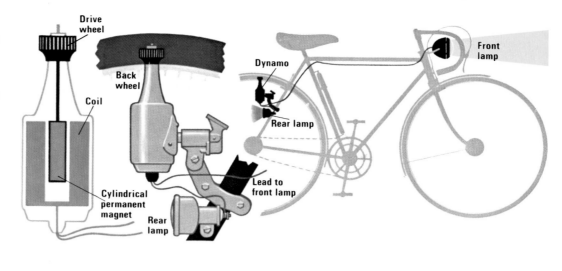

Drive wheel

Coil

Back wheel

Dynamo

Front lamp

Rear lamp

Cylindrical permanent magnet

Rear lamp

Lead to front lamp

Gauss

at points on rivers where there is a fall of level, usually at a natural waterfall. A dam is built to restrict the waterfall and the water is led through a large pipe to the lower level where it rotates a water turbine. In all cases the turbo-generator is a means of converting the energy of motion (mechanical energy) into electrical energy.

Fleming's Right Hand Rule

Fleming devised a rule, Fleming's Right Hand Rule, to work out in which direction the current flows in a conductor when it is moved through a magnetic field.

If the conductor is in the shape of a coil, the current is obviously going to change direction as the coil rotates. So the current produced by this type of machine is going to vary from nothing, to a maximum in one direction, falling again to nothing when the coil is vertical. The current then reverses direction and builds up to a maximum in the opposite direction, finally returning again to zero. This series of event is called an alternating current. The number of times this cycle changes in one second is called the frequency.

In small machines such as a bicycle dynamo the magnetic field is produced by a permanent magnet. In the large machines the electromagnet is rotated inside the coil of wire instead of the other way round. The effect is exactly the same. The electricity is generated in the stationary coil (stator) by the changing magnetic field produced by the rotating magnet (rotor).

153

POWER AND GENERATORS

The water-wheel and the windmill were for many thousands of years people's only sources of mechanical power. The water-wheel was a very large wheel placed in a flowing river. The rim was very wide and the spokes were broad and extended beyond the rim so that they formed large flat paddles. As the river water flowed over the wheel, it moved the paddles, thus making the whole wheel turn. The wheel was attached to the side of a mill and the axle was connected to large millstones for grinding corn. As the wheel turned, so did the millstones. The windmill worked in a similar way, using the force of the wind to move the sails to provide a turning force for the axle.

Hydroelectric generators

In the nineteenth century the water turbine was developed from the simple water-wheel, and was much more efficient. In a turbine, the paddles of the wheel are bucket-shaped. Water, poured from above, fills up these buckets and the weight of this water moves the wheel round. As the paddles reach the lowest position, the buckets empty themselves. With the discovery of electricity, water turbines were used to turn generators to produce electricity for light, heat and power (see page 152). These are called hydroelectric generators. The power supply for hydroelectric stations is made continuous by building dams to store large quantities of water.

People are finding other ways of turning the energy of water into electricity. For example, there are huge amounts of energy in the tidal movements of seas and rivers, and in the movement of waves.

In hotter parts of the world, the sun's energy can be turned directly into electricity. In windy areas, groups of windmills called wind farms can create enough electricity for a small town.

However, at present all these methods produce only a tiny proportion of the

Below
The principle of a thermal power station. Coal or oil is burnt in a boiler to produce steam. The steam drives a turbine which is coupled to a generator.

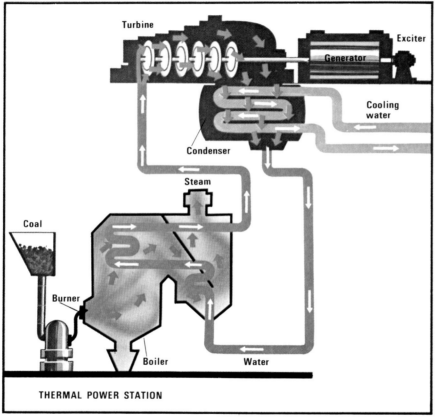

THERMAL POWER STATION

Right
Solar cells are used in spacecraft to provide energy. Light from the sun is converted directly into electricity by these cells. Solar cells are used in hot countries to provide hot water in houses.

world's electricity. Most of it is produced from fuels. These are coal and oil, formed from plant and animal fossils millions of years ago, and nuclear fuel. Coal and oil are burnt to give heat. Nuclear power stations use the heat produced when atoms are made to split into two parts. This is called nuclear fission (see page 192). It is the same process as in the atom bomb, but it is very carefully controlled so that it does not occur too quickly and cause an explosion.

The heat from the coal, oil or nuclear fuel is used to produce steam and drive a steam turbine. This turns a generator which makes electricity.

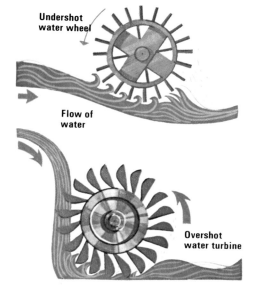

Undershot water wheel

Flow of water

Overshot water turbine

Left
Water turbine. The simplest kind of water turbine is the undershot water wheel in which the paddles dip into the flowing stream of water and are made to rotate. In the overshot turbine water falls into bucket-shaped paddles. The weight of the water turns the wheel. This type of turbine needs a difference of level in the flowing water.

MAKE A SMALL WATER TURBINE
You will need: cork ● knitting needle ● 6 pen nibs ● wire coathanger ● plastic bottle ● nail ● water

Push a knitting needle lengthways through the middle of the cork. Do this carefully – knitting needles are sharp. Stick 5 or 6 nibs into the cork evenly spaced, so that they stick out at right-angles. Your turbine rotor is now complete.

Make a stand for the rotor using wire from an old wire coathanger. Bend the wire to form a cradle for the needle, using a pair of pliers if necessary. (Watch your fingers again!) Place the rotor in the cradle, and your turbine is ready for action.

You can make the turbine spin just by placing it under the tap. But it can be done more effectively using a water jet from a large plastic bottle. Pierce a hole near the bottom of the bottle with a nail. When you fill the bottle, the water spurts out of the hole in a jet. Arrange your turbine so that the jet strikes the rotor blade at right-angles. Many hydroelectric power stations have this kind of arrangement.

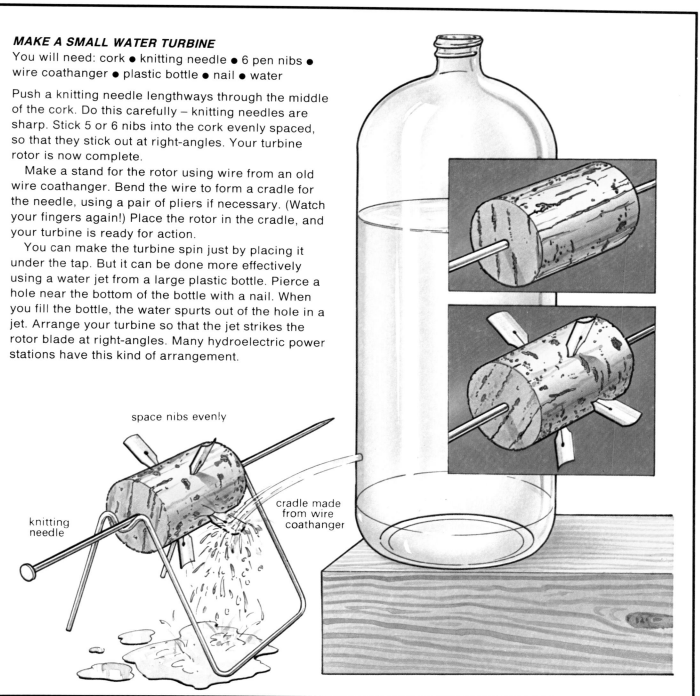

space nibs evenly

knitting needle

cradle made from wire coathanger

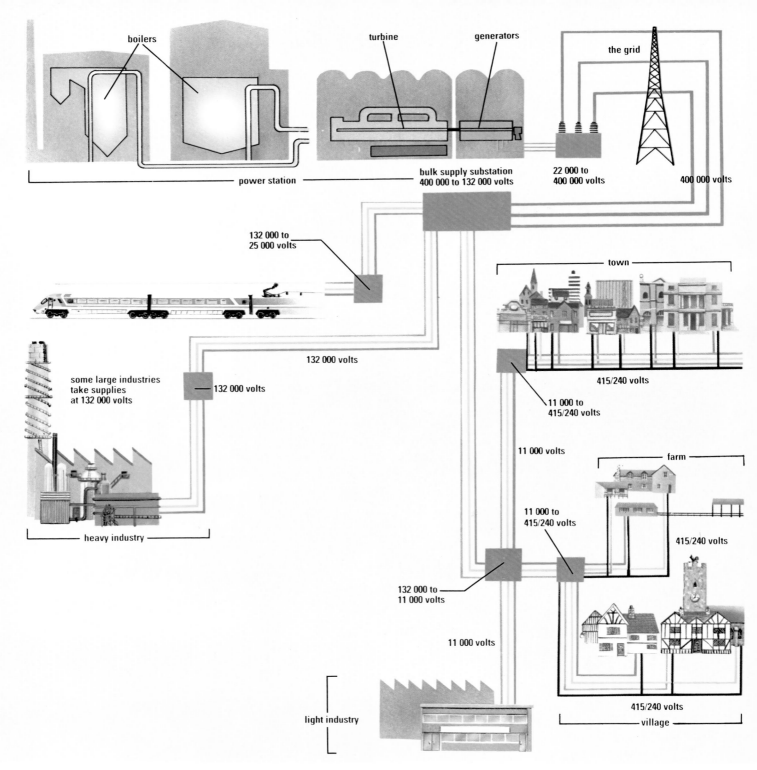

boilers

turbine

generators

the grid

power station

bulk supply substation
400 000 to 132 000 volts

22 000 to
400 000 volts

400 000 volts

132 000 to
25 000 volts

132 000 volts

some large industries
take supplies
at 132 000 volts

132 000 volts

town

415/240 volts

11 000 to
415/240 volts

11 000 volts

farm

11 000 to
415/240 volts

415/240 volts

heavy industry

132 000 to
11 000 volts

11 000 volts

light industry

415/240 volts

village

Above

The manufacture and distribution
of electricity. Inside the power
station, steam is produced in
boilers and sent into steam
turbines which drive the electricity
generators. After it is used, the
steam is converted back into water
and recycled to the boilers. The
electricity generators send out an
electric current at 22,000 volts to

the power station substation
which increases it up to 400,000
volts for transmission over the grid
system, since less electric power is
lost at high voltage. The voltage
has to be lowered by substations
to 132,000 volts for main
distribution. For general use a
415/240 volt service is provided by
small substations.

MAINS SUPPLY ELECTRICITY

In our homes we use a large number of
electrical appliances, including electric
lights, cookers, washing machines,
mixers, drills, fires, and television. These
and many more are operated by mains
supply electricity. The mains supply is
generated in power stations and transmit-

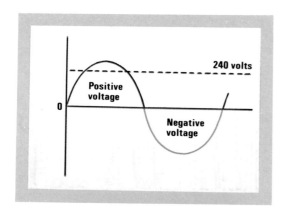

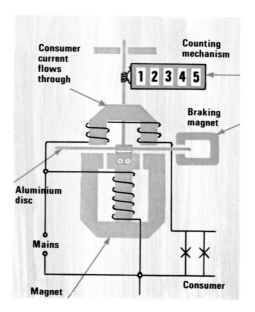

Left
Electricity meters consist of a special kind of electric motor which drives a counting device. This shows the number of units (kilowatt-hours) used. The aluminium motor disc must not rotate after the current has ceased. A braking magnet is used to stop the disc.

Far left
The mains electricity supplied to homes is alternating current. This means that the voltage rises from zero to a maximum value of about 340 volts; it then declines to zero again. This is called half a cycle. The remaining half cycle is a negative voltage, the minimum voltage being −340 volts. The average of each half cycle is 240 volts. The number of times this cycle is repeated in one second is called the frequency. In Britain this is 50 hertz (1 hertz is a freqeuency of 1 cycle per second). In the USA it is 60 hertz.

ted by wires to homes, offices and factories. There is a network of these wires running throughout the country and this is called the grid. The British grid consists of 235 power stations and has 13,000 km (8,000 miles) of wires. The voltage carried by these wires is very high, sometimes as high as 400,000 volts. The wires are mostly carried on pylons that are a familiar sight in the countryside. These high-voltage wires carry the current to sub-stations where the voltage is reduced by transformers (see page 151). This reduced voltage is transmitted to the users, usually by underground cables, but sometimes by overhead wires.

Alternating and direct currents

In most countries the mains supply is alternating current (ac for short). This means that the voltage varies up and down and is not steady as it is in direct current (dc). Alternating current is used because its voltage can be changed by a transformer. Direct current cannot be changed in this way.

When the electricity enters a home or factory it has to be metered because we have to pay for the electricity we use. The more we consume the more we pay. A meter consists of a special type of motor connected to a counting device. It has a little dial that shows the number of units used. At regular intervals throughout the year someone from the electricity company comes to read the meter and then a bill is sent to the consumer. The bill is

worked out on the number of kilowatt-hours used. If you have a 2 kilowatt heater and you keep it on for one hour you will be charged for 2 kilowatt-hours. For a 3 kilowatt heater burning for 2 hours the consumption would be 6 kilowatt-hours.

The price of electricity, in most countries, depends on the time at which it is used. It is usually cheaper at night than in the day. So some heaters, called storage heaters, are heated by electricity during the night and give out their heat during the day.

Below
Many industrial machines work on mains electricity. Heavy machines require special installations.

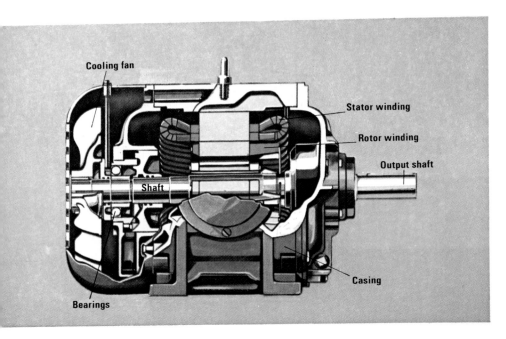

Cooling fan
Stator winding
Rotor winding
Output shaft
Shaft
Casing
Bearings

Above
An electric induction motor. The rotor and the stator have identical windings. The two windings behave rather like a transformer. The magnetic field induced in the rotor causes it, and the attached drive shaft, to rotate.

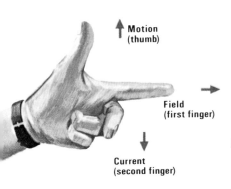

Motion (thumb)

Field (first finger)

Current (second finger)

Above
Fleming's left hand rule gives the direction of motion for motors. The first finger gives the direction of the magnetic field, the second finger indicates the direction of the current, and the thumb then gives the direction of motion.

Right
A vacuum cleaner uses an electric motor to suck up dust. The motor drives a fan which sucks in the air through the dust bag. The motors are usually ac synchronous motors as no change of speed is needed.

ELECTRIC MOTORS

Electric motors depend on the same principle as the generator invented by Michael Faraday (see page 152).In the generator, a current is produced in a conductor by moving it through a magnetic field. In the motor, a current is passed through a conductor placed in a magnetic field. This produces a force on the conductor which tends to make it move. Again, as in the generator, the most convenient arrangement is to make the conductor into a coil of wire and place it between the poles of a magnet.

The commutator

The current has to be supplied to the coil through a device called a commutator.

The commutator reverses the direction of the electric current after the coil has made half a rotation. If there were no commutator, the coil would come to rest after half a turn, with the coil horizontal. The change in direction of the current makes it rotate through another half rotation, and so on.

On a large motor there is not one coil but a series of coils, each displaced by a small angle from the previous one. The commutator, too, has many segments, one for each separate coil. The current is fed to each segment of the commutator by the carbon brushes as it rotates between them.

Electric motors have a wide variety of uses, from tiny fraction-of-a-kilowatt motors that drive electric shavers, to enormous motors that drive trains and industrial machinery. Some motors are designed to run on alternating current

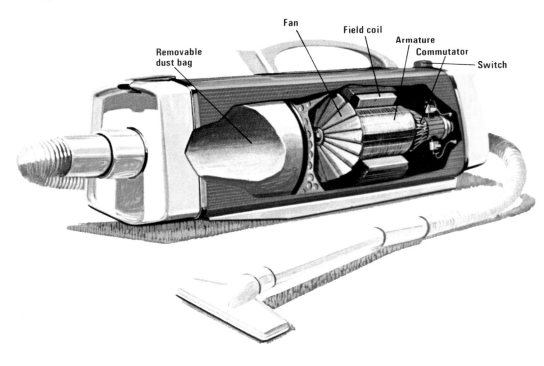

Fan
Field coil
Armature
Commutator
Switch
Removable dust bag

Right
Electric trains use large electric motors. In the London Underground, the current is picked up from a live rail. On the Continent and in America an overhead line and a pantograph are used.

(ac), some on direct current (dc), and some can be used on either (universal motors). The dc motors used in electric trains are the same type as the model described, except that the permanent magnet is replaced by an electro-magnet.

Synchronous ac motors run at a constant speed that depends on the frequency of the supply. They are therefore not used when it is necessary to vary the speed to any great extent.

The ac induction motor, which is widely used in industry, has rotatory windings (the rotor) very similar to the stationary winding (the stator). The two windings behave rather like a transformer (see page 151). Some of these motors will not start themselves and therefore need a separate starter motor.

Electric motors are a very convenient and clean means of obtaining mechanical energy. Electric cars would reduce the pollution in our cities enormously. They produce no exhaust fumes and are much more silent than cars driven by internal combustion engines.

One of the advantages of electric motors is that they produce rotary motion directly. In a petrol engine the back and forward motion of the piston has to be converted into rotary motion.

Some electric motors, called linear motors, do not produce rotation. They are a type of induction motor in which the stator and rotor are both straight and parallel. This type of motor may one day be used to provide economic intercity transport by monorail. One winding would be on the vehicle, the other winding would be on the single track used.

MAKE AN ELECTRIC MOTOR
You will need: a large cork ● No 26 SWG insulated copper wire ● a knitting needle ● rubber bands ● stout pins ● nails ● two small bar magnets ● empty matchboxes

Take a large cork and wind on to it, lengthways, 25 turns of copper wire. Hold this winding in place by two or three rubber bands. Make connections to the two ends of the wire using two stout pins which must be left protruding from the cork by about 2cm. Now pass a knitting needle through the centre of the cork and support the whole device on two crossed nails at each end. The magnetic field is produced by two bar magnets supported on matchboxes. A 6 volt battery is connected by two wires to two bent paper clips held in position by drawing pins. The pins from the cork must just touch the paper clips. The motor is not self-starting. To start it, rotate the cork.

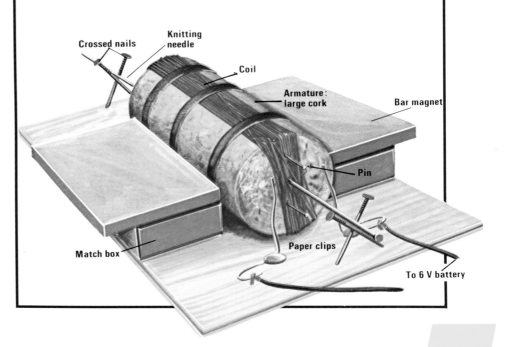

Below

Edison's original tinfoil phonograph, invented in 1877, recorded the human voice by making sound impressions on a piece of tinfoil wrapped tightly around a bass drum. The drum had to be turned by hand.

Bottom

Thomas Alva Edison, the American inventor, was born in 1847 and died in 1931. Among his many inventions is the talking machine, later called by various names including gramophone, phonograph, and record player.

RECORDING ON TAPE AND DISC

One of the many uses of magnets and electromagnetism is in tape players. Magnetic recording of sound was first achieved in 1898 by a Danish inventor, Valdemar Poulsen. He used a reel of steel wire instead of the tape used in modern recorders. The use of tapes was introduced in the 1920s.

Tape recorders

In tape recorders a magnet is used to record sounds on to the tape. The tape is a strip of plastic with a coating of a powdered material called iron oxide. This is magnetic. To produce a tape recording the sound is first converted into electrical signals by a microphone. In the microphone the varying pressure of air which is the sound is changed into a varying electric current. This is taken through wires to the recording head where the electrical signal is recorded on the magnetic tape.

The recording head is a curved piece of iron wound with a coil of wire to make an electromagnet. The iron has a very narrow gap between the ends. As the electric current flows through the coil a magnetic field is produced across the gap between the two poles of the electromagnet. The tape is passed along very close to the gap. The iron oxide on the tape is magnetized by the magnetic field on the recording head. When the current through the coil is large the magnetic field is strong. The tape is then strongly magnetized. When the current is small the tape is weakly magnetized. In this way the changes in the current are recorded on the tape.

When the recording is being played back the tape moves past a similar head called the reproducing head. The magne-

Right

Compact discs are read by a laser beam rather than by a needle. This means that the disc is never touched by anything other than a beam of light and so is very long-lasting.

Edison

tic parts of the tape produce a weak magnetic field in the reproducing head. As the tape goes past, this magnetic field changes. The magnetic field causes a small current in the coil. This changes as the field changes. It is made stronger by an amplifier. The varying electric current is identical to the one produced by the microphone during recording. When it is passed into a loudspeaker the original sound is reproduced.

Records and record players

The first machine to reproduce the human voice, the talking machine, was very different from a tape player. It was invented in 1877 by an American, Thomas Alva Edison, and was the fore-runner of the record player. A modern record is a flat plastic disc with a spiral groove on each side. Marks or indentations run along the grooves representing the recorded sound. Thousands of copies of a record are made from one master disc. The master disc has ridges instead of grooves. The first mass-produced records were made of shellac in heated presses. The master was stamped against the surface of the soft shellac leaving grooves identical to those cut in the original recording.

The play-back needle travels in these grooves and vibrates against the bumps in the grooves thus reproducing the original sound. The play-back needle vibrates in the pick-up which converts the vibrations to electric currents. These currents are fed to an amplifier which increases their power so that they can operate a loudspeaker.

Improvements in recording, electronics, and loudspeakers have led to sound reproduction which is very close to the original sound. This high fidelity sound is usually called hi-fi.

Compact discs

A big step forward has been the development of the compact disc. These smaller, silvery-looking discs are played in a similar way to the video disc (see page 181).

Below
A video cassette recorder. This can record television programmes for later viewing. The electric signals that make up a television programme's picture and sounds are changed into magnetic signals in the video recorder. These signals are then recorded on tape as magnetic patterns in the tape. When the tape is played, the magnetic patterns reproduce the original electric signals, and these go into the television set to give a picture and sound. A long-playing video cassette recorder has over half a kilometre of tape in it.

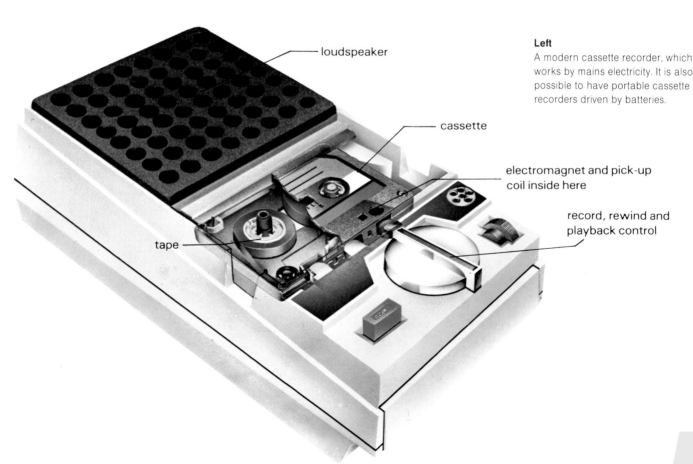

loudspeaker

cassette

electromagnet and pick-up coil inside here

record, rewind and playback control

tape

Left
A modern cassette recorder, which works by mains electricity. It is also possible to have portable cassette recorders driven by batteries.

Fresnel

Young

Above

The wave theory of light, proposed by the Dutch scientist Christiaan Huygens (1629–95), was studied by both Augustin Fresnel (1788–1827) of France and Thomas Young (1773–1829) of England. Young proved the theory in 1801.

Planck

Above

Max Planck (1858–1947), a German physicist. Many processes, including absorption and emission of light, could not be explained by wave theory. In 1900, Planck suggested that electromagnetic radiation could also be thought of as a stream of small bundles of energy, called quanta. Each quantum, travelling at the speed of light, has an energy proportional to the frequency of the radiation. A light quantum is called a photon.

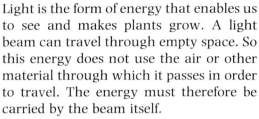

Using Waves and Electrons

WAVES

Light is the form of energy that enables us to see and makes plants grow. A light beam can travel through empty space. So this energy does not use the air or other material through which it passes in order to travel. The energy must therefore be carried by the beam itself.

We can tell from the sharp edges of shadows that rays of light travel through air along a straight path. They cannot bend round corners.

People therefore thought of light rays as straight lines. They helped to explain reflection and refraction. Then in 1680, Huygens suggested that light rays were in fact waves. Over a century later his theory was shown to be true.

crest and one trough it has travelled one wavelength. The wave has completed one cycle of its motion and is ready to repeat itself. The number of cycles in one second is called the frequency of the wave.

Waves move at tremendous speed. The speed is always the same in one particular medium such as air, but decreases when waves enter denser material, such as glass or water. This change in speed causes refraction of the light beam producing an increase in wavelength. The speed of a light wave in any medium equals its wavelength multiplied by its frequency. The greatest speed of light is in a vacuum, such as outer space. The speed in air is very close to this value. The maximum speed is equal to 300,000 km per second. No object moving in a vacuum can travel faster than this speed.

Each light wave has its own wavelength and each of these wavelengths corresponds to a slightly different colour. Red light has almost twice the wavelength of violet light. Yellow, green and blue light have wavelengths between these values.

Wavelengths

Light travels in one direction but the ray itself is moving up and down in continuous crests and troughs. This wave has a similar shape to ripples on a pond. As it moves through space, there is always the same distance between two neighbouring crests or troughs. The distance is called the wavelength. It is an extremely tiny distance measured in minute fractions of a metre. The height of a crest or the depth of a trough is called the amplitude. The greater the amplitude of the wave, the greater its energy. As the energy decreases, the amplitude grows less and less.

After the wave has gone through one

Electromagnetic radiation

Light is not the only form of energy transmitted in waves. Radio waves, infrared and ultraviolet radiation, X-ray, and gamma rays also travel as wave motions. All these waves move at the speed of light. However, the wavelengths (and hence frequencies) are very different. It is the different wavelengths that give each type of radiation its special properties. They are all examples of electromagnetic radiation, and they all travel as electromagnetic waves.

The chart showing the different electromagnetic radiations in order of increasing wavelength (or decreasing frequency) is called the electromagnetic spectrum.

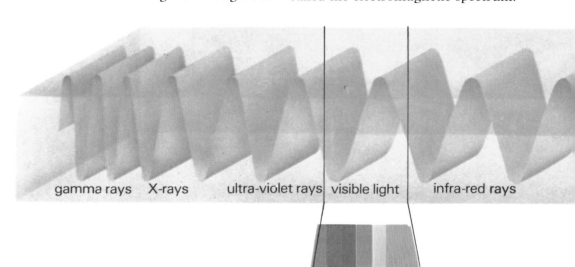

gamma rays   X-rays   ultra-violet rays | visible light   infra-red rays

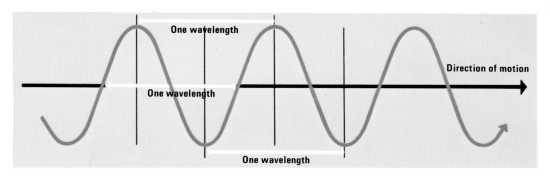

One wavelength

One wavelength

Direction of motion

One wavelength

Left

The wavelength of red light is almost twice that of blue light. The frequency is that number of complete wave cycles in one second. As the wavelength increases, the frequency decreases. Red light has almost twice the wavelength of blue light, while its frequency is almost half that of blue light.

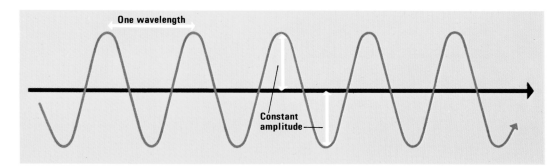

One wavelength

Constant amplitude

Left

The amplitude, or maximum height, of a crest or trough, remains the same if the wave's energy stays the same. If the wave loses the energy, the amplitude decreases. The square of the amplitude (amplitude times amplitude) gives a measure of the energy.

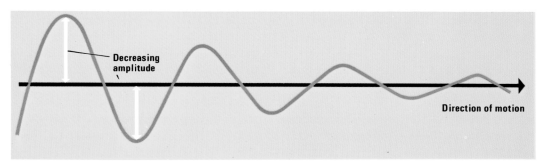

Decreasing amplitude

Direction of motion

Below

The electromagnetic spectrum. Radio waves have much longer wavelengths than light waves which in turn have greater wavelengths than X-rays and gamma rays. We can only see a very narrow part of the spectrum.

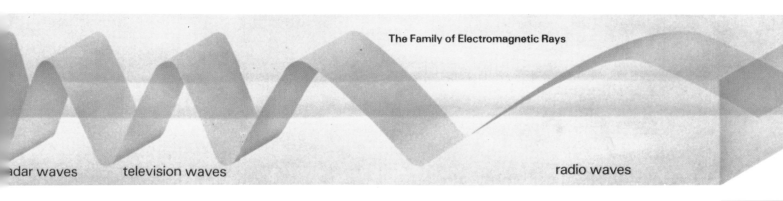

The Family of Electromagnetic Rays

adar waves   television waves   radio waves

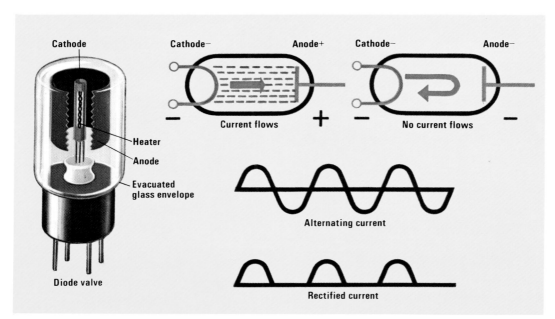

Cathode

Heater

Anode

Evacuated glass envelope

Diode valve

Cathode−   Anode+

Current flows   +

Cathode−   Anode−

No current flows   −

Alternating current

Rectified current

Below

Wilhelm Konrad Roentgen (1845–1923), a German physicist. He discovered X-rays in 1895 and studied many of their properties. The discovery of X-rays started a new era in physics and medicine.

Roentgen

Fleming

Above

Sir John Ambrose Fleming (1849–1945) an English physicist. He invented the diode valve in 1904.

X-RAYS

Like light, X-rays also move as waves, but the wavelength is very much smaller. Unlike light waves, they are invisible. The energy of X-rays is very high. They can travel a great distance inside an object and sometimes they are able to pass straight through it.

X-rays are produced in an X-ray tube when a narrow stream of electrons emitted from a heated cathode is strongly attracted towards the anode. The anode is at a very high voltage. This means that the electrons move very fast towards the anode and therefore have a large amount of energy. The anode contains a small disc of heavy metal such as tungsten. When the electrons strike the tungsten atoms, they give up their energy to electrons in the atoms. To get rid of this excess energy, the atoms emit X-rays.

X-rays have various uses in medicine. X-rays, like light, can produce an image on photographic film. If a person stands between a low-energy source of X-rays and a film, a photo of the bone structure is obtained. Broken or badly formed bones can be seen.

CT scanner

A more advanced type of X-ray machine is the computerized tomographic (CT) scanner. A CT scanner uses a computer to produce highly detailed pictures of the inside of a patient's body. The computer in a CT machine is fed data on how the different tissues in the body absorb X-rays. As a patient is scanned, the computer compares this data with the amount of radiation actually absorbed by the patient's body. The computer is able to build up a very detailed picture of the tissues in the body.

To produce a CT scan, X-rays are only passed through a thin slice of the body at one time. This also helps produce a clearer picture. The X-ray tube travels around the patient's body, making $1\frac{1}{2}$ million exposures as it travels. Sensitive detectors also travel around the body opposite the X-ray tube. The detectors are linked to the computer which builds up the detailed picture on a television-like screen. Today's scanners can examine slices of the body from 2 mm to 13 mm thick, as easily as if they were slices of bread.

NMR scanner

Another type of body scanner is called an NMR scanner. This uses a process called nuclear magnetic resonance (NMR) to produce detailed pictures of the inside of a patient's body. The patient lies in a strong magnetic field produced by an electric

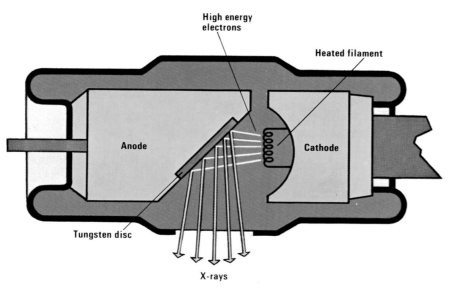

High energy
electrons

Heated filament

Anode

Cathode

Tungsten disc

X-rays

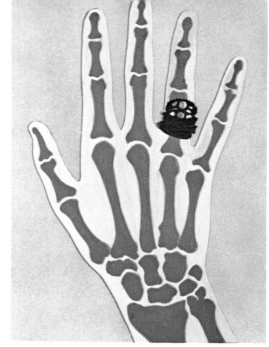

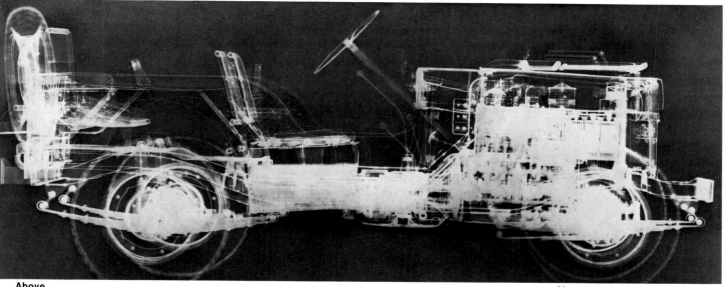

Above
An X-ray photograph of a jeep.
Engineers use photographs of this
type to detect faults in assembly or
to show up some types of defect in
the metal.

current flowing in a superconducting coil.
Radio signals are beamed into the area of
the body being investigated. The nuclei, or
central parts, of the atoms of the body
produce tiny magnetic signals which are
picked up by detectors. A computer is used
to form a picture of the inside of the body
from the magnetic signals.

X-rays are also used in scientific
research to find out how atoms and
molecules are arranged in crystals and
how they are grouped together in some of
the giant chemical compounds found in
the body, such as DNA. This type of
research is called X-ray crystallography.

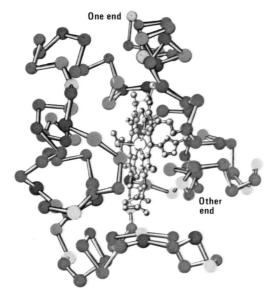

One end

Other
end

Above top
An X-ray photograph of a hand
with a ring. Dentists take X-ray
photos to check that your teeth
are growing correctly and to see if
you need any fillings. Only bones
and teeth show up on the negative
of the film. The film is blackened
by X-rays which are able to pass
straight through skin and air.
Bones and teeth absorb most of
the X-rays and therefore appear
whitish on the negative and dark
on the print, as shown above.

Left
The chemical structure of
cytochrome C. This is a giant
molecule present in the cells of the
body. Its complicated structure
was unravelled by the use of X-
rays. Each coloured ball
represents a different group of
atoms. Knowing its structure helps
scientists to learn about how it
works.

ELECTRON MICROSCOPES

The electron microscope is a powerful instrument used to examine very small objects. Instead of using light to illuminate the object, a beam of electrons is used. Electron microscopes are powerful enough to produce images, or pictures, of single atoms about 30 millionths of a millimetre across. There are many fields of science, such as medicine, chemistry and physics, where the electron microscope is a valuable tool.

Different types

There are several different types of electron microscope: the transmission electron microscope, the scanning electron microscope, the field ion microscope, and the scanning tunnelling microscope.

The transmission electron microscope was first developed by a German scientist, Ernst Ruska, in 1932. A beam of electrons is produced by heating a thin coil of wire to a high temperature. The electron beam passes through a thin slice cut from the object being studied. The electrons bounce off the atoms and molecules making up the thin slice. They are then focused by special magnets, called magnetic lenses, to form an image of the object on a television-like screen.

In the scanning electron microscope a fine beam of electrons moves across, or scans, the surface of the object. Some of the electrons bounce off the atoms in the surface. These are picked up and focused by magnetic lenses to form an image of the surface on the microscope screen.

The field ion microscope is also used to examine the surface of an object. The specimen to be examined is first cut or etched, using chemicals, into a sharp needle point. This is placed in a chamber in front of a fluorescent screen. A small amount of helium gas is let into the chamber and a high voltage applied to the needle. Helium atoms close to the tip of the needle lose electrons and become electrically charged. The screen attracts the helium atoms, and they form a greatly magnified image of the needle tip on the screen.

The scanning tunnelling microscope also uses a fine needle. The needle hovers just above the surface of the specimen

Right
The huge CIBA factory in Switzerland where drugs are manufactured. Millions of pounds are spent every year by the various drug manufacturers on research and new drugs are discovered and tested all the time. This is one reason why medicine has been described as the art that makes use of all the sciences.

being examined. There is a voltage between the needle and the specimen. This causes an electric current to flow across the gap between the needle and specimen. As the needle moves over the spectrum, the current is kept constant by moving the needle up and down. In this way, the needle traces the minute hills and valleys in the surface. A computer converts the movements of the needle into a picture of the atoms on the surface of the specimen.

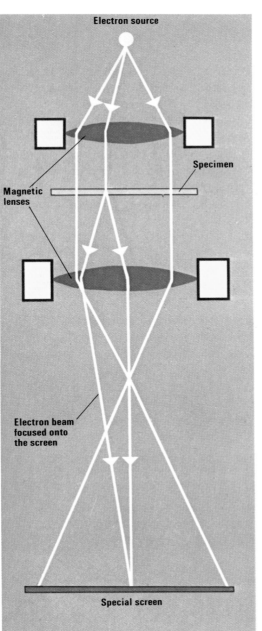

Electron source

Magnetic lenses

Specimen

Electron beam focused onto the screen

Special screen

Above
An enormous electron microscope in Japan.

Above
Seen through a simple microscope, this fly's wing looks ten times its real size.

Left
A diagram of a transmission electron microscope. The image is formed in a similar way to that in the optical microscope, but the magnification is much greater. A tiny part of an animal can be shown in great detail. Images of nerves, blood cells, and viruses, for example, are used to find out how these living things work.

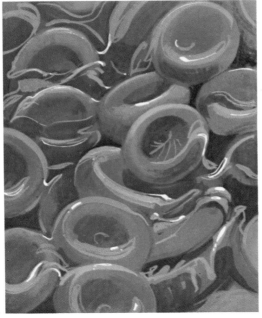

Left
Red blood cells, magnified 5000 times. Blood contains a large number of red cells, as well as many other substances. The red cells here were magnified by a scanning electron microscope, a slightly more complicated form of the ordinary electron microscope. It produces more life-like images.

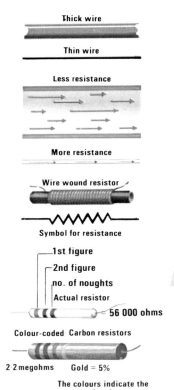

Thick wire

Thin wire

Less resistance

More resistance

Wire wound resistor

Symbol for resistance

1st figure
2nd figure
no. of noughts
Actual resistor
= 56 000 ohms

Colour-coded Carbon resistors

2·2 megohms   Gold = 5%

The colours indicate the amount of resistance offered by the resistor

Colour code		
black		0
brown		1
red		2
orange		3
yellow		4
green		5
blue		6
violet		7
grey		8
white		9

Variable resistors

Knob

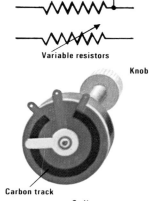

Carbon track

X ——WWWW—— X

Above
Wire-wound resistors and the colour-code. A resistor controls the amount of current in a circuit. It is made of a material that slows down the flow of electrons. When you turn down your radio you increase the resistance and the signal to the loudspeaker becomes weaker.

ELECTRONICS

Electronics is concerned with the movement of electrons. Circuits are complete pathways for electrons to travel along while they do useful work. This work ranges from lighting a torch bulb to running a huge computer. These pathways are connected to various electrical components that each perform different functions. The components include valves, transistors, resistors, capacitors, and inductors.

The diode valve

The diode valve was invented by John Fleming in 1904. It consists of two electrodes, a cathode and an anode, in a sealed glass tube from which the air has been removed. It can convert alternating current (ac) to direct current (dc).

When the cathode is heated, electrons are emitted. These are attracted towards the positively charged anode. A current therefore flows through the valve, but only in one direction – towards the positive anode. If the anode becomes negatively charged, no current flows.

The triode valve has an anode, a cathode, and a third electrode called the grid. The flow of electrons from cathode to anode is affected by the charge on the grid. As the grid becomes more positive a greater number of electrons flow through it. The voltage on the grid therefore controls and can also increase (amplify) the current flowing from cathode to anode.

During the middle of the twentieth century scientists found that the flow of electricity through certain solid materials called semiconductors could be controlled without using a vacuum. The solid material, germanium or silicon, is made very pure. Then carefully controlled amounts of boron, arsenic, phosphorus, or indium are added. The silicon is now doped. These

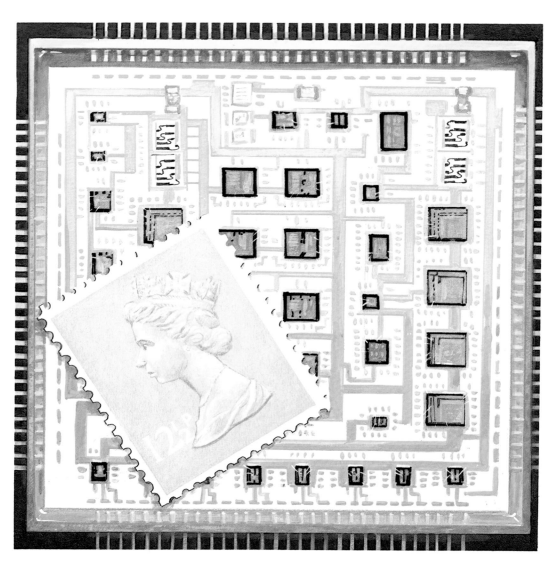

impurities alter the way that the current flows through the solid.

Transistors

These solid devices called transistors quickly replaced valves in many circuits. Unlike valves they require no heaters, are small, and need much less voltage to run them. Because they are so small they are put in containers to protect them. These containers are made of plastic or metal.

Gradually transistors were made smaller and cheaper. Soon several were packaged together to make a chip.

Chips

The next development was to put a complete circuit on a chip. This is called an integrated circuit. Integrated circuits are light, long lasting, cheap, and reliable.

In order to make a chip, the circuit is first drawn on a very large scale with the help of computers. It is then reduced and etched on to a slice of silicon. The chips are then tested. This is done using very fine probes under a microscope. After testing, the chips are put into their containers.

The chip is connected by wires of very thin gold or aluminium to pads around it. These pads are joined to the connectors or pins of the container. They are now ready for use.

Calculators were one of the first products to use silicon chips. Now integrated circuits are used in numerous devices, including many household appliances.

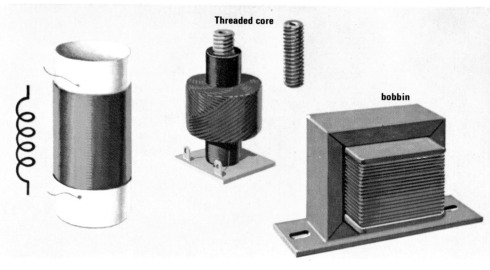

Threaded core

bobbin

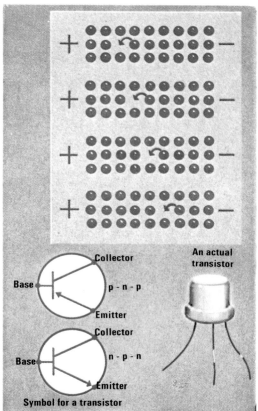

Collector

Base

p - n - p

Emitter

Collector

Base

n - p - n

Emitter

Symbol for a transistor

An actual transistor

Above
A coil or inductor consists of wire wrapped round a piece of metal or non-metal. It produces electro-magnetic inductance. It has many uses such as smoothing out the ripples of current from a diode valve that has changed alternating current (ac) to direct current (dc).

Left
A transistor consists of a sandwich of semiconductor material. There are two types of semiconductor: the n-type will produce a flow of electrons from negative to positive; the p-type will produce a movement of gaps in the electron structure from positive to negative (as in the upper part of the illustration). Transistors can have an n-type base with p-type emitter and collector, or vice-versa.

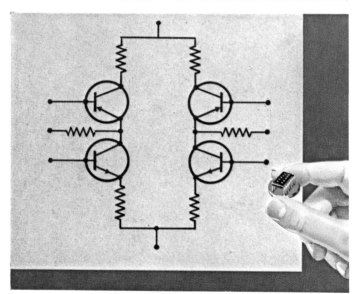

Left
Silicon chips are so tiny that several of them together are still smaller than a postage stamp.

Left
An integrated circuit. Transistors and other electrical components can now be made extremely small. Thousands of components, forming many hundreds of circuits, can be permanently fixed on to a tiny piece of semi-conductor material. This is called an integrated circuit. It is very light, long-lasting, and cheap and is therefore widely used.

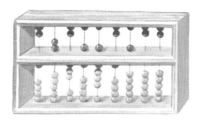

Babbage

COMPUTERS

Throughout the ages people have used calculating machines to help them work out their sums. One of the very earliest was the abacus. This simple, cheap device is still used in many Asian shops and banks to make calculations at very great speed. Much more complicated machines have now been built that can do a much wider range of highly complex tasks.

The first computer

The fastest, most accurate, and most useful machine is the computer. Charles Babbage built the first computer in the early nineteenth century. It was worked by cogs and levers. It carried out a long series of calculations and printed out the results. He invented a more modern

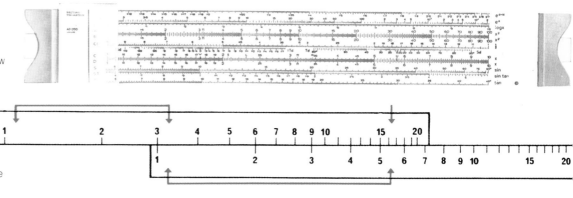

Decimal numbers	Binary numbers			
	2^3 (=8)	2^2 (=4)	2^1 (=2)	2^0 (=1)
				1
1			1	0
2			1	1
3		1	0	0
4		1	0	1
5		1	1	0
6		1	1	1
7	1	0	0	0
8	1	0	0	1
9	1	0	1	0
10	1	0	1	1
11	1	1	0	0
12	1	1		

Punched tape

on this data is carried out in the processor. Once the computer has processed the information it is sent to the output. This might be magnetic tape, disc, or printer.

Programming languages

Computers have to be told exactly what to do with the information they receive. This is the job of people known as programmers. To write the program they have to use special languages such as Basic, Fortran, Cobol, and Alcol. These languages are not interchangeable. If the programmer makes a mistake the computer will not operate as expected. If the computer gives a silly answer it is the program or the input that is wrong, not the computer.

Opposite bottom
The binary system and computers. A simple switch has only two positions: on and off. These can easily be represented in computers as 1 and 0. Computers then carry out all of their mathematical calculations using only these two numbers (binary arithmetic) rather than the 10 numbers that we use (decimal arithmetic). 2 is written as 10, 3 as 11, and 4 as 100.

Below
The four main units of a computer are the input unit, in which information is fed into the computer; the memory, which stores the information as well as the computer program that tells the computer how to use the information; the central processing unit (CPU), which processes the information to get results; and the output unit which produces results in a form people can use.

computer but it was never built because of lack of interest.

Modern computers rely on electronic devices. The first computers were built with valves but these were later replaced by transistors (see page 168). The development of the integrated circuit revolutionized the computer industry.

The numbers we use every day belong to the decimal system based on groups of ten. Computers are electronic, using electricity. The simplest way to send an electrical signal is to switch the electricity on and off. For this reason, computers use the binary system based on groups of two. Computers consist of billions of switches which can be on or off. This is the only signal a computer uses thousands and thousands of times as it does its operations.

Before a computer can do anything it needs two things. First it needs instructions for what it is going to do. This is the program. Secondly, it needs the information or data that it is going to work on. These inputs can be made in a variety of ways. The information is often fed from magnetic tape or disc. Keyboard systems looking like a typewriter are very common. These are usually linked to a visual display unit or VDU so the operators can see what they are doing.

The data go first to the computer's memory. Each piece of data is put in a particular place which is labelled. This is the address. When the control unit works through the instructions it removes the data from the store as required. The work

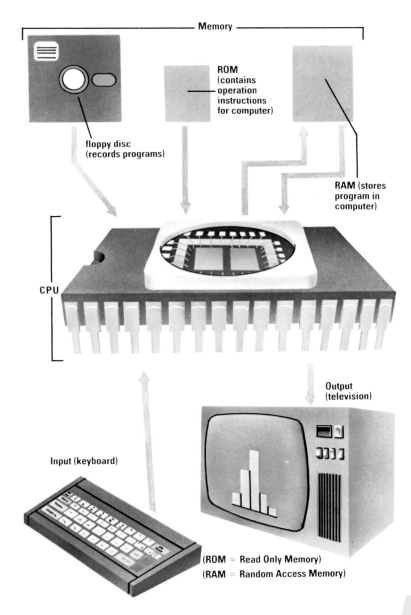

Memory

ROM (contains operation instructions for computer)

floppy disc (records programs)

RAM (stores program in computer)

CPU

Input (keyboard)

Output (television)

(ROM = Read Only Memory)
(RAM = Random Access Memory)

COMPUTERS AT WORK

Once integrated circuits had been developed they were soon widely used. Compared with valves, they were cheaper, more reliable, and did not break easily. As techniques improved, the chips became more powerful and cheaper. Nowadays many homes, offices, and factories use equipment that contains silicon chips.

ROM and RAM

Perhaps you have seen or used video games. These contain a chip programmed with instructions to play the game. This is the read only memory or ROM. Another chip receives the information you supply, for example by moving the control lever to move a monster. This is the random access memory, RAM. This information is processed by the microprocessor or silicon chip and the result is fed to the television screen. All this happens in a fraction of a second. The computer then waits for you to give the next instruction.

Some domestic appliances now use microprocessors. A modern mechanical sewing machine has more than a thousand parts. Some of these, perhaps a half, can be replaced by a microprocessor. Because this reduces the number of moving parts, there will be less wear, the machine will be more reliable, and it will last longer.

As computers have become cheaper people have been able to buy them to use at home. With these, you can play video games, look after the family budget, or do the accounts for a small business.

In big business, computers are often used for working on large amounts of information. Banks use them to control their customer's accounts which contain millions of pieces of information held on databases. Customers can use the cash points which are really VDUs (see page 171) to supply cash or to tell them details of their account via the computer.

Computer networks

Soon you will be able to carry out more

Above
Computer-guided robots at work in a car-assembly plant. Robots can be programmed to perform a series of repetitive tasks and so can work on assembly lines with minimal human supervision.

Right
Modern sewing machines contain advanced micro-circuits that enable them to carry out already programmed stitch settings. The microprocessor also reduces the number of moving parts needed by a half.

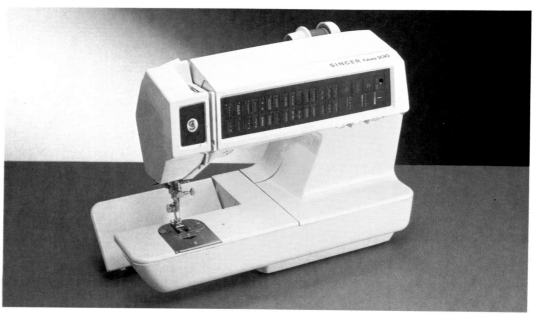

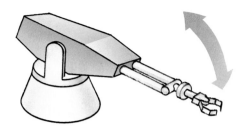
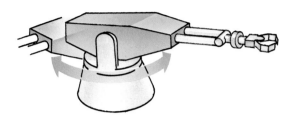

Left
A robot can be programmed to make a variety of movements. The arm can move in and out, be raised and lowered, and be swung from side to side. The hand can move in lots of different ways too.

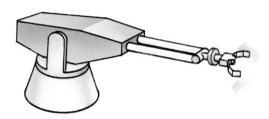
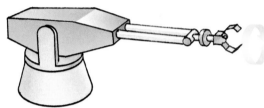

tasks through such terminals. Shops will have a bank terminal instead of a till. When you buy something you will give a bank card or number and the money will be transferred from your account to the shop's account. Soon shops, homes, and banks will be linked and you will be able to order and pay for goods and pay your bills without leaving home. They will be part of a computer network.

Companies as well as individuals have access to such networks. At present many office workers use computers in place of typewriters. These are called word processors. Messages can be sent very quickly from one computer to another without having to write a letter. This may lead to the paperless office.

In industry, microprocessors are used to control equipment. Some work is even done by robots. They are very good at doing the same job over and over again without making a mistake. In an increasing number of car-assembly plants, production line robots spot-weld parts of the car body together. They are also used for unpleasant jobs such as paint spraying.

Computers have revolutionized the retail trade. Before the computer, it was very difficult to keep track of the stock of the many items sold in large stores. Now a laser scanner at the checkout reads information about the items sold from bar codes on the items. The stock records are automatically updated by computer and more stock ordered when necessary.

Below left
In the paperless office, each desk has a computerized workstation. This combines a telephone, computer and keyboard. The workstation is connected to a central computer containing all the company records, and to other workstations.

Below
A bar code. These can often be found on packets of food and on books. The spacing and thickness of the lines can be read by a laser and identifies the product. The information can be fed to the till to work out the customer's bill and to a central computer to keep a check on the stock.

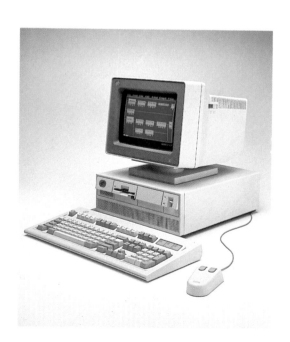

TELECOMMUNICATIONS

Communications is the sending of messages between places. There are many ways of doing this. In Africa messages were sent over short distances by beating on drums. The Indians of North America used smoke signals. Signals were sent between ships using coloured flags, and semaphore signals were also used by sailors.

The telegraph

Today we can send messages over much greater distances using electrical devices and waves. This is called telecommunications. The first practical system for electrical signalling was the simple telegraph invented by the Russian Baron Schilling in 1823. A wire carrying an electric current made a compass needle move when a message was sent. An American, Samuel Morse improved on this type of telegraph. He sent messages by using a code of short and long electric pulses. Morse code proved to be fast and reliable. It is still used today for some radio communications.

The telex

The modern equivalent of the telegraph is the telex system. This has a special typewriter with keys that send a code for each letter along the wires. A receiver at the end of the wire picks up the coded signal and types the letter.

The telephone

In 1876, the telephone was invented by Alexander Graham Bell. This carried speech along a wire. At first each telephone was connected to every other one. When the number of telephones increased, each telephone was instead connected to a telephone exchange. This connected the call to the number required. The first long distance telephone line was set up between Boston and New York in 1884. Since then great changes have taken place in telecommunications.

It is now possible to call anywhere in the world cheaply and quickly. Cables under the oceans connect the telephones in all countries. However a phone does not have to be at the end of a cable. There are

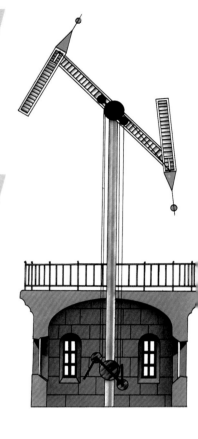

Above
The semaphore telegraph invented by Claude Chappe in 1793.

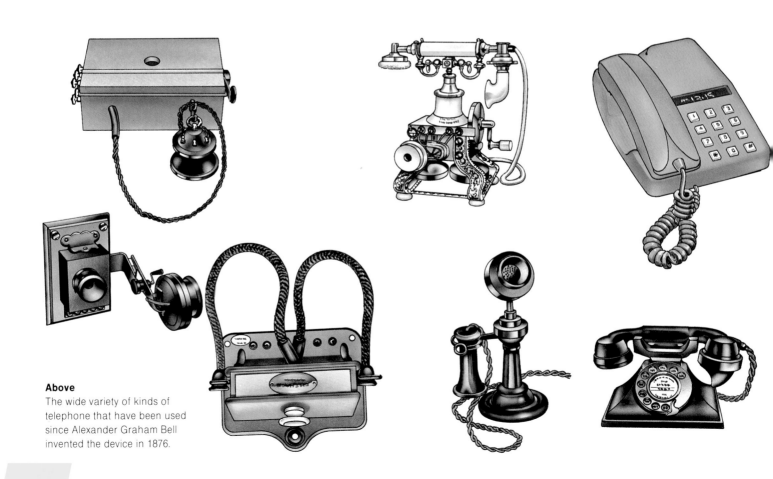

Above
The wide variety of kinds of telephone that have been used since Alexander Graham Bell invented the device in 1876.

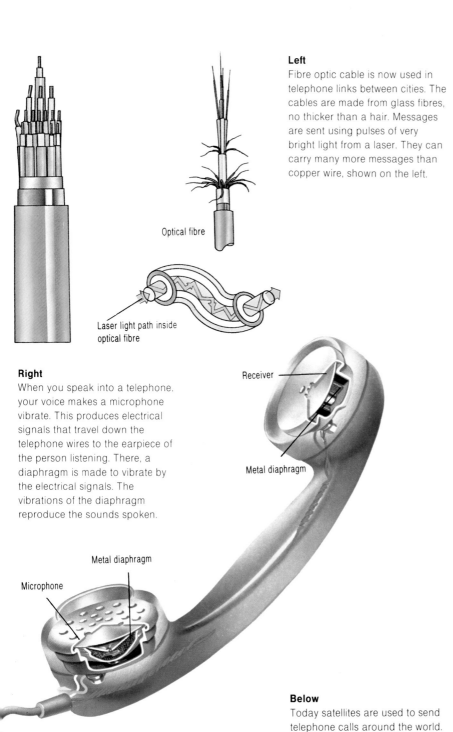

Left
Fibre optic cable is now used in telephone links between cities. The cables are made from glass fibres, no thicker than a hair. Messages are sent using pulses of very bright light from a laser. They can carry many more messages than copper wire, shown on the left.

Optical fibre

Laser light path inside optical fibre

Right
When you speak into a telephone, your voice makes a microphone vibrate. This produces electrical signals that travel down the telephone wires to the earpiece of the person listening. There, a diaphragm is made to vibrate by the electrical signals. The vibrations of the diaphragm reproduce the sounds spoken.

Receiver

Metal diaphragm

Metal diaphragm

Microphone

Below
Today satellites are used to send telephone calls around the world.

cordless telephones which use radio waves. Many telephone calls travel as radio waves now. Communications satellites, high in space, are linked to the telephone system by microwaves, a kind of radio.

Short-range cordless telephones have a small radio transmitter nearby, usually on the wall. This sends out radio signals that are picked up by the handset. Long-distance radio phones, such as in-car phones, do not need to be connected to the telephone system at all. Their signals are carried through a network of radio transmitters. Each transmitter covers a small area, called a cell. Calls travel from one cell to another until they reach the transmitter nearest the receiving phone.

Another important development has been the use of digital signals to send telephone conversations along the wires. These signals consist of a code of brief pulses. A digital system changes the electrical signal produced by the telephone mouthpiece into a digital signal. Using digital signals produces a clearer conversation with no noise on the line.

The cables that telephone signals are sent along have changed too. These used to be made of copper wire but now optical fibres are being used. These are hair-like strands of very pure glass. Telephone signals are sent along the fibres using a laser light which travels inside the fibre. Optical fibres are not affected by the electrical noise that can spoil normal telephone messages. Optical fibres will reduce the number of cables needed, too. Each fibre can carry about 2,000 conversations at the same time. Only thirty conversations can be carried on a ordinary copper wire.

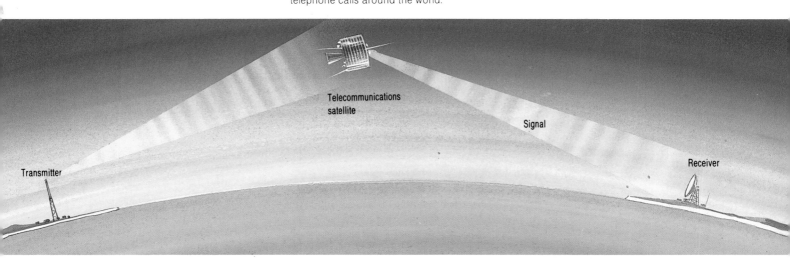

Telecommunications satellite

Signal

Transmitter

Receiver

Right

Transmitting radio waves. A. Ground waves following the curvature of the earth for a relatively short distance.
B. Sky waves reflected from the ionosphere, over 80 kilometres high, and sent back to earth. Several bounces are possible and the radio signal may be sent all the way around the world.
C. Sky wave passing straight through the ionized layer. It may continue out into space, getting weaker and weaker, or be received and transmitted back to earth by a special communications satellite.
D. A communications satellite relays radio waves that pass through the ionosphere back to earth.

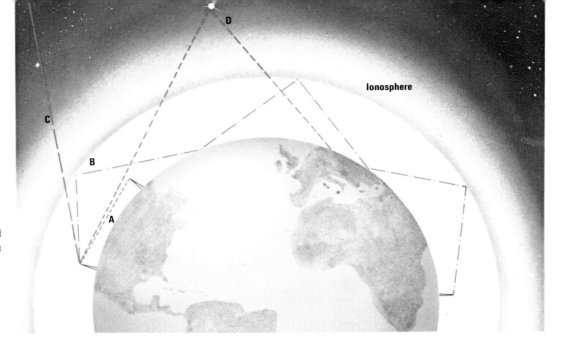

Right

Heinrich Hertz (1857–1894), a German physicist, demonstrated the existence of radio waves in 1886. He found that radio waves behave much the same as light waves. Hertz played an important role in laying the groundwork for the invention of wireless telegraphy.

Below

Guglielmo Marconi (1874–1937) an Italian electrical engineer who invented wireless telegraphy in 1895. He came to England in 1896 and succeeded in transmitting a wireless signal for a distance of 14.5 kilometres. In 1901 he was able to receive a wireless signal (the letter S in Morse Code) sent across the Atlantic, from Cornwall to Newfoundland. He was awarded the Nobel prize for physics in 1909.

Hertz

Marconi

RADIO

Every hour of every day all over the earth there are millions of radio waves travelling through the air at the speed of light – 300,000,000 metres per second (or 186,000 miles per second). In order to hear them we must have a radio set, which changes the electric signals picked up by the receiving aerial into sounds that we can hear through a loudspeaker. These radio waves can be transmitted on many different frequencies or wavelengths.

At first, radio transmitters were a series of dots and dashes representing in Morse Code the letters of the alphabet. Then the invention of the microphone, which changes sounds waves into electrical waves, and the electronic valve (see page 168), allowed music and voice to be transmitted by radio.

Radio waves

There are two types of radio waves. The ground wave can follow the curvature of the earth for a short distance of about 350 km. Ground waves cannot therefore be used for transmitting radio waves between distant countries or even between cities separated by a large distance in the same country. Radio waves can be made to travel much greater distances by being bounced off an electrically-charged layer in the atmosphere. This layer, called the ionosphere, is over

80 km above the ground. The reflected radio waves are called sky waves.

When short-wave radio waves are transmitted, they are reflected off the ionosphere. These waves can be received by radio sets many hundreds of kilometres from the transmitting sets. The waves can then be bounced back to the ionosphere and be reflected back to earth over and over again in a series of bounces or skips. This is how a radio signal from London is able to be heard in Australia, for example, thousands of kilometres away.

Communications satellites

Not all sky waves are reflected by the ionosphere. Some high-frequency waves (short wavelengths) pass through the ionosphere into outer space. When short wave radio waves are being transmitted over a great distance they have to be reflected back to earth by a communications satellite. A television programme is broadcast over a great distance by using a communications satellite to reflect the high-frequency waves.

Radio telescopes on earth pick up radio waves from distant stars which can pass through the earth's atmosphere (see page 184).

Radio broadcasts give us information, music, and other forms of entertainment. Radio is also extremely useful for two-way communications between aeroplanes and control towers, and for ship-to-shore links.

Below
A simple radio receiver. The signal from the transmitting station is picked up by the receiving aerial and is tuned in by the circuit containing the variable capacitor and coil. The signal then passes through the diode which detects or demodulates the signal so that it can be heard in the headphones.

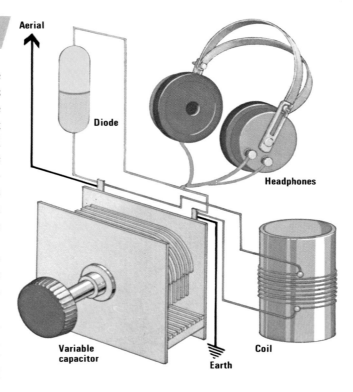

Above
The Post Office Tower in Central London is used for mounting radio and TV aerials. A high tower is a good place for aerials as they can transmit ground waves much further than aerials mounted at ground level.

Left
The basic radio wave broadcast is called a carrier wave. It is varied or modulated to add the signal. In amplitude modulation (AM), the strength of the carrier wave is varied. In frequency modulation (FM), the frequency of the carrier wave is varied. Inside the receiving radio, the signals are separated from the carrier wave and turned back into sound.

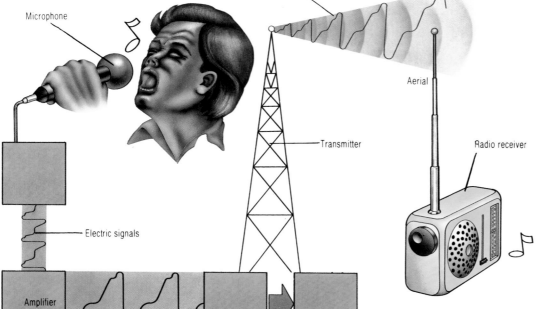

TELEVISION

Television shows still pictures. The pictures appear to move because they are shown one after the other at high speed. To give this impression, there are thirty pictures per second.

Black-and-white television

Each picture is divided into 625 lines. In a black-and-white television picture each line contains several thousand bits of light or dark. To make a good picture the lines are separated into tiny bits – as many as 200,000 bits altogether. The television camera contains a signal plate covered with dots of a chemical that are sensitive to light (photosensitive dots). Each dot corresponds to one of the 200,000 tiny bits. An electron beams crosses the plate line by line and transmits the signals picked up from the dots. Brighter dots cause a stronger signal than darker dots. The signals are amplified and then transmitted.

In the television set in your home the signals are received, amplified, and shown on the picture tube (or cathode-ray tube). In the cathode-ray tube, another electron beam is produced. This beam is made to cross the screen 625 times, so making the 625 lines. At the end of each line the beam flies back and starts the next line. These 625 lines are produced in $\frac{1}{30}$ second and each set of 625 lines is called a frame. As the beam crosses the back of the picture screen it gets weaker and stronger in accordance with the signals picked up from the photosensitive dots in the camera. The tube contains a special fluorescent screen, coated with chemicals, which glow under the impact of the electron beam. The stronger the beam, the brighter the light. The set also contains a loudspeaker for producing the sound and a synchronizing system for keeping the sound and picture together.

Baird

Left
John Logie Baird was born in 1888 and died in 1946. When ill health prevented him from working as an electrical engineer he turned to studying television. He produced the first practical system. His system was used for a short while but then better ways of televising were found. His system used infrared rays.

Below
The picture tube, or cathode-ray tube, consists of an electron gun which produces the electron beam, and a number of magnetic coils for focusing the beam and making it scan the screen. The screen is coated with a fluorescent substance that emits light when struck by the electron beam.

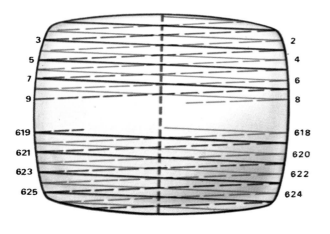

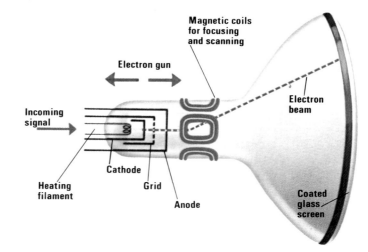

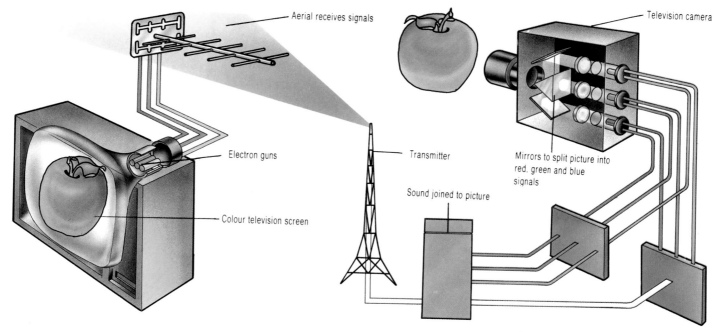

Aerial receives signals

Television camera

Electron guns

Transmitter

Mirrors to split picture into red, green and blue signals

Sound joined to picture

Colour television screen

Colour television

Colour television works in a similar way. There are three electron beams each of which carries the signal for one of the colours, red, blue, and green. The screen of the picture tube is coated with $1\frac{1}{4}$ million tiny dots of phosphor, arranged in groups of three. A phosphor is a substance that emits light when an electron beam falls on it. Each of the three phosphors used emits only one of the three colours red, blue, and green. So the blue phosphor emits blue light when the electron beam carrying the blue signal falls on it, and so on. These three colours can be combined in different proportions to give all the other colours of the original scene (see page 84).

Cable television

Instead of being transmitted as waves, programmes can be sent along wires. This is the basis of cable television. Customers have their set connected by wire or cable to a transmission centre and they pay to receive programmes. There is a wide choice as the cable is able to carry many channels.

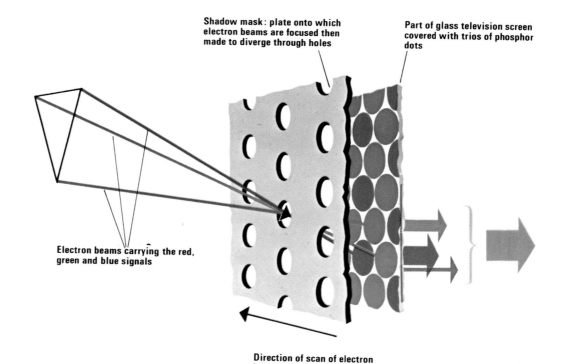

Shadow mask: plate onto which electron beams are focused then made to diverge through holes

Part of glass television screen covered with trios of phosphor dots

Electron beams carrying the red, green and blue signals

Direction of scan of electron beams

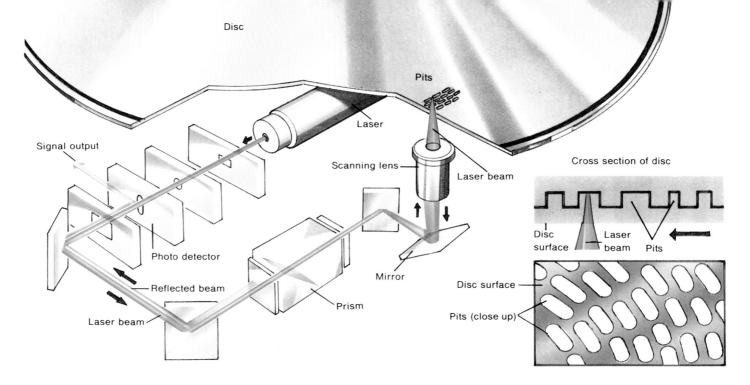

Disc

Pits

Laser

Scanning lens

Laser beam

Signal output

Photo detector

Reflected beam

Mirror

Prism

Laser beam

Cross section of disc

Disc surface

Laser beam

Pits

Disc surface

Pits (close up)

VIDEO

The word "video" means "I see". A video recorder records pictures which can be shown on a television set. John Logie Baird, the Scottish scientist who invented an early type of television, also invented a video recorder. His video recorder stored pictures on a flat disc like a music record. Most modern video players use magnetic tape, called video tape, to store pictures. Pictures are also stored on discs that are similar to the compact discs used to record music.

Video tape players

To record a scene or picture on a video tape player, the picture must be changed into an electrical signal. This is done by the video camera. Light from the scene enters the camera and goes into a glass tube, called a vidicon tube. The light is focused on to a flat plate at one end of the tube. An electron gun at the other end of the tube fires a beam of electrons at the plate. As the beam moves across the plate, it is converted into an electrical signal of the scene. The signal is fed to the player and recorded on tape.

Video tapes

Video tapes are similar to the tapes used to record sounds. They are made of tough plastic and are covered with fine needle-shaped particles of iron-oxide material. The electrical signal of the scene is used to magnetise the iron particles on the tape. The tape stores the magnetic pattern of the scene.

Video tape is wider than audio or music

Above
A video disc has a silvery surface covered with small holes, or pits. A laser beam reads the patterns of pits, and builds up picture and sound signals from the pattern.

Below
In a video cassette recorder, a series of rollers guides the tape. When recording, the tape first moves over the erase head which removes any sound and picture previously recorded. Then the tape moves past a video head drum which records the picture signal as diagonal tracks across the tape. The sound is recorded along the top of the tape by the sound head.

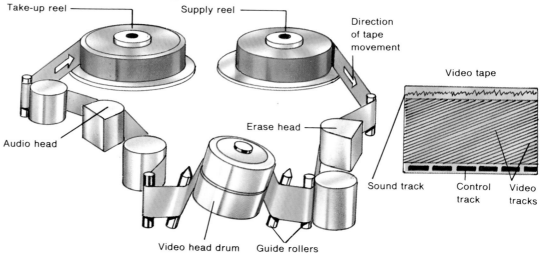

Take-up reel

Supply reel

Direction of tape movement

Video tape

Audio head

Erase head

Sound track

Control track

Video tracks

Video head drum

Guide rollers

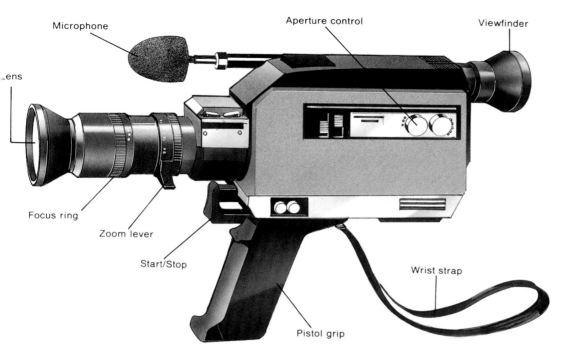

Microphone
Aperture control
Viewfinder
Lens
Focus ring
Zoom lever
Start/Stop
Pistol grip
Wrist strap

tape. This is because more information needs to be recorded to produce a picture than to produce sound only. The picture signals are recorded in diagonal lines across the tape. This enables the tape to hold more information. If a straight line was used, it would take 33 kilometres of tape to record the pictures in a one-hour programme.

To play the tape, you put the cassette containing the tape into the video player. The pattern of magnetism on the tape produces an electrical signal when the tape moves past the video and sound heads. This goes into the television set to give picture and sound.

Video discs

A video disc stores pictures, too. However, you cannot record on discs at home. The pictures are put on them when they are made. The pictures are recorded as a pattern of small pits, or holes, in the silvery disc surface. When the disc is placed in a video disc player, a narrow beam of laser light reads the pattern of pits and reproduces the pictures. Video discs are very useful for storing large amounts of information, such as encyclopedias, or catalogues. Any picture or piece of information on video disc can be found very quickly.

Recently, modern electronics has produced a new way of storing pictures. This is the charge-coupled device, or CCD. It is semiconductor chip consisting of alternate layers of silicon and metal. It stores a picture as a pattern of electric charges on its surface. CCDs are so sensitive that astronomers use them to record the faint light from faraway stars.

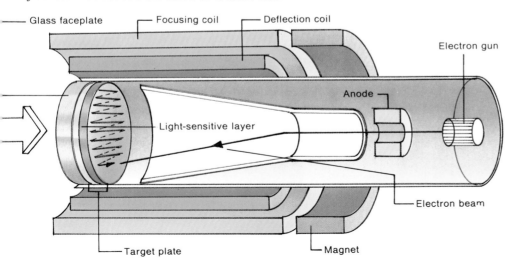

Glass faceplate
Focusing coil
Deflection coil
Electron gun
Anode
Light-sensitive layer
Electron beam
Target plate
Magnet

RADAR

The name radar comes from the initial letters of the phrase RAdio Detecting And Ranging. Radar is a radio transmitting and receiving system that uses radio waves of only a few centimetres in wavelength. Such short radio waves are known as microwaves. The waves are transmitted from a special type of aerial. The aerial, with a dish-shaped reflector behind, can point in any direction. It receives signals strongest when pointing in the direction of the incoming radio waves. Usually, radar aerials turn automatically and constantly in a complete circle, so they can send and receive signals in any direction.

How radar works

Ordinary radio waves are so long that they pass round solid objects. The very short waves used by radar tend to bounce off most objects. Radar makes use of this to find out how far away an object is, and, in the case of a moving object, in what direction it is travelling and at what speed.

Any radio waves sent out by the transmitter hit an object which is reflected back to the radar station in a fraction of a second. During this brief time the transmitter is shut off and the aerial is used to receive the reflected waves and pass them to a special cathode-ray tube resembling a TV picture tube. On this tube, a picture or image is formed of the reflected waves or signal.

Certain objects, especially those made of metal, reflect back a strong signal. This forms a bright image on the radar screen. Other objects, especially those not made of metal, reflect back weaker signals and form less bright images on the screen. A bigger object reflects back more radio waves. With experience, an operator can tell if he or she is seeing a flight of birds or a group of jet planes.

Signals are reflected back more quickly from nearby objects than distant objects. The time taken for a signal to be reflected back by an object shows the distance of the object.

Great technical improvements were made in radar by the British in 1940. They developed a special transmitting tube called a magnetron. This can produce very high-powered signals at the extremely short wavelengths needed for radar. This made it possible for smaller aerials to be used, which made radar capable of being used in aircraft.

Use of radar

Radar is used to aid navigation by both aircraft and ships, as well as to tell them if they are about to enter an area of bad weather or collide with another craft or vessel. During the Second World War radar was first used to track enemy aircraft and provide automatic guidance control for anti-aircraft guns. The great advantage of radar over sight is that it works at night and in fog or clouds.

Right
Whether a radar beam will be reflected by an object depends partly on its height above ground and partly on the angle at which the radar aerial is pointed. A plane may escape being detected by flying very low.

Far right
The cathode-ray tube shows the reflected radar signal (echo) and tells the operator the distance away of an object or storm as well as its speed and direction. The spiral at the top of the screen is a hurricane. The smaller light areas show heavy rainfall.

Right
One of the important uses of radar is at airports to help aircraft land, especially during bad weather. Two different signals are transmitted from the ground. One signal indicates to the pilot the correct direction of approach for the aircraft. The other shows at what height the plane should be flying. Pilots can therefore tell exactly where they are at every moment during their approach to the runway.

Right
Most radar stations use the same aerial to transmit as to receive. During a very brief instant, between each radar pulse being transmitted, the receiver is turned on to receive the returning signal by means of an automatic switch. This switch changes the aerial connections from the transmitter to the receiver.

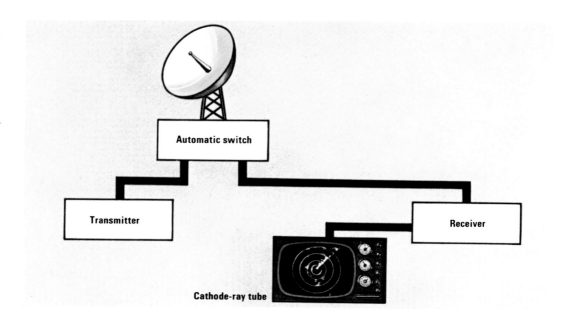

Automatic switch

Transmitter

Receiver

Cathode-ray tube

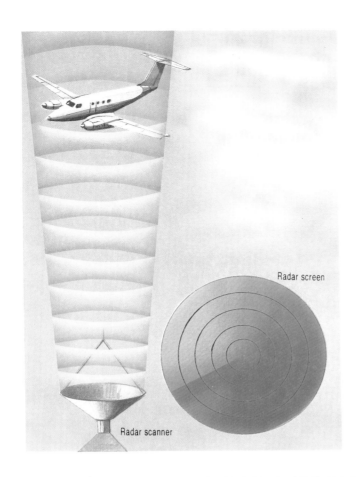

Radar screen

Radar scanner

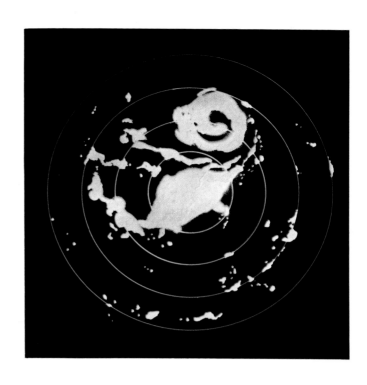

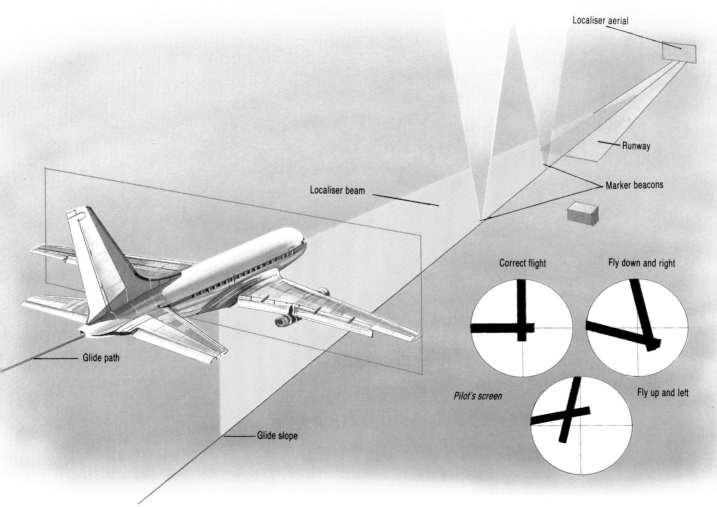

Localiser aerial

Runway

Marker beacons

Localiser beam

Glide path

Glide slope

Correct flight

Fly down and right

Pilot's screen

Fly up and left

RADIO ASTRONOMY

The sound you hear on radio has been carried through the air by radio waves. These waves travel between the broadcasting station and the radio receiver which may be several thousand kilometres apart. Radio telescopes pick up waves which are travelling through the air from much further away. These radio waves come from stars in different parts of the universe. They can travel for millions of years before they reach the earth and are picked up by the telescopes.

Radio waves from space were first discovered by accident in 1932 by Karl Jansky. He was using a radio receiver with a movable aerial. When he pointed the aerial towards the Milky Way he received signals from the stars.

Radio telescopes

Most radio telescopes are built in isolated places where they will not be too disturbed by radio waves from earth. Some radio telescopes, like the one at Jodrell Bank near Manchester, England, are made of sheets of metal joined together in a bowl shape. This bowl is called the reflector. In the centre of the bowl is the aerial. The bowl is fixed to a rotating stand which enables it to move in all directions.

The reflector is made of shiny metal similar to the metal behind an electric fire. They both work in the same way. The bars of the fire give off heat rays and the metal reflects back. The reflector of a radio telescope receives radio waves travelling through the air and reflects them to the central aerial.

There are a number of designs of aerial used in radio astronomy. Some look rather like television aerials. The aerial picks up the radio waves and sends them back through wires to the receiver. The receiver changes the radio waves into a special kind of picture.

Radio astronomers study the patterns of

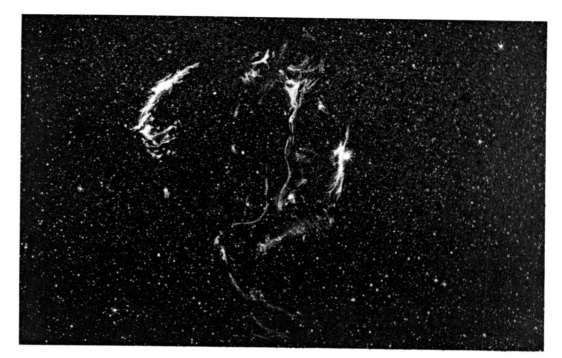

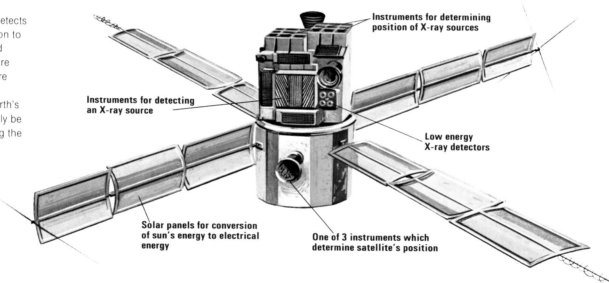

Instruments for determining position of X-ray sources

Instruments for detecting an X-ray source

Low energy X-ray detectors

Solar panels for conversion of sun's energy to electrical energy

One of 3 instruments which determine satellite's position

lines made by the radio waves using instruments such as computers to help them. From the patterns they can learn many facts, such as how hot a star is or how fast it is moving.

Quasars and pulsars

Many stars send out radio waves, including the sun. These signals are often very difficult to detect. However, special radio sources exist, called quasars and pulsars, which give out strong signals. Pulsars, first discovered in 1967, are tiny stars that rotate extremely rapidly and regularly.

They give out a pulse of radio waves at each rotation and so the pulses are emitted at very regular intervals. Pulsars are a type of dying star. The remains of the star that exploded in 1054 forming the Crab Nebula is a pulsar. It is about 30 km in diameter and makes one complete rotation in about three hundredths of a second.

Very little is known about quasars. They seem to be star-like objects at enormous distances from us. The radio signals given out by them must be extraordinarily strong since they are easy to detect even after travelling great distances through space.

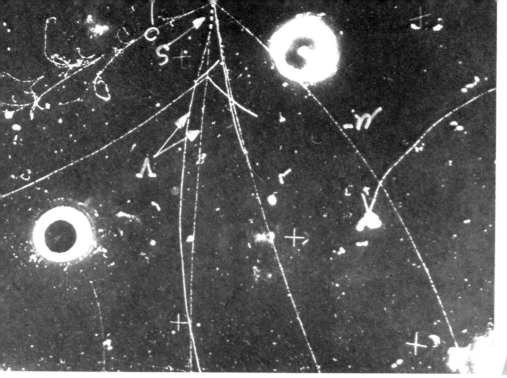

proposed that atoms could not be divided into anything smaller. This is now known to be incorrect. Atoms are composed of a central nucleus around which move electrons. The nucleus contains protons and neutrons. Protons and neutrons are composed of even smaller particles called quarks. Quarks and electrons are elementary particles. This means that they cannot be divided into smaller particles. They are the basic units of matter.

Although these particles cannot be subdivided, some can change or decay into other elementary particles. They are therefore unstable, and only last for a certain time.

Photons and neutrinos

When the neutron is outside the nucleus it is unstable. It lasts about 15 minutes then changes into a proton, an electron, and another elementary particle called the neutrino. These three particles are all stable and do not decay into other particles. The neutrino is a strange particle. It has no mass and no charge. It is a tiny bundle of energy. It is therefore extremely difficult to detect, and was only discovered in 1956.

The photon is an elementary particle. Like the neutrino, it is stable, has no mass or charge and is a bundle of energy. Radio waves, light, and X-rays can all be thought of as a stream of photons (see page 162). These types of radiation only differ in the amounts of the energies of the photons.

There are a large number of elementary particles apart from those already mentioned. They are all unstable, some of them decaying in minute fractions of a second. Elementary particles can react together to produce other particles, but reactions can only occur if certain laws are obeyed. The total charge of the particles reacting together (or decaying) must equal the total charge of the particles formed. When a neutron decays, its zero charge is balanced by the positive charge of the proton and the equal but negative charge of the electron. This is called the conservation of charge. Many other properties of the particles reacting together must also be conserved.

Below
Cosmic rays from outer space. This high-energy radiation consists mainly of protons and some alpha particles. These particles collide with molecules in the air and produce other elementary particles. At sea level about one particle per square centimetre arrives every minute. The source of cosmic rays is uncertain. They possibly come from exploding stars (supernovas).

Inside the Atom

ELEMENTARY PARTICLES

Matter consists of groups of atoms. In the early nineteenth century John Dalton

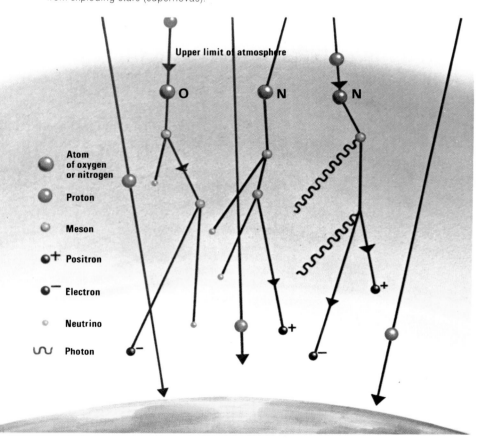

Upper limit of atmosphere

O   N   N

- Atom of oxygen or nitrogen
- Proton
- Meson
- + Positron
- − Electron
- Neutrino
- Photon

Particle accelerators

The properties and reactions of elementary particles are studied by nuclear physicists. They use particle accelerators to produce beams of high energy particles. The first of these machines were built in the 1930s. Since then machines have been built that produce particles which have an energy many thousands of times greater than those of the original accelerators. Some of these machines are very large. The Fermilab machine near Chicago is a ring some 6.5 km across. These very energetic beams of particles are made to collide with atoms, which are usually

hydrogen. This happens in a bubble chamber. When charged particles move through the bubble chamber a trace is produced. This trace is photographed and the type of trace tells the scientists what type of particle caused it. They use this information to build up a picture of the structure of matter.

The particles are grouped by their mass. The names of the groups are from the Greek words for light, medium, and heavy. The light particles are called leptons and include the electron. The medium mass particles are called mesons. The heavy particles are the baryons of which the most notable are the proton and the neutron.

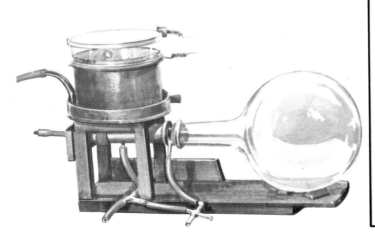

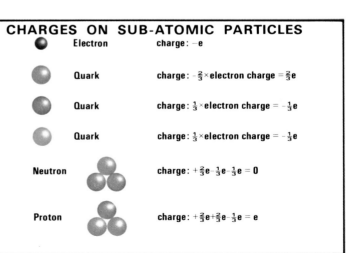

CHARGES ON SUB-ATOMIC PARTICLES

Electron		charge: $-e$
Quark		charge: $-\frac{2}{3} \times$ electron charge $= \frac{2}{3}e$
Quark		charge: $\frac{1}{3} \times$ electron charge $= -\frac{1}{3}e$
Quark		charge: $\frac{1}{3} \times$ electron charge $= -\frac{1}{3}e$
Neutron		charge: $+\frac{2}{3}e - \frac{1}{3}e - \frac{1}{3}e = 0$
Proton		charge: $+\frac{2}{3}e + \frac{2}{3}e - \frac{1}{3}e = e$

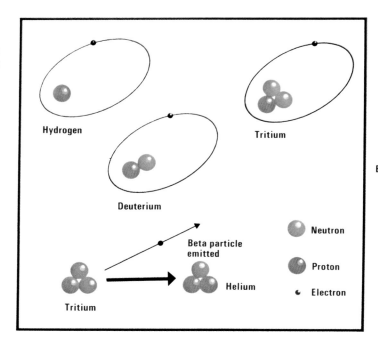

RADIOACTIVITY

An atom consists of a number of electrons moving around a central nucleus. The nucleus contains tiny particles called protons and neutrons. The nuclei of any particular element, such as a carbon, always have the same number of protons, equal to the number of orbiting electrons. The positive charge of the protons is thus balanced by the negative charge of the electrons. However, the number of neutrons in the nucleus of an element can vary. Atoms of an element with the same number of protons in their nuclei but a different number of neutrons are isotopes of that element. Every element has several isotopes.

The nuclei of many isotopes always remain unchanged. They are stable isotopes. Other nuclei are unstable. At any moment they can emit energy, in the form of radiation, in order to reduce this instability. These are nuclei of radioactive isotopes, called radioisotopes for short. Radioactivity was first reported in 1896 by Becquerel. He found that some form of energy was being emitted by uranium salts. It was found that this emission came from the nucleus, and did not involve the orbiting electrons.

Alpha and beta particles

A radioisotope can lose energy in various ways, but two important processes are the emission of an alpha particle and the emission of a beta particle. An alpha particle consists of two protons and two neutrons. It is actually the nucleus of a helium atom. After its nucleus has emitted an alpha particle, a radioisotope is changed into the isotope of another element having two less protons. The weight of the nucleus is reduced by losing the alpha particle.

A beta particle is an electron. There are no electrons in a nucleus, however, so where does it come from? It results from the sudden changes or decay of a neutron into a proton, an electron and another

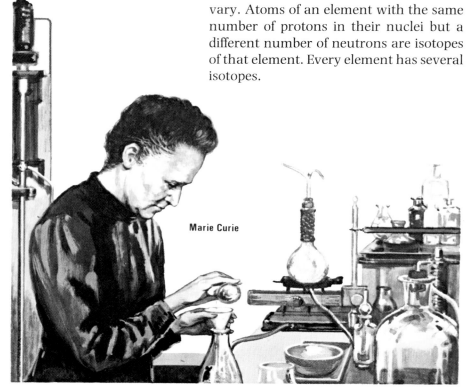

Marie Curie

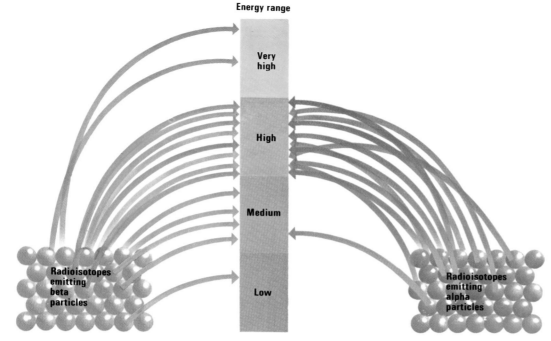

Very high

High

Medium

Low

Radioisotopes emitting beta particles

Radioisotopes emitting alpha particles

Left
The energy of particles emitted by different radioisotopes can vary widely. The particles and rays emitted will also travel very different distances. The beta particle will be stopped by a thin sheet of perspex, whilst the alpha particle would not pass through a sheet of paper. Gamma rays need thick steel, concrete, or lead to stop them.

Below
The radioactive series of uranium starts with the disintegration of a radioisotope of uranium containing a total of 238 protons and neutrons (92 protons). It ends in the production of a stable isotope of lead. Half-lives are shown for some of the disintegrations.

particle called a neutrino. This decay only occurs in nuclei of radioisotopes, never in the nuclei of stable isotopes.

After the emission of a beta particle, the radioisotope is transformed into an isotope of another element having one more proton than the original. The weights of these two isotopes are about equal, since the neutron and proton have approximately the same weight.

During the decay, radioisotopes may emit electromagnetic radiation. This can include X-rays and the more powerful gamma rays.

A radioisotope often decays into an isotope that is also radioactive. In turn, the second isotope may decay into a third radioisotope, and so on. This process will continue until a stable isotope is formed. The radioisotopes involved form a radioactive series.

The time taken for half of the nuclei of a radioisotope to disintegrate is called its half-life. The values of the half-life for different radioisotopes vary from a tiny fraction of a second to many million years. In radioactive material the number of nuclei of the radioisotope present grows less and less as more of them decay.

The activity of a radioactive material is measured by the number of disintegrations in a second. It therefore decreases with time, the rate depending on the half-life of the radioisotope.

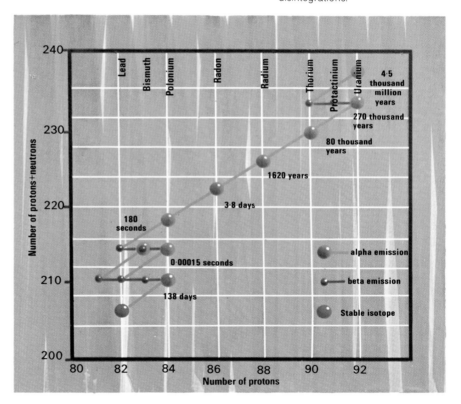

Lead · Bismuth · Polonium · Radon · Radium · Thorium · Protactinium · Uranium

Number of protons+neutrons

4·5 thousand million years
270 thousand years
80 thousand years
1620 years
3·8 days
180 seconds
0·00015 seconds
138 days

alpha emission
beta emission
Stable isotope

Number of protons

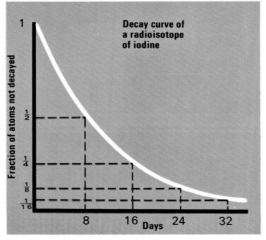

Decay curve of a radioisotope of iodine

Fraction of atoms not decayed

Days

Left
The decay curve of a radioisotope of iodine, having a half-life of eight days. After 16 days only a quarter of the original number of nuclei remain. This fraction is reduced to an eighth after 24 days and to a sixteenth after 32 days.

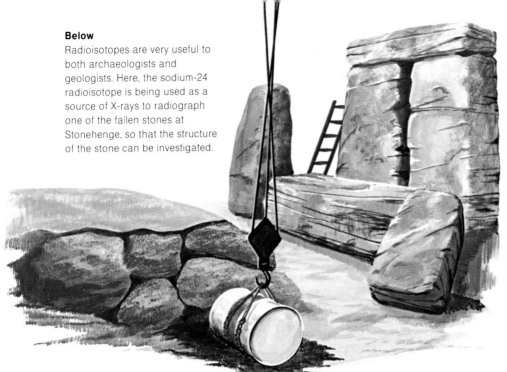

RADIOISOTOPES

Several radioisotopes occur naturally in the rocks on the earth's surface. One out of every 100,000 atoms of potassium is radioactive. Many rocks, including granite, contain potassium compounds. The radioisotope of potassium decays into a stable isotope of argon, the half-life being over 1,000 million years. By measuring the amounts of these two isotopes present in a particular rock it is possible to calculate the time at which the potassium isotope first started to decay. This is the time at which the rock was formed. By finding the age of rocks it is possible to estimate the age of the earth. This method, called radioactive dating, gives the age of the earth as being 4,000–5,000 million years.

Radiocarbon dating

Radiocarbon dating can be used to find the age of objects several thousand years old. These objects must be made from material that was once living, such as wood. All plants obtain carbon from the carbon dioxide in the atmosphere. This carbon contains a very small but constant proportion of a radioisotope with a half-life of 5,730 years. The absorption of carbon from the atmosphere stops when the material dies. The radioisotope of carbon, however, continues to decay. By determining the amounts of stable carbon and the radioisotope present in the object, its time of death can be found.

Radioisotopes occurring naturally on earth all have extremely long half-lives. Radioisotopes with short half-lives probably disappeared from the earth by decay thousands of millions of years ago.

Isotopes with short half-lives are very useful in medicine, industry, and scientific research. So scientists produce their own supply. They are called artificial radioisotopes. Most are formed by bombarding elements with low-energy neutrons.

Certain elements, such as iodine, collect in one particular part or organ of the body. If the organ is not working properly, too much or too little collects there. A radioisotope has the same chemical properties as the stable isotopes of the same element. If a radioisotope is introduced into the human body, by injection say, it will

Right

A picture (scan) of the amounts of a radioisotope present in different areas of the liver. The colours dark blue, green, through to red represent increasing amounts. The greatest quantity of radioisotopes should collect in the centre of the liver. The dark blue area near the centre of the scan indicates the presence of a cancer tumour.

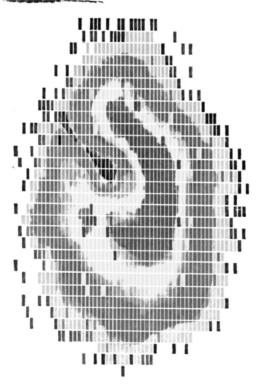

Below

Radioisotopes can be used to control the thickness of a piece of metal being produced as a long thin sheet. The amount of radiation reaching the counter will change if the thickness of the sheet changes. An electrical signal is then sent to correct the spacing of the rollers.

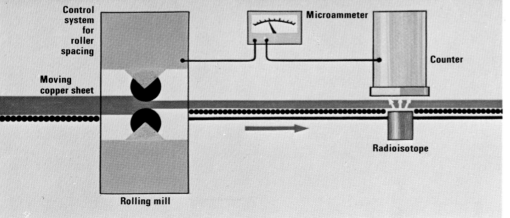

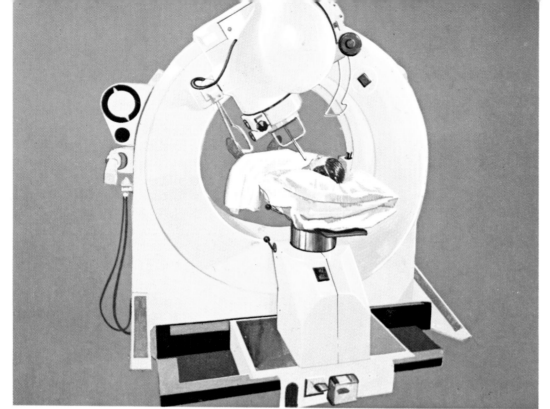

follow the same path as a stable isotope of the same element.

The amount of radiation emitted by the radioisotope can be measured very accurately. So, doctors can use radioisotopes to trace the path of elements in the body. This may help them to diagnose a disease, such as cancer.

The streams of alpha or beta particles emitted by a radioisotope charge or ionize the material through which they pass. X-rays and ultraviolet rays also ionize. These rays and particles add electrons to or remove them from the atoms or molecules of the material. This gives the atoms or molecules a negative or positive charge. The ionizing action of rays and particles is used in medicine to treat cancer.

Many molecules in the body have very complicated structures which can be damaged by ionizing radiation. It prevents the molecules from controlling processes going on in the cells, and the cells eventually die. Cancer cells are dangerously overactive and ionizing radiation can be used to kill them. Ionizing radiation is therefore useful, but it is a dangerous tool and great care has to be taken with it.

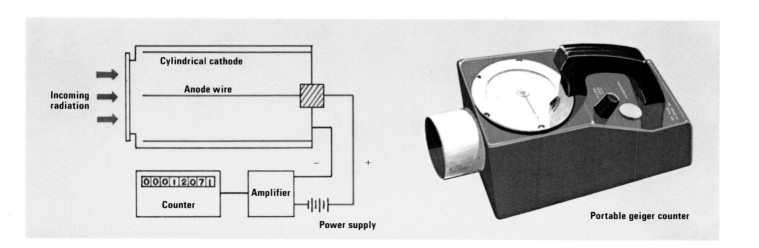

Cylindrical cathode

Anode wire

Incoming radiation

0 0 0 1 2 0 7 1

Counter

Amplifier

Power supply

Portable geiger counter

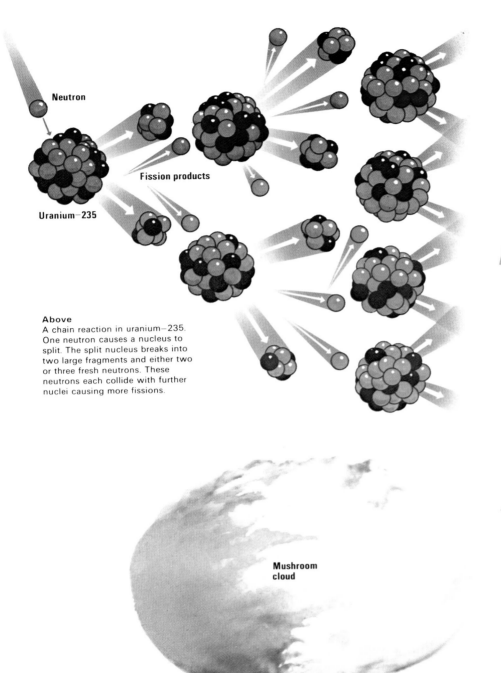

Above
A chain reaction in uranium–235. One neutron causes a nucleus to split. The split nucleus breaks into two large fragments and either two or three fresh neutrons. These neutrons each collide with further nuclei causing more fissions.

Neutron

Fission products

Uranium–235

Mushroom cloud

Right
Fissile uranium–235 and plutonium –239 can be stored safely if the quantity is small (less than a few kilograms). This is because so many neutrons escape from the surface of the material that the chain reaction cannot continue. This smallest quantity capable of maintaining a chain reaction is called the *critical mass*. Above the critical mass enough neutrons are kept inside the material to keep the chain reaction going. In an atom bomb two masses smaller than the critical mass are brought together to make one lump above the critical mass.

1 critical mass

2 subcritical masses

NUCLEAR FISSION

When the nucleus of an atom breaks up, the pieces into which it breaks fly apart with great speed. The kinetic energy (energy of motion) of these fragments is huge. When the particles hit matter, their kinetic energy is changed into heat energy. This heat can be put to useful work in power stations. It can also be used for destructive purposes in the atom bomb.

Chain reaction

To make this energy available it is necessary to start a chain reaction in a radioactive material. A chain reaction starts when the fragments from one atomic nucleus collide with another nucleus causing it to split. The fragments from this nucleus cause other nuclei to split, and so on.

A large radioactive nucleus, like uranium, is split by bombarding it with atomic particles. This splitting is called fission. A neutron is the atomic particle usually used as it has no charge and is therefore not repelled by the nucleus. When a neutron strikes the nucleus of certain isotopes of uranium, the uranium nucleus splits into two approximately equal large fragments and either two or three neutrons. These neutrons fly off and cause two or three more uranium nuclei to break up. This is how the chain reaction starts.

In the atom bomb all the energy of this nuclear reaction is released in a fraction of a second, in the form of a tremendous explosion. To make this happen the fuel must consist of pure uranium–235 or plutonium–239. Both of these isotopes are

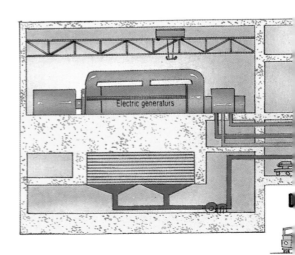

Electric generators

fissile, that is, they split up when struck by a neutron.

In a nuclear reactor arrangements have to be made to slow down the devastating explosion that takes place in a bomb. This is done by using a mixture of the fissile isotope of uranium and the more plentiful, but much more stable isotope, uranium–238.

Natural uranium is one of the most valuable and sought after minerals on earth. When it comes from the ground, it contains only 7 fissile uranium–235 atoms in every 1,000. It is not possible to build up a chain reaction in this material. In order to start a chain reaction it is necessary to increase the percentage of uranium–235 atoms in natural uranium – or to add plutonium to it. This is called enriching the natural fuel.

Nuclear reactors

There are various types of reactor. In thermal reactors the fuel is mixed with a substance called a moderator. This is a substance consisting of light atoms, such as carbon or water. The neutrons emitted during fission collide with the atoms of the moderator. These collisions slow down the neutrons so that more are able to cause fission of the uranium–235 isotope. This process generates a large amount of heat.

The core of a nuclear reactor contains the uranium fuel and the moderator. The heat produced is used to heat up a liquid called the coolant. The coolant becomes very hot and is able to make water boil. The steam produced is used, as in coal or oil-fired power stations, to rotate a turbine which drives a generator. Many countries today have nuclear power stations to supply the growing demand for electricity.

Fast reactors involve the interaction of fast neutrons with the nuclei. Steps are being taken to develop fast breeder reactors. These use plutonium–239 as fuel mixed with uranium–238. Some of the fast neutrons produced by the plutonium–239 fission are absorbed by the uranium–238 to produce or breed plutonium–239. In this way the much more common uranium–238 can be used to produce energy. This would enable uranium reserves to last far longer.

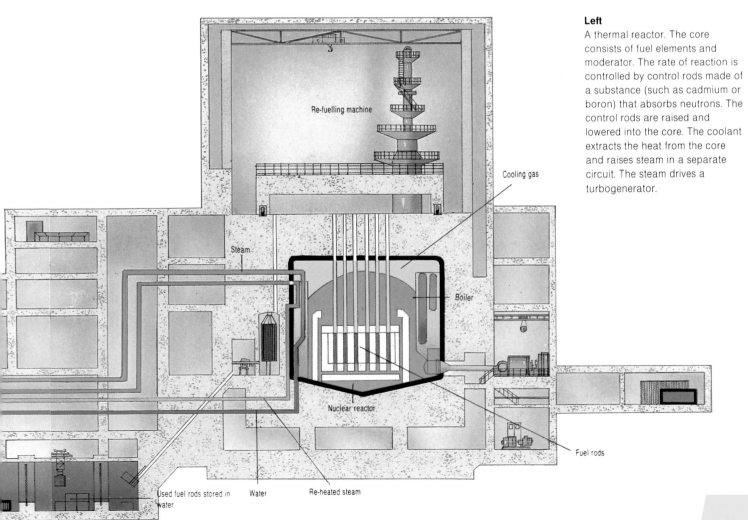

Left
A thermal reactor. The core consists of fuel elements and moderator. The rate of reaction is controlled by control rods made of a substance (such as cadmium or boron) that absorbs neutrons. The control rods are raised and lowered into the core. The coolant extracts the heat from the core and raises steam in a separate circuit. The steam drives a turbogenerator.

Re-fuelling machine

Cooling gas

Steam

Boiler

Nuclear reactor

Fuel rods

Used fuel rods stored in water   Water   Re-heated steam

NUCLEAR FUSION

The fission of heavy nuclei is one way to obtain nuclear energy. Another way is the fusion (or joining together) of light nuclei. Deuterium is an isotope of hydrogen, sometimes called heavy hydrogen. Two atoms of deuterium can join together to form helium. This releases an enormous amount of energy. When 1 kg of deuterium is converted to helium the energy released is six times greater than the energy released by the fission of 1 kg of uranium.

Thermonuclear reactions

These thermonuclear reactions, as they are called, will only take place if the deuterium atoms collide with great energy. This means that they must be moving very rapidly which, in turn, means that they must be at a very high temperature – millions of °C. Temperatures as high as this do not normally occur on earth. However they do occur in the interior of stars.

The energy of the sun and other stars is derived from thermonuclear reactions. In the interior of the sun, hydrogen is being converted into deuterium, and deuterium into helium. The gravitational attraction in the centre of the sun forces all the hydrogen atoms (protons) close together. This creates the high pressure and high temperature needed for fusion.

When a neutron collides with a proton a deuterium nucleus is formed. When two deuterium nuclei collide, a series of reactions occurs leading to the formation of helium. The total mass of helium formed is less than the total mass of deuterium. This difference in mass, called the mass defect, is converted into energy. Einstein showed that a small amount of mass is equivalent to a huge amount of energy. This is why thermonuclear reactions produce so much energy.

It is extremely rare for the high temperatures required for thermonuclear reactions to occur on earth. The atom (fission) bomb is one way of producing such temperatures. It is used to create the conditions for fusion in the hydrogen bomb.

If it were possible to make a fusion reactor this would have very great advantages over the fission reactor. Hydrogen is

Einstein

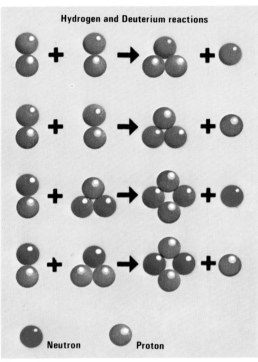

Hydrogen and Deuterium reactions

Neutron   Proton

Left
Thermonuclear reactions occur between deuterium nuclei. A deuterium nucleus consists of one neutron and one proton. In the first reaction two deuterium nuclei fuse to produce a helium–3 nucleus (two protons and one neutron) and one spare neutron. In the second reaction, which also can occur, the hydrogen isotope called tritium (one proton and two neutrons) is formed. In the last two reactions tritium and helium–3 react with deuterium to form helium–4.

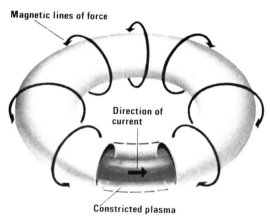

Magnetic lines of force

Direction of current

Constricted plasma

Left
One problem of thermonuclear reactions is to keep them in a vessel. One solution relies on magnetic fields to keep the reaction away from the walls of the tube. At the high temperature of a thermonuclear reaction the atoms lose their electrons and become a collection of electrons and positively charged nuclei. A gas in this state is called a plasma. In a toroidal (ring-shaped) reaction vessel the plasma is created by passing an enormous current through the gas. This current also produces a strong magnetic field which keeps the plasma to the centre of the tube and away from the walls.

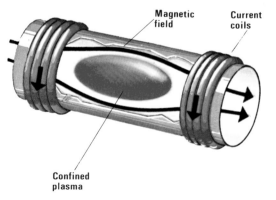

Magnetic field   Current coils

Confined plasma

Left
Some experimental reaction vessels are straight. The plasma is stopped from touching the ends by magnetic mirrors (strong magnetic fields round the end of the tube). In some experiments the material is turned into a plasma using the energy of a laser beam.

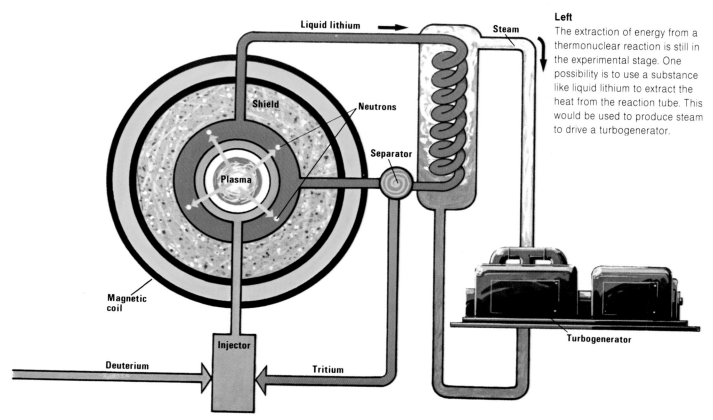

Left
The extraction of energy from a thermonuclear reaction is still in the experimental stage. One possibility is to use a substance like liquid lithium to extract the heat from the reaction tube. This would be used to produce steam to drive a turbogenerator.

much easier and cheaper to obtain than uranium. Two out of every three atoms of water are hydrogen and 15 out of every 100,000 hydrogen atoms are deuterium atoms. Sea water would therefore provide plenty of fuel.

There is another great advantage. A fission reactor produces very dangerous radioactive waste. This is at present stored in tanks until a way to store it permanently is developed. A fusion reactor would produce very little radioactive waste.

Scientists in many countries are trying to make fusion reactors work but none so far have succeeded for more than the smallest fraction of a second. A temperature of about 100 million degrees is needed for fusion to happen. At this temperature the material is a plasma and would vaporize any container. So the problem is not only reaching a high enough temperature, but also containing the material. To overcome this, people have tried containing the plasma inside a magnetic field. Many of the reactors are ring shaped. They are called Takomak reactors after the first one developed in the USSR.

Left
In the fusion process, atoms of two light elements are squeezed together and fuse to form a heavier element. They release energy as they do so.

195

Industry and Transport

FUELS

The main fuels are coal, oil, and natural gas. All three were formed from the remains of animals and plants that lived millions of years ago. Until the middle of the twentieth century coal was by far the most widely used fuel. Oil and natural gas are now being used more and more.

The Carboniferous period

Most of the world's coal began forming in the Carboniferous period. This is the name given to the time from 345 to 280 million years ago. The remains of swamp forests were buried under a great weight of sands and other material which was laid down on top of them. The dead vegetation turned into coal and the layers (or seams) of coal are divided by other rocks. There are various forms of coal. These range from the younger brown coal, lignite, to the older hard anthracite.

Oil was formed under great heat and pressure, and is found in certain types of rock formation. Great sunken parts of the earth's crust (geosynclines), where sedimentary rocks occur, often contain oil. It is held in rocks that are full of tiny holes called pores and therefore act as sponges.

These rocks are trapped between impervious layers which neither hold any liquid nor let it pass through them.

Natural gas also occurs underground, usually lying above a layer of oil-bearing rock. Both oil and gas are recovered by drilling down through rock. Large amounts of oil and gas have been found underwater, for example, under the North Sea. This makes drilling more difficult, because it has to be done from a ship or floating rig.

In its natural or crude form, oil is useless. In an oil refinery it is divided into its components and most of these can be used. The process is basically that of heating the crude oil. The components change into gases at different temperatures. There are separated from each other in a tall tower called a fractionating

Bottom
A coal mine showing the ventilation shaft on the left and the lift shaft on the right. There are three coal seams running across. The lowest one was formed earliest and the highest one latest.

Below
A North Sea gas rig. Weather conditions in the North Sea can be very hazardous for those working on the oil rig. The rigs are reached by helicopter.

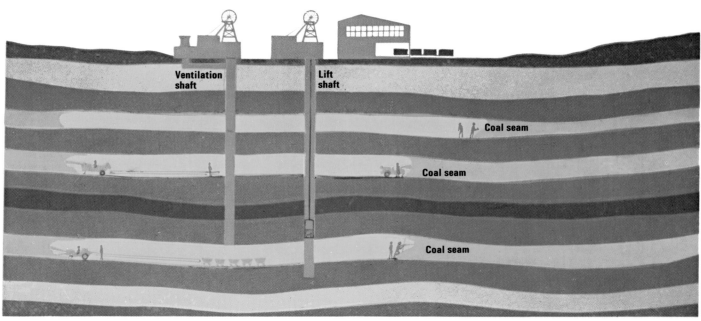

Ventilation shaft

Lift shaft

Coal seam

Coal seam

Coal seam

column (see page 23). The lighter fractions of the crude oil rise to the top, and the heaviest fractions remain at the bottom.

Petrol for motor vehicles is an important product obtained from crude oil. There are many others, ranging from tar and lubricating oils at the heavy end to aircraft fuel and paraffin at the lighter end.

Coal, oil, and natural gas are all used as fuels for producing heat both in the home and in industry. Many years ago, electricity generating stations in Britain used only coal as the fuel for their steam turbines. Then some started using oil instead. Today electricity is also produced using another type of fuel – uranium. This radioactive element is found in certain rocks. It is used in nuclear power stations (see page 192).

The petrochemical industry

A new industry has grown up in recent years as a by-product of oil refining. This is the petrochemical industry. The chemical industry has always been closely associated with the coal mining industry and gas works in the past, because coal is an important source of chemicals; modern petrochemical plants are on a much larger scale. The fuels are the source of chemicals for a wide range of products which we use every day. These include plastics, artificial fibres (nylon, etc.), paint, fertilizers, explosives, and many others.

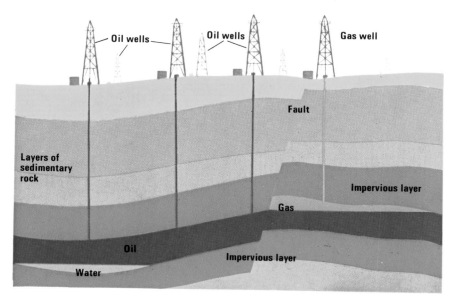

Above
A typical rock formation containing oil and natural gas. When a well is sunk, the oil can spout out under pressure or sometimes it is pumped out.

Left
A fractionating column in a refinery.

Below
Drilling the coal face in a mine. The more modern the colliery, the more elaborate is the machinery used.

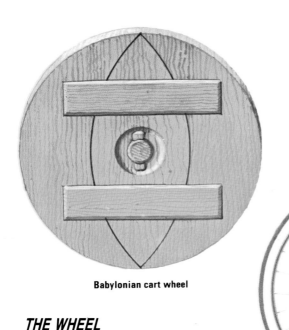

Babylonian cart wheel

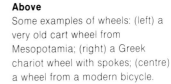

Modern bicycle wheel

THE WHEEL

Imagine living in a lonely place with no trains, buses, cars, or bicycles. You would have to walk everywhere. This is what life was like in primitive times. Gradually, many thousands of years ago, people started to live in groups near rivers. They built huts to live in and began to grow crops in the land around their settlements. People had learnt to be farmers. At first animals were used to carry people and their goods. With the invention of the wheel people could move about much more easily. It made a tremendous difference to the way people lived.

You can get an idea of how useful wheels are by putting a heavy book on a table and pushing it along. Then take some round pencils and rest the book on them. It is much easier to move the book by making the pencils roll underneath it. There is less friction when things roll than when they slide. The large stones at Stonehenge were probably moved on tree trunk rollers.

The first use of the wheel

Nobody knows who first had the idea of using wheels. In Asia, about 4000 BC, people had carts with wheels that were solid circles of wood. Two wheels on either side of the cart were joined by a pole which we now call the axle. The axle was joined to the cart. These carts were first pushed by people. Later they were pulled by animals.

By 1750 BC, the Ancient Egyptians were using spokes on their wheels. The spokes came out of the hub at the centre of the wheel. They were attached to an outer rim which moved over the ground. The wheels, made of wood, were much lighter than the older, solid wheels. Vehicles could therefore move much faster. Egyptian chariots with spoked wheels were

Above
Some examples of wheels: (left) a very old cart wheel from Mesopotamia; (right) a Greek chariot wheel with spokes; (centre) a wheel from a modern bicycle.

Below
The first wheels were made of wood. In the sixteenth century the first tyre was made. This was a band of iron in the shape of a hoop, which was made to fit tightly around the wheel. These wheels were lighter than solid iron wheels and lasted almost as long. Wheels were also made with a saucer shape. They were held on the cart as shown in the diagram. This made them stronger. They were called dished wheels.

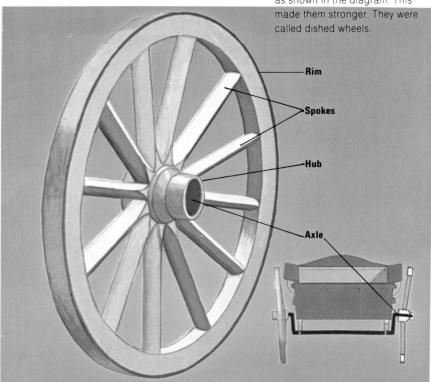

Rim

Spokes

Hub

Axle

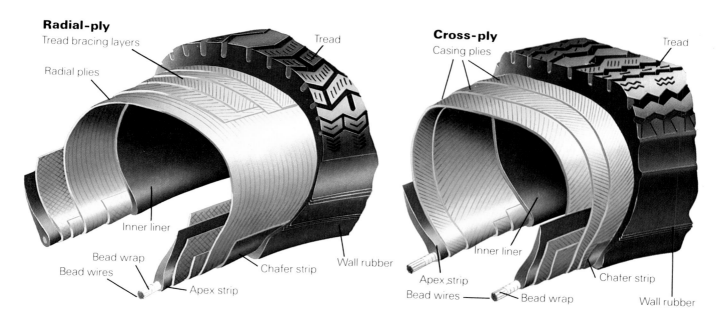

Radial-ply
Tread bracing layers
Radial plies
Tread
Inner liner
Bead wrap
Bead wires
Apex strip
Chafer strip
Wall rubber

Cross-ply
Casing plies
Tread
Inner liner
Apex strip
Bead wires
Bead wrap
Chafer strip
Wall rubber

greatly feared by opposing armies because of the speed at which they could move. Instead of wood, the Romans used iron to make their spoked wheels. These last much longer but were very heavy. Modern wheels are much lighter and springier. They have rubber tyres filled with compressed air, sometimes called pneumatic tyres.

How a wheel works

When a wheel is turning it moves on the axle, which goes through a hole in its centre. The point where the axle goes through the wheel is called the bearing. When the wheel moves, the axle is fixed and the hub of the wheel rubs against the axle. This friction makes it more difficult for the wheel to go round and the parts quickly wear out. It also makes the hub and axle very hot when the wheel turns quickly.

To make it easier for the hub to slide on the axle it is coated with grease or oil.

Early people probably used animal fats for this.

Ballbearings were first used in the nineteenth century. They are used in many modern wheels. A number of steel balls are held between the inside of the hub and the axle. Instead of sliding on the axle the hub rolls around it, just as the book moves along the rollers. Because the balls roll instead of sliding, the wheel turns more easily.

Above
The two main types of tyre in use today. Radial-ply, the most commonly used, have casing cords that run radially, and additional piles that strengthen the tread. The cross-ply tyre has fabric cords that are stretched diagonally to brace the tread.

Ball bearings

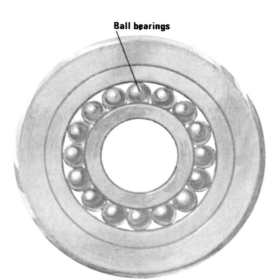

Left
Ballbearings make the wheel move more easily on the axle.

Below
It is much easier to push a book along on rollers. This is because the surfaces in contact roll over one another rather than sliding. This causes much less friction.

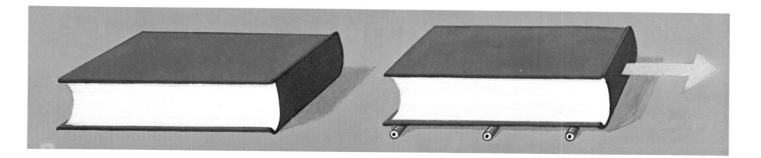

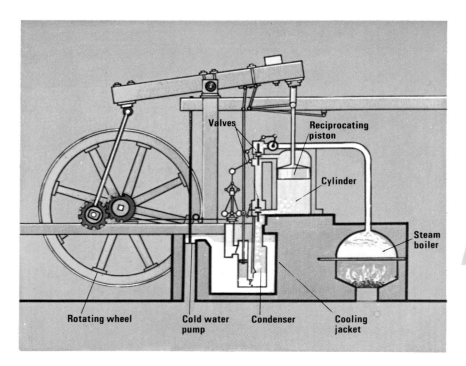

Valves

Reciprocating piston

Cylinder

Steam boiler

Rotating wheel

Cold water pump

Condenser

Cooling jacket

ENGINES FOR TRANSPORT

It is almost impossible to imagine now how difficult it used to be to move about the country. Before the railways were developed in the nineteenth century, land transport depended entirely on the horse. Seas were crossed by sailing ships. The need for the horse and the sail were abolished by the invention of an efficient steam engine by James Watt.

Invention of the steam engine

Watt was born in 1736, in Greenock, Scotland. At seventeen he learnt to make mathematical instruments and had a job as mathematical instrument maker to Glasgow University. One of the jobs they asked him to do was to repair a model of Newcomen's steam engine. This rather inefficient engine was used to pump water out of mines.

Watt improved on Newcomen's design and then he completely altered it. His new engine used only a third of the fuel that Newcomen's engine required. Watt also made his engine capable of rotary movement, using a crank and gear wheels. By 1782 his engine was working up to 40 machines in a factory. This was the beginning of the Industrial Revolution when workers began to be replaced by machines.

The earliest steam engines were stationary. The first attempt to use them for transport was in 1786, when the American John Fitch built a steamship. By 1850 propeller driven steamships were regu-

Top
Watt's steam engine. Steam from the boiler enters the cylinder through a valve and pushes the piston down. At the bottom of the stroke another valve opens and steam pushes the piston up. The up-and-down (reciprocating) motion of the piston is converted to round-and-round (rotary) motion by a system of cranks and gears.

Above
John Fitch's paddle steamboat. It worked but was not financially successful. Fitch died unknown.

Right
George Stephenson's steam locomotive called the *Rocket*. It won a competition in 1829 covering 12 miles in 53 minutes.

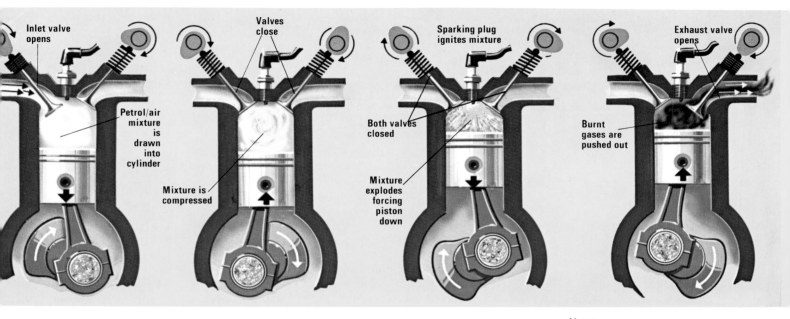

Inlet valve opens

Valves close

Sparking plug ignites mixture

Exhaust valve opens

Petrol/air mixture is drawn into cylinder

Mixture is compressed

Both valves closed

Mixture explodes forcing piston down

Burnt gases are pushed out

larly crossing the Atlantic. The first successful steam train was built by George Stephenson in 1814. This began the era of land travel by railway.

The internal combustion engine

The steam engine has the great disadvantage that it is necessary to carry coal or wood around to make the fire. The search began for a lighter fuel and an engine in which to burn it. The result was the internal-combustion engine. A gas version of this was made by the Frenchman Etienne Lenoir in 1860. The modern engine we use in our cars is based on the four-stroke engine, built by Nikolaus Otto in 1876. The cycle of strokes on which it works is called the Otto cycle. Modern car engines have 4, 6, or 8 cylinders. The

more cylinders they have, the more smoothly the engine runs. The first practical petrol cars were built in Germany in 1885 by Gottleib Daimler and Carl Benz.

In 1892 the German engineer Rudolf Diesel built an engine using oil as the fuel. This engine does not need sparking plugs. Instead, the explosion takes place when the oil is sprayed into the cylinder which contains highly compressed air. Diesel engines are used in buses, taxis, lorries, and some trains and boats.

Small petrol and Diesel engines are often two-stroke engines. In this type of internal-combustion engine there are no valves. The piston uncovers parts or holes in the cylinder wall as it moves up and down. Some motor cycles, cars, and lawnmowers have two-stroke engines. You can recognize them by the "pop-pop" noise they make at each stroke.

Above
The Otto cycle. On the first stroke the piston goes down and the inlet valve opens. Air and petrol vapour is sucked into the cylinder. On the second stroke the piston rises, compressing the mixture. The sparking plug fires and the mixture explodes. This pushes the piston down for the third stroke. On the fourth, upward, stroke, the exhaust valve opens and the gases are pushed out. The cycle is then repeated over and over again.

Below left
The Diesel locomotive is not as smooth as the electric train but is cheaper to run because an electrified rail or overhead wire is not required.

Below
In the Diesel engine the air is heated before the fuel is let in. The fuel is sprayed in, in fine drops which ignite spontaneously in the hot air. In the petrol engine the petrol and air mixture is ignited by the sparking plug. Not all the mixture is burned.

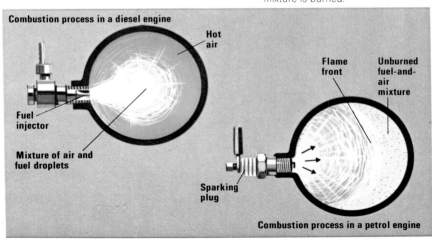

Combustion process in a diesel engine

Hot air

Flame front

Unburned fuel-and-air mixture

Fuel injector

Mixture of air and fuel droplets

Sparking plug

Combustion process in a petrol engine

Below

This petrol-driven car was invented by Siegfried Marcus in 1874. Though it could be driven under its own power it was heavy and clumsy. It was not a commercial success.

Bottom left

In 1873, Bollée's L'Obéissante was the first car to have pivoted front wheels, instead of the whole axle moving. This meant that it was more easily steered and manoeuvred. The car was very elaborate. Its steam engine was placed at the back. The wheels were moved by the steam in much the same way as pedals move a bicycle – by turning gear wheels.

Bottom right

The 1911 Ford Model T was the most popular car made at the time. Between 1908 and 1927, fifteen million were sold.

CARS

After Newcomen had invented the steam engine in 1712, attempts were made to harness this device to a cart in place of the horse. It was only with Watt's improved engine that this became possible. The first successful power-driven cart was built in 1769 by Nicholas Cugnot. From then on, all over the world a great variety of extraordinary steam-powered vehicles were produced.

The 'horseless carriage'

The first practical steam vehicles, called 'horseless carriages', were built in 1820. Good roads had been built by Telford and McAdam for horse-drawn vehicles. The hard surfaces were ideal for steam carriages.

The early vehicles resembled stage coaches and carried goods and passengers in the same way. They travelled at about 30 mph. However in the 1865 Road Locomotives Act (called the Red Flag Act), the Government restricted their speed to 4 mph. This Act slowed down car development in Britain very considerably.

In the nineteenth century, the trend was to develop light vehicles, which were easy to manoeuvre. One problem with a steam engine is that it requires a furnace of some sort to raise steam. This means carrying large quantities of heavy and bulky coal. With the development of the oil industry, inflammable liquids such as petrol became available. These made it possible to do away with external combustion in engines. Internal-combustion engines were built, in which the petrol vapour explodes inside the cylinder.

The first successful gas engine was built by Etienne Lenoir in 1860. This inspired a German, Nikolaus Otto, to build a four-stroke internal-combustion engine in 1876.

The world's first practical petrol-driven cars were produced in 1885. In 1889

Marcus petrol car

L'Obéissante

Ford Model 'T'

petrol cars were imported into Britain and the speed limit was raised to 12 mph.

At the beginning of the twentieth century steam engine cars were still being produced. In 1906 the Stanley brothers in America built the Stanley Rocket capable of travelling at 127 mph. However, steam cars were clumsy and expensive to run and gradually disappeared.

Petrol-driven cars

Instead, people concentrated on improving petrol-driven cars. In 1907, Sir Henry Royce produced his first famous Silver Ghost. Between 1907 and 1930 car bodies became stronger and more stream-lined. Front suspension was added and syncromesh gears were invented. Shock absorbers, windscreen wipers, and indicators became standard equipment on every car. Major developments since 1930 include the use of automatic gears and the invention of the Wankel engine.

Electric cars

The first electric cars appeared in 1891, made possible by Gaston Plant's invention of a storage battery. Though popular, they could only go short distances before the battery needed recharging. When petrol cars became self-starting, electric cars went out of favour. They are still used today for milk floats and other delivery vehicles. Interest in electric cars has revived because they do not pollute the air. It is hoped that new lighter types of batteries or fuel cells can be developed which will last as long as a full tank of petrol.

Below
The Wankel and two-stroke engines work in a similar way. However, in the two-stroke, the piston moves up and down. In the Wankel engine the triangular-shaped piston compresses the air and petrol mixture within an elliptical cylinder.

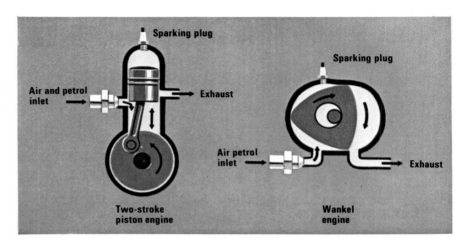

Below
A cutaway diagram of a modern motor car.

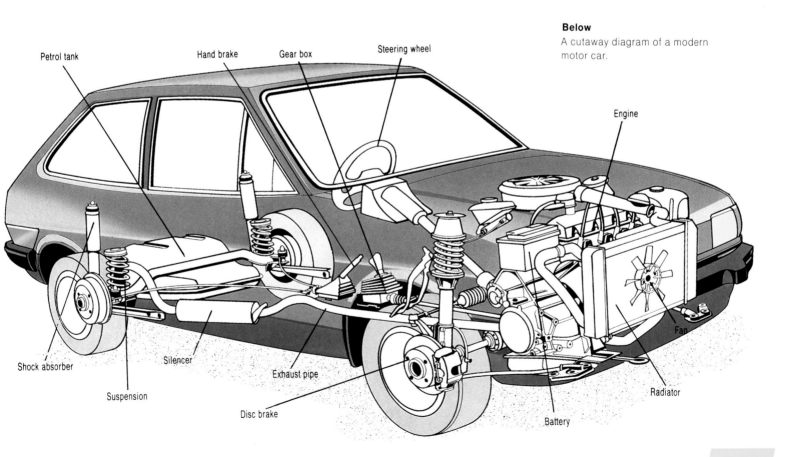

The first people to travel by water probably used logs as simple boats. They sat astride the log and used a piece of wood to paddle along. About 5,000 years ago, the Egyptians began to build proper boats. Their first boats were made from bundles of reeds. Later they made stronger and bigger ships from short planks of wood. They learnt to use a sail so that the wind could push their ships along. They fixed a paddle near the back of the ship to steer it. In these ships, the ancient Egyptians made long journeys.

Over the years, ship design was improved. More masts and sails were added until the ships could move very fast. The fastest of all sailing ships was called the clipper. It was long and narrow and had three tall masts, with up to six sails on each mast. The *Cutty Sark*, a famous clipper, sailed from Australia to England in 69 days. The usual time was 100 days.

The steamship was the next improvement in ship design. An American, John Fitch, used a steam engine to drive a ship in 1786. His ship, the *Experiment*, had oars that were driven by steam. Soon afterwards paddlesteamers were used. These had a paddle wheel, like the wheel of a water mill, at the side or back of the ship.

In 1894, a British engineer built a new kind of steamship engine. It was called the steam turbine. Steam turbines use less fuel and go faster than paddlesteamers. The first steam turbine ship crossed the Atlantic in 1904. Soon all large ships were using turbines as engines.

Steam turbines are still used in some ships today. Another type of engine often used is called the Diesel engine. The Diesel engine also powers some land vehicles, such as lorries and buses.

Below

A Roman galley. These were among the earliest efficient sailing ships, and could also be rowed by tiers of slaves. Ships like this one were the warships of the Roman Empire.

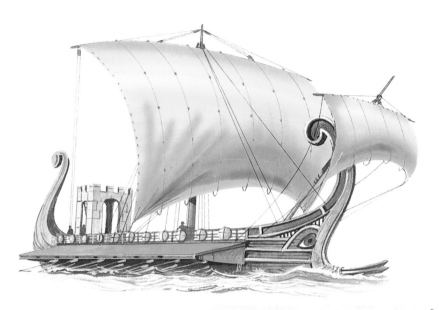

Right

A nineteenth-century clipper, the ultimate in sailing ships. Long and narrow, it had three tall masts with up to six sails on each mast. The clipper was the fastest sailing ship the world had seen.

The hovercraft and the hydrofoil

Some of the ships used today are quite different from the ships of 100 years ago. These are the hovercraft and the hydrofoil. The hovercraft floats on a cushion of air which lifts it above the water. The hovercraft is driven forward by large propellers that spin in the air above the craft. Hovercraft can travel on both land and sea. The hydrofoil has small wings on its underside. These lift the craft out of the water when it is moving.

Other ships have to push through the water and this slows them down. Hovercrafts and hydrofoils can move more swiftly because they travel above the water. They cannot travel over rough seas, and so are used for short journeys in quiet waters.

Submarines

Under the sea, the submarine is used. The first submarine was built by David Bushnell in 1775. It was used during the American Revolution when the Americans tried to attach a mine to the hull of a British ship. It was moved along by propeller-like screws that were turned by hand from within the submarine.

The most modern submarines have small nuclear reactors which use plutonium or uranium as fuel. They boil water to turn turbines which drive the propeller. The great advantage of a nuclear reactor is that it uses only a tiny quantity of fuel to produce a lot of power. So nuclear submarines can travel completely around the world without surfacing.

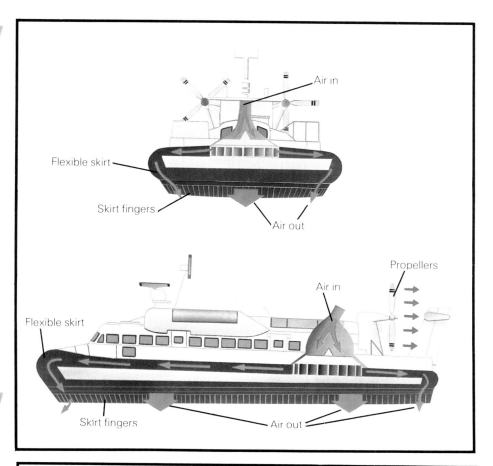

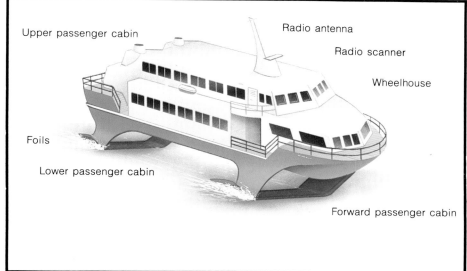

Top right
Front and side views showing the flow of air through a hovercraft. A hovercraft travels on the cross-Channel service between England and France. It can travel at speeds up to 90 kph (56 mph) and the journey takes about 40 minutes.

Above right
A hydrofoil with surface-piercing foils, which lift the craft out of the water when it is moving.

Right
A nuclear-powered submarine breaks through the Arctic ice.

Right

The first historic flight made by the Wright brothers on 17 December, 1903. They made four more flights that day.

Below

The first manned flight of the Montgolfier hot-air balloon took place on 21 November 1783.

Bottom

In 1981 the *Solar Challenger* became the first solar-powered aircraft to cross the English Channel. The journey of 290 km (180 miles) took 5½ hours.

AIRCRAFT

People have always dreamt of being able to fly. Many flying machines and devices have been tried. The first successful balloons were launched by the Montgolfier brothers in 1782. They were filled with hot air, which being lighter than the cooler surrounding air lifted the balloon off the ground. In 1783 their balloon carried people through the air for the first time, although the balloon was tethered to the ground. In 1785 Blanchard and Jeffries crossed the Channel in a hydrogen-filled balloon. Hydrogen is lighter than air and so rises up through the air.

Gliders, copying the principle of flight used by birds, were tried at the end of the nineteenth century. The wings of a glider are shaped so that as they pass through the air an upward force called the lift is created. A wing with this shape is called an aerofoil.

Gliders rely on the wind to give them the force or thrust to move forwards. The invention of the internal combustion engine made powered flight possible.

The Wright brothers

The Wright brothers learnt to fly gliders and they used this experience to make aeroplanes powered by petrol engines. Their first successful flight took place on the 17th December 1903. The plane flew for 12 seconds covering 40 metres at a height of about 3 metres. The plane had a wood and canvas frame built round the engine.

At first flying was regarded as a dangerous sport. Planes were built for enthusiasts. In the First World War, however, they were used for dropping bombs. After the war it was realized how valuable they were. Planes were soon improved, wood and canvas giving way to metal, particularly aluminium. Instead of being open they had enclosed bodies, with seating for a passenger as well as a pilot.

In 1919 Alcock and Brown were the first to fly the Atlantic nonstop. In 1934 a DC2 was used to carry passengers from England to Australia. In 1939 Pan American Airways provided the first transatlantic passenger service.

The Second World War and after

During the Second World War, planes were the most vital part of the fighting

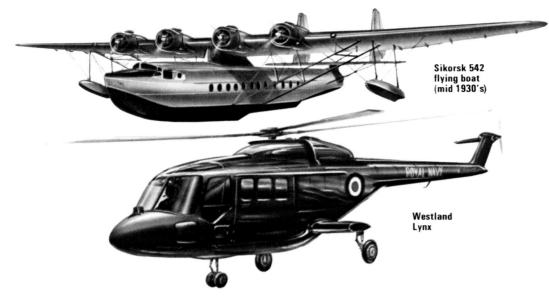

**Sikorsk 542
flying boat
(mid 1930's)**

**Westland
Lynx**

force. During these six years, necessity led to great advances in the development of aircraft. The main advances were the use of monoplanes (single wing) in place of biplanes (double wing) and the development of the jet engine. By the end of the war both sides were using jet fighters.

After the war all these developments were used to provide modern passenger aircraft. For example, the Boeing 707 was a development of the B29, the aircraft used to drop the atom bomb on Japan.

In fixed wing aircraft, lift is obtained from stationary wings. A propeller or jet produces the forward thrust. These aircraft need long runways and have high landing speeds.

Supersonic aircraft can fly faster than the speed of sound, which is about 760 mph (1200 km per hour). *Concorde* can fly at twice the speed of sound.

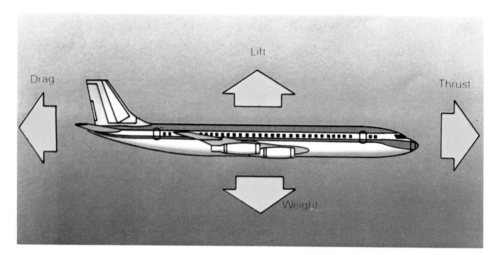

JET ENGINES

During the Second World War it became very important to make aeroplanes fly faster. So the British Government decided to develop a jet engine that had been patented in 1930 by Frank Whittle. By the end of the war Britain, America, and Germany had several types of jet propelled fighters. Since then jet engines have become the source of power for most large aircraft.

Jet propelled aircraft do not have propellers. They obtain their thrust from the reaction to a high-speed jet of gas produced by burning fuel.

In a jet engine, high-pressure gas is produced by burning a fuel such as paraffin. The air needed for burning the fuel is drawn in from the front of the engine. The burning takes place in a series of combustion chambers arranged around the engine. The hot gases escaping from the combustion chambers rotate a turbine and then pass out of the jet nozzle at the rear.

The turbine consists of a number of blades attached to a shaft. This is connected to another turbine-like device at the front of the engine which compresses the incoming air. As the gases rotate the turbine, the turbine drives the compressor which forces air into the combustion chambers. In this way large quantities of fuel can be burnt.

Supersonic flight

Without jet engines supersonic flight would not be possible. *Concorde* has specially developed jet engines that enable it to cruise at twice the speed of sound.

The simplest type of jet engine is the ramjet. It has no moving parts and consists of a long tube. So it is sometimes called a flying drainpipe. The centre of the tube serves as the combustion chamber and the tail as the jet nozzle. A ramjet can only work if the craft is already moving rapidly. As the tube flies through the air, air is forced into the combustion chamber and fuel is injected. The burning of the fuel in the air makes hot gases flow out of the jet nozzle at a higher speed than the air flowing in. This produces the thrust to force the ramjet through the air.

Below right
The ramjet, or flying drainpipe, has no moving parts. It only works when the pipe is flying through the air fast enough to produce a high pressure in the centre portion. In this wider centre portion the air is slowed down and the pressure increases. Fuel is added and burnt at high pressure. Hot gases flow out of the rear nozzle pushing the ramjet forwards. Rocket assisted ramjets have been used in some guided missiles.

Below
Jet engine. Air enters at the left end. It is compressed by the compressor blades, and then enters the combustion chambers. The fuel burns in the compressed air and passes out of the jet nozzle, turning the turbine on the way. The turbine turns the compressor. In some jet engines, the turbine also turns a propeller. Engines like these are called turboprops.

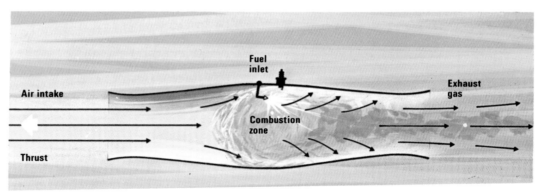

Air intake   Fuel inlet   Exhaust gas

Combustion zone

Thrust

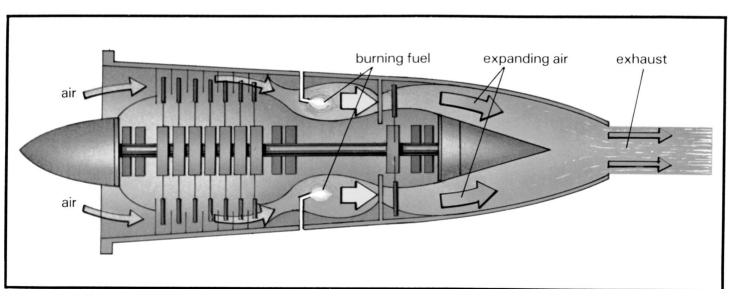

air   burning fuel   expanding air   exhaust

air

JET-PROPELLED SPEEDBOAT

You will need: old cigar tube ● balsa wood ● nail ● stiff wire ● candle

ASK AN ADULT TO HELP YOU DO THIS. Your jet-propelled speedboat will be driven by a jet of steam which you will be able to make in a boiler. For this you can use a metal tube (such as a cigar tube) or a small tin with a tight-fitting lid. Use a nail to pierce a small hole in one end of the tube (or tin). Saw a piece of wood into the shape of a boat hull and make a hole near each corner.

Make a four-legged cradle for the tube out of stiff wire. Wind the wire around both ends of the tube, and push the feet into the holes in the wood. Half fill the tube with water and fit the lid on tightly. Place a candle underneath the tube, and light it. Now launch the boat on the water, taking care not to touch the tube, which will be getting hot.

The water in the tube will soon start to boil, and a jet of steam will spurt out of the hole. As the steam escapes backwards, your speedboat will shoot forwards. It will carry on travelling until it runs out of steam.

The jet-propelled speedboat works according to the law of reaction. The force (action) of the steam, going backwards, sets up an equal force (reaction) going forwards, and it is this force that propels the boat.

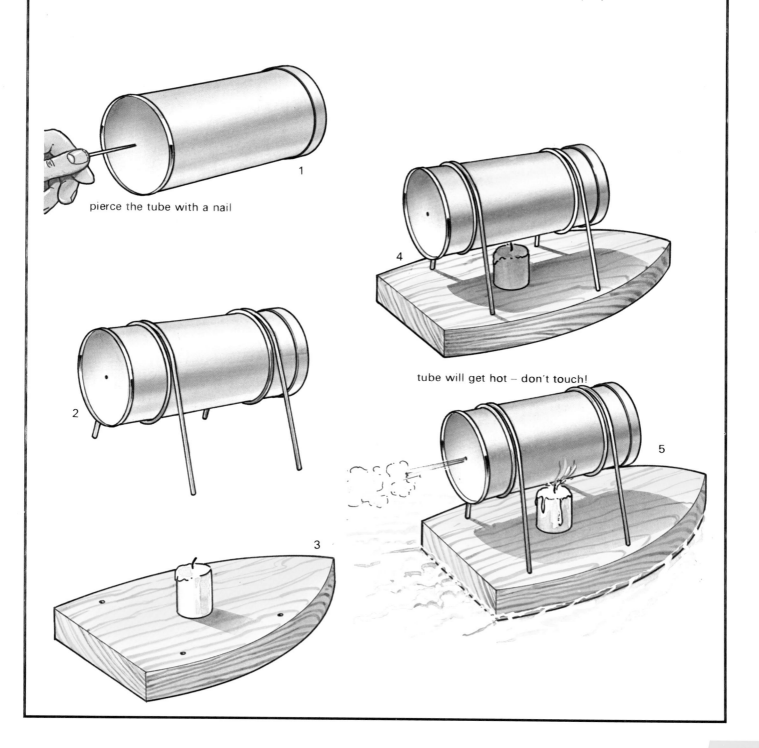

pierce the tube with a nail

1

2

3

4

tube will get hot – don't touch!

5

ROCKETS

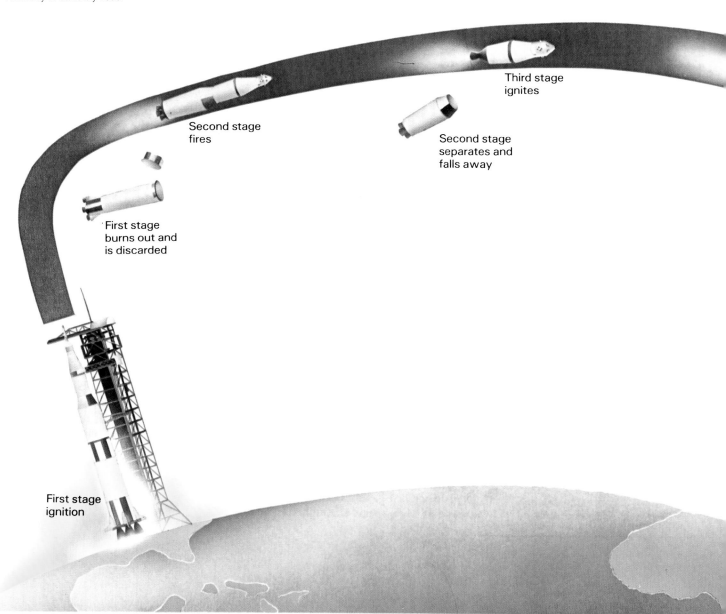

Von Braun

Above

Werner Von Braun. He studied engineering and during the Second World War he perfected the V2 rockets. After the war he worked for the Americans and was responsible for the *Explorer* satellite, launched from Cape Kennedy in January 1958.

As early as the eleventh century the Chinese used war rockets. In the nineteenth century the use of rockets in war was advanced by the studies made by Sir William Congreve. Towards the end of the Second World War, the Germans designed huge V2 rockets to bombard London. After the war these rockets were adapted for space travel by scientists in the USA and USSR.

Rockets are propelled in a similar way to jet-propelled aircraft (see page 208). The fuel is burnt in a combustion chamber and the hot gases flow out of a nozzle. The reaction to the fast moving gases produces the forward thrust. The difference between a jet aircraft and a rocket is that the jet needs the oxygen in the air to burn the fuel. The rocket carries its own oxygen, usually in liquid form. This means that a rocket can fly outside the earth's atmosphere where there is no air. It is the only means of propulsion in space at present.

To launch a satellite into an orbit round the earth a rocket must reach a speed of about 8,000 metres per second (18,000 mph). This speed is achieved by using a launching system in parts or stages. When the first stage motor has used up its fuel it drops off. So the second stage motor does not have to carry its weight.

To escape from the earth's gravitational pull, the speed must be increased to about 11,200 metres per second (25,000 mph). As the moon's gravitational pull is much less than the earth's, the launching speed

Third stage
ignites

Second stage
separates and
falls away

Second stage
fires

First stage
burns out and
is discarded

First stage
ignition

from the moon is only about 2,400 metres per second (5,300 mph).

The Space Shuttle

The Space Shuttle, which carries things into orbit, is made up of three parts. There is a very large fuel tank for the main engine that burns liquid hydrogen and liquid oxygen. Strapped to this are two solid-fuel booster rockets, the first to be used for manned space flight. They are released from the rocket after their fuel is burnt and are re-used. The third part is the Space Shuttle Orbiter. This manoeuvres in space by using small rockets in the nose and tail.

Orbiting satellites can be used to find out what space is like just outside the earth's atmosphere and for surveys of the earth.

In meteorology (weather forecasting) use can be made of satellites. They carry special instruments for this. They can observe the formation of clouds from above and relay the pictures back to earth.

An important part of space travel is studying the effects of space travel on human beings. The high acceleration, the vibration, and the noise can have a bad effect on astronauts. More important are the effects of the high temperatures involved, and the radiation in the outer atmosphere. Massive doses of radiation can be fatal. Weightlessness is yet another hazard.

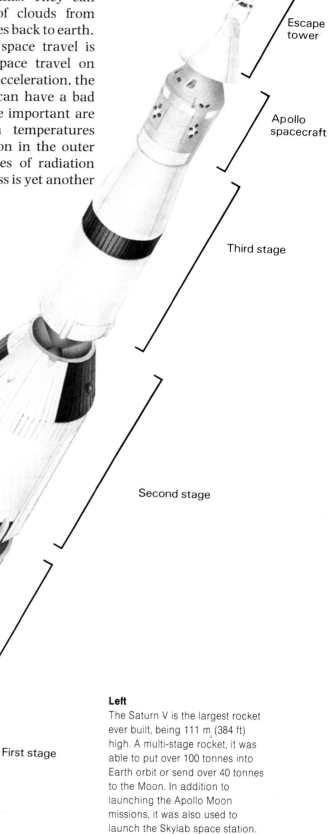

Escape tower

Apollo spacecraft

Third stage

Second stage

First stage

Third stage
continues firing
until payload
is in orbit

Left
The Saturn V is the largest rocket ever built, being 111 m (384 ft) high. A multi-stage rocket, it was able to put over 100 tonnes into Earth orbit or send over 40 tonnes to the Moon. In addition to launching the Apollo Moon missions, it was also used to launch the Skylab space station.

SPACE TRAVEL

People have long wanted to journey beyond the earth, but it is only quite recently that space travel has become reality.

In order to escape from the gravitational pull of the earth, the modern rocket (see page 210) has been developed. People began to investigate space by using rockets to shoot small objects, called artifical satellites, into orbit round the earth. The first one, *Sputnik 1*, was launched by the USSR in 1957. These complicated devices are used for various purposes: to obtain information about the sun, stars, and others things in the universe, to study weather patterns in the earth's atmosphere, or to act as communication and navigation devices.

Telstar 1, a communications satellite launched in 1962, made possible the first direct television link between Europe and America. Today *Intelsat* satellites send messages all over the world.

Manned space flight

In 1961, the first manned space flight was made by Soviet cosmonaut Yuri Gagarin. He made one orbit of the earth. John Glenn was the first American to be put into orbit round the earth.

The Soviets began to study the moon using a series of space vehicles called *Lunik*. In 1959, *Lunik 3* sent back to earth photographs of the hidden side of the moon. During the 1960s, the USSR concentrated on solving the problems of orbital space flight. They also continued their moon studies with the unmanned *Lunik* series.

The Americans, however, turned their efforts to becoming the first people on the moon. In their *Mercury* (one-man) and *Gemini* (two-man) orbital space flights, they studied the conditions in space and the problems, such as weightlessness, that would face people.

The unmanned *Ranger* and *Surveyor* probes were launched on a path towards the moon, in preparation for the manned *Apollo* missions. In 1969, Neil Armstrong and Edwin Aldrin of *Apollo 11* became the first men to walk on the moon.

In 1971, the USSR made a major breakthrough when it launched the *Salyut*

space station. In 1972, *Skylab*, an American experimental space station, was launched. This fell to earth in 1979, scattering debris across western Australia. The Soviets launched the *Mir* space station in 1986. This has a number of docking ports and separate modules for scientific experiments. In 1988, two cosmonauts set a new record by spending 365 days in orbit in the *Mir* space station.

Unmanned space probes

Both America and the USSR have sent out many unmanned space probes. The American *Mariner 10* probe photographed Mars. It then flew on to Venus and Mercury. *Vikings 1* and *2* actually landed on Mars but failed to find signs of

Above
An American astronaut from *Apollo 16* standing on the moon's surface, next to the lunar module and the lunar rover. They used the lunar rover to travel over the surface and collect samples of lunar rock.

Below
This diagram shows how satellites in synchronous earth orbit such as Telstar and Early Bird can relay communications throughout the world.

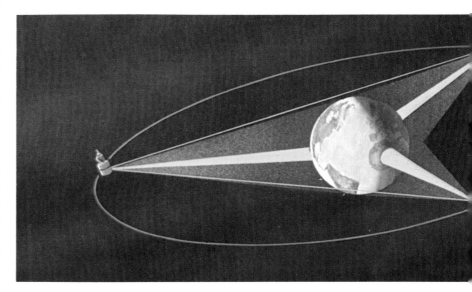

life. Both American *Pioneer* and the USSR's *Venera* probes have landed on Venus.

The outstanding study of the planets so far is that carried out by *Voyagers 1* and *2*. They showed the moons of Jupiter in 1979, and Saturn and its many rings in 1981. *Voyager 1* sent back about 17,000 pictures. *Voyager 2* explored Uranus in January 1986 and Neptune in August 1989.

The *Space Shuttle* was first launched by the Americans in 1981. It can return to earth for re-use. It is used to carry astronauts and satellites into orbit. Future activities include satellite repair and refuelling space stations. The European Space Agency's *Giotto* probe flew to Halley's Comet in 1986 and sent back many pictures of the comet close up.

Right
The solar telescope satellite is designed to observe the sun.

Right
The Space Shuttle had its first flight in April 1981. It is designed to take off like a rocket, fly in orbit like a spacecraft, and return to Earth like a conventional aircraft.

Below right
Spacelab is designed to fit in the cargo hold of the Space Shuttle. On board, up to four scientists will be able to conduct a wide variety of experiments.

SPACE SHUTTLE

Arm to launch and recover satellite

Computerised navigational controls

Flight deck

Accommodation compartment

Temperature control panel

Bay to hold Spacelab

Payload bay doors

Main rocket engines

Instrument to undertake geological surveys of Earth

Device using laser beams to sound the atmosphere

pressurised laboratory

Tunnel linking Spacelab with Orbiter cabin

SPACELAB

Right

Blast furnace. Trucks carry the ore, coke, and fluxes (mostly limestone) to the top of the furnace, which may be 70 metres high. Hot air (about 800°C) is blown into the brick-lined furnace causing the coke to burn and produce carbon monoxide. This acts on the ore and raises its temperature to about 1600°C. The molten iron falls to the bottom and is drawn off and run into sand moulds to form pig iron. The slag floats on the iron and is run off at a higher level.

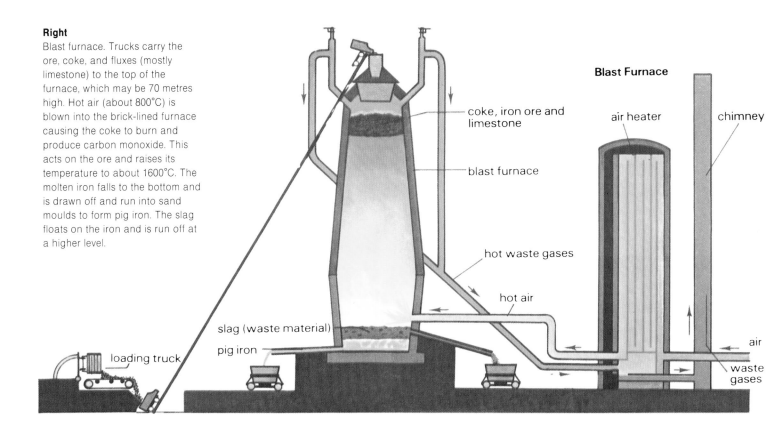

Blast Furnace

coke, iron ore and limestone

blast furnace

hot waste gases

hot air

slag (waste material)

pig iron

loading truck

air heater

chimney

air

waste gases

Below

Henry Bessemer (1813–98) developed his process for making steel from iron because cast-iron cannon balls were too weak to be used in the rifled cannons he had invented.

Bessemer

IRON AND STEEL

People made the first tools and weapons from bones and stones or from wood. Gradually they discovered that metals – the hard shiny materials they found on meteorites or sometimes in the ashes of a fire – could be made into sharper and tougher tools. The first metal to be obtained in any quantity was copper. This was too soft except when it was found mixed with tin. A mixture of copper and tin is called bronze. About 3500 BC the Egyptians were using bronze tools and weapons. This was the beginning of the Bronze Age.

The Iron Age

Iron had been known for as long as bronze, but the only source was the occasional meteorite. Then somewhere in Asia, about 1500 BC, people found that by heating certain minerals called iron ores with wood they could make iron themselves. The Hittites were the first to have an army using iron weapons. They soon defeated the armies who had bronze weapons, as bronze swords are no match for iron ones.

This was the start of the Iron Age, which we are still in today. Iron and steel are still the most important metals of construction. Cars, factory machinery, agricultural machinery, and weapons are all made mostly of iron and steel. Large buildings have steel frameworks. Hundreds of millions of tonnes of iron and steel are used throughout the world every year.

Today we obtain most of our iron from the iron ores called haematite and magnetite. These occur in many places all over the world and are easily mined from the earth. The iron is extracted from the ore in a blast furnace. There the ore is burnt with coke and limestone to produce liquid iron. This is run off into moulds and allowed to set into slabs. It is called pig iron and can be used to make cast iron.

To make 100 tonnes of iron takes about 190 tonnes of ore, 100 tonnes of coke and 50 tonnes of limestone. At the same time

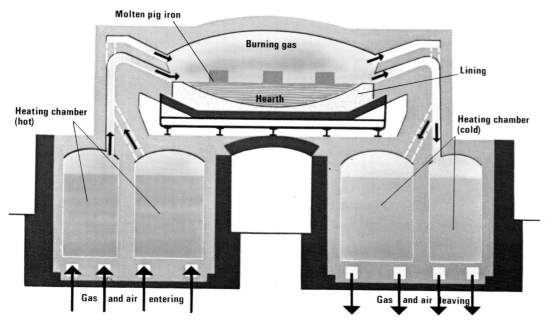

Molten pig iron

Burning gas

Lining

Hearth

Heating chamber (hot)

Heating chamber (cold)

Gas and air entering

Gas and air leaving

Left
The open-hearth steel-making furnace. Air and gas are heated by being passed over hot bricks. The gas and air burn over the molten pig iron removing carbon and other impurities. The burnt gases are used to heat the bricks to warm the incoming gas and air. The furnace is lined with special bricks that absorb some of the sulphur and phosphorus in the iron.

Far left
All these objects are made of plain steel: nail; horse-shoe; wire-wool.

50 tonnes of slag are produced. This is used to make cement and concrete.

The Bessemer process

Pig iron is not pure iron. It contains 3–4 per cent of carbon, which makes it rather brittle. The most useful form in which iron is used is steel. Steel is iron with most of the carbon removed, leaving only 0.2–1.5 per cent. A cheap way of doing this was discovered by Henry Bessemer in 1856. A blast of air is sent through the molten iron so that most of the carbon forms carbon dioxide with the oxygen in the air. Today the Bessemer process has been replaced by the open-hearth and basic oxygen methods of steel-making.

Steel is much stronger and more versatile than iron. By adding other elements it can be made stronger, or rust-proof, or able to stand higher temperatures. If 13 per cent of manganese is added to steel it becomes much harder. Nickel and chromium added to steel give the stainless steels which do not rust.

Left
These objects are made of steel alloys. Manganese steels are used for safes, chrome-vanadium steel is used in cars, stainless steel is used for cutlery. Chrome-tungsten steel is used for tools like this chisel. Tungsten, silicon, or cobalt steels are used to make magnets.

CLOTHING MATERIALS

Spinning and weaving are two of the world's oldest industries. The earliest piece of cloth dates back to about 4500 BC. There are many types of woven materials such as matting, fencing, or wicker for baskets. The most important one, however, is cloth.

The thread for cloth must first be spun from fibres. Wool is made from the hair of goats, sheep, and llamas. Cotton comes from the fluffy seed pods of cotton plants, and linen from the stalks of a plant called flax. Silk is made by a kind of caterpillar called a silkworm. It spins the silk to make a cocoon inside which it changes into a moth. Besides these natural fibres we also use artifical fibres. Rayon is made from wood and Terylene, Acrilan, and nylon are made from oil.

These threads are often dyed. Natural fibres are easily dyed by dipping. Artificial fibres are not easily dyed and they are usually coloured when they are being made into thread.

Spinning and weaving

In Europe the spinning was done by hand up to the fourteenth century. The spinner would draw out a piece of fluff from a mass of wool or cotton, then twist it, overlapping the ends of several bits to form a thin long thread. This was wound onto a stick called a spindle. The process became faster when the spindle was rotated by the foot treadle of a spinning wheel. This produced thread of a more even thickness.

Thread is woven into cloth using a loom. Early looms consisted of two wooden bars. Threads were tied between the bars to form the warp. A long thread called the weft was wound on to a shuttle. This was passed over one thread and under the next, over the next, and so on. On the way back the shuttle was passed over a thread that it had previously gone under and vice versa. The threads were thus interlaced at right angles to each other. Gradually this process was automated so that modern power looms can weave many metres of cloth in a day. This can be of a complicated pattern under computer control.

The first sewing machine

Clothes were made by sewing the material together by hand. In 1882 an American, Walter Hunt, built the first sewing machine. In a sewing machine there are two pieces of thread. One length is on a

Crompton

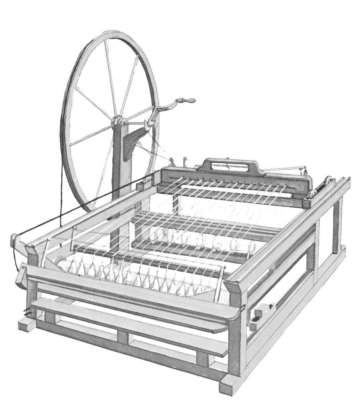

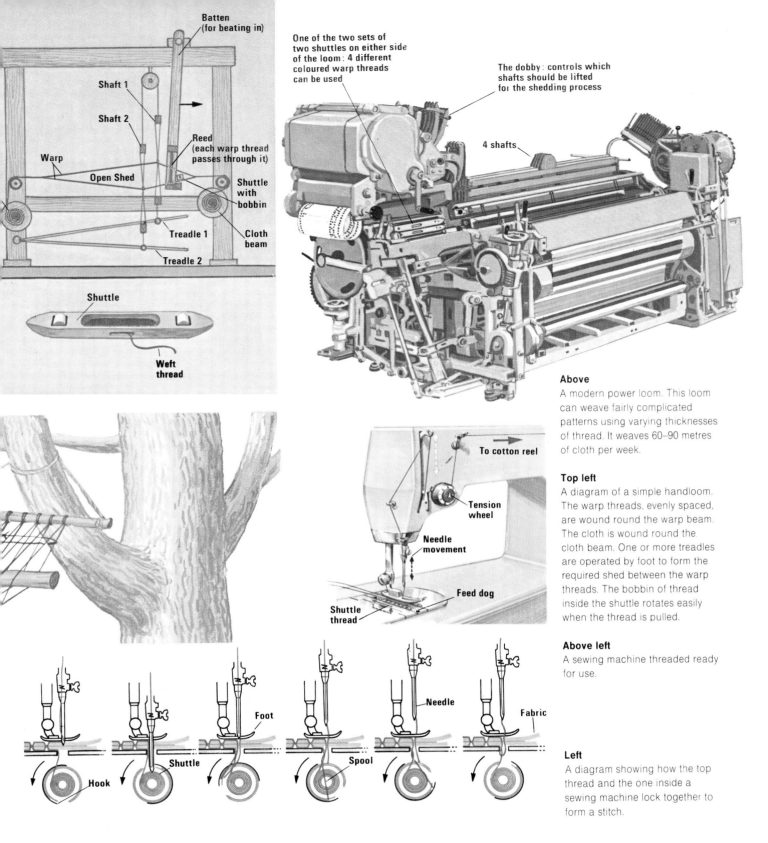

Batten (for beating in)

One of the two sets of two shuttles on either side of the loom: 4 different coloured warp threads can be used

The dobby: controls which shafts should be lifted for the shedding process

Shaft 1

Shaft 2

Warp

Open Shed

Reed (each warp thread passes through it)

4 shafts

Shuttle with bobbin

Treadle 1

Cloth beam

Treadle 2

Shuttle

Weft thread

To cotton reel

Tension wheel

Needle movement

Feed dog

Shuttle thread

Foot

Shuttle

Hook

Spool

Needle

Fabric

Above
A modern power loom. This loom can weave fairly complicated patterns using varying thicknesses of thread. It weaves 60–90 metres of cloth per week.

Top left
A diagram of a simple handloom. The warp threads, evenly spaced, are wound round the warp beam. The cloth is wound round the cloth beam. One or more treadles are operated by foot to form the required shed between the warp threads. The bobbin of thread inside the shuttle rotates easily when the thread is pulled.

Above left
A sewing machine threaded ready for use.

Left
A diagram showing how the top thread and the one inside a sewing machine lock together to form a stitch.

special bobbin inside the machine. The other is on a reel on top of the machine. This is threaded through a moving arm and then through the eye of the needle. In a sewing machine the eye is at the pointed end. The cloth is made to move under the needle which moves up and down. As the needle goes through the material it carries the thread with it. This is looped round the other thread inside the machine to make the stitch. Under the material are two rows of blunt teeth called the feed dog which carry the material along. Modern sewing machines are able to produce very complicated stitch patterns by using micro-chip technology.

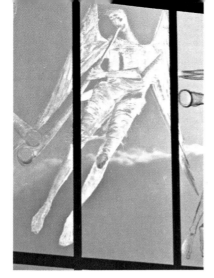

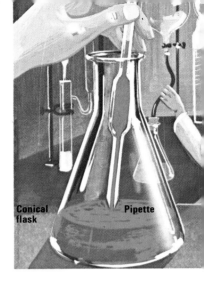

Conical flask **Pipette**

Above
These two cathedral windows show different ways of decorating glass.
Right The beautiful stained glass rose window in the Cathedral of Chartres in France, built in the twelfth century. *Left* The Flying Angel etched on the Great Glass Screen in Coventry Cathedral, England, finished in 1961.

Above
Glass has always been prized for its beauty. This wine goblet is decorated with diamond-point engraving. It was made in 1686.

Right
Some everyday uses of glass: sheet of plate glass; light bulb; milk bottle; jam jar; windscreen; thermometer.

GLASS

Today people make many materials such as nylon, perspex, and bakelite. These are not found naturally, like wood and stone. They are artificial materials. The oldest artificial material is glass, which was first used about 3,000 years ago.

Glass is made from a mixture of sand, soda, and limestone. These are ground together and heated to about 1,500°C. They form a clear jelly-like substance. When this cools it sets into a hard brittle glass. To produce coloured glass, small amounts of other chemicals can be added. Sand always contains some iron, which, if not removed, gives glass a greenish colour.

Glass is used for making jars, bottles, and other vessels. About 2,000 years ago it was found that a piece of hot soft glass on the end of a metal tube could be blown out into a bubble which could then be shaped. Nowadays glass-blowing can be done by machine. Glass is also used in windows. At first only small pieces were made. These were joined together on lead frames. Later windows were made by blowing a piece of glass into a large bubble and flattening it, so that it formed a plate. Windows made like this have a lump in the middle where the bubble was joined to the glassblowing tube.

Today bottles and jars are nearly all made by machine, in moulds. Modern window glass is usually made by the float

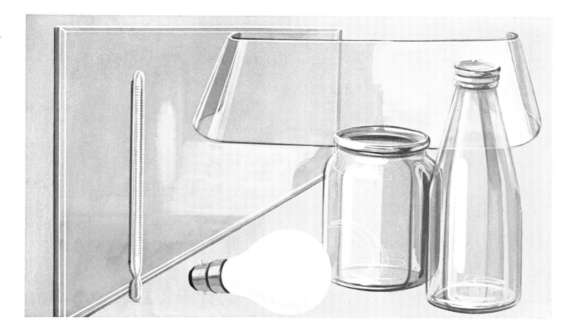

Flask

Test tube

Beaker

glass process. Molten glass is poured on molten metal where it forms a thin, very flat layer before it is cooled (see page 43).

Pyrex, Pyrosil and fibreglass

Different kinds of glass can be made by adding other substances to the normal mixture. The glass in a car windscreen is very strong. When a windscreen cracks it breaks into many small pieces. These do not have sharp edges, so the driver does not get cut. Glass can be made to withstand heat. Ordinary glass would crack if it were heated but Pyrex glass does not. Neither does it break as easily when it is dropped. It is therefore used for making cooking dishes. When rockets and spacecraft are sent into space they have to stand extremely high temperatures. They are therefore covered with a special glass called Pyrosil. This is also used to make cooking dishes now.

Glass can be made into very fine threads. This is called fibreglass. It is used to make a type of felt for insulating homes. It can be woven into cloth which is hard wearing and does not burn. The glass fibres can also be mixed with plastic to make a very light but strong material. It does not rust like iron or rot like wood, so hulls of boats are often made from it.

In our modern world there are many substitutes for glass, such as perspex and other plastics. These are lighter than glass and do not break easily. Many bottles are now made of plastic. But plastics are not as heat-resistant as glass and are affected by chemicals.

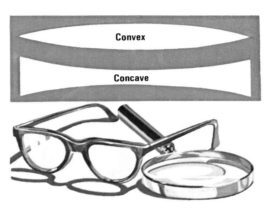

Convex

Concave

Left
Glass is used for making lenses. As light passes through the lens its direction is changed. The amount the light is bent depends on the type of glass used and on its shape. Lenses are used in spectacles and in many instruments such as telescopes, binoculars, microscopes, and cameras. The glass used for making these lenses has to be of very good quality and have no flaws. It is called optical glass.

Below
Making plate glass and bottles. The glass for bottles is blown into a mould. This can be opened up when the bottle has cooled.

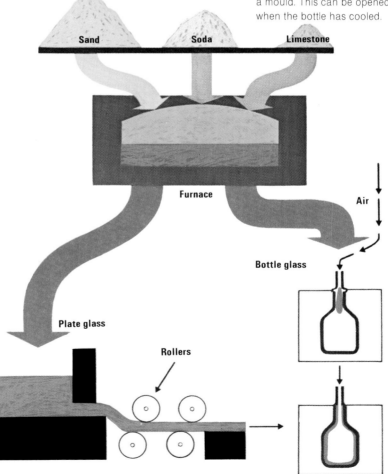

Sand

Soda

Limestone

Furnace

Air

Plate glass

Bottle glass

Rollers

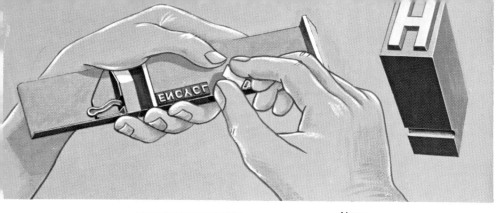

PRINTING

Before the invention of printing, books had to be written by hand. It took months, often years, for a person called a scribe to make a single copy of a book.

Printing in its most simple form was invented in China over 2,000 years ago. Parts of a flat wooden block were cut away to form raised letters or designs. The raised surface was covered in ink and a sheet of paper pressed down on to it to print on the paper. This was very slow and expensive.

Johann Gutenberg

In the fifteenth century a German printer, Johann Gutenberg, made it possible to print books faster and cheaper. Instead of carving an entire page out of one block of wood, he carved each letter separately on small blocks of wood of the same height. These pieces, called characters, could be placed in any order to form words and sentences. When the printing was completed, the pieces of type could be used again to make new words. Instead of pressing a piece of paper against the inked type by hand, a mechanical press was used to force the paper against the type. Even with this improvement, it was still slow.

William Caxton

William Caxton was one of the first English printers. After learning the art of

Above
Separate pieces of type were selected by hand to form words. They were placed in a special tray called a composing stick.

Left
The ancient Chinese method of printing from wood or stone blocks. The modern hobby of lino cutting is done in a similar way, using lino blocks.

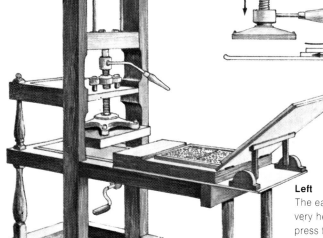

Left
The earliest printing presses were very heavy wooden machines. To press the paper down on to the inked type the printer had to tighten a big wooden screw. This forced down a heavy wooden plate on to the paper.

Inking rollers

Damping roller

Plate cylinder, carrying type or illustration

Impression transferred to blanket cylinder

Reel of paper

Tension rollers

Yellow printing

Magenta printing

Cyan printing

Caxton

printing in Europe in 1471, he returned to London and set up his own press in Westminster. Early books were mainly on law and religion. Caxton also printed books on other subjects. In the 500 years since Gutenberg first used separate pieces of type, many improvements have been made in both the speed and quality of printing.

Modern printing

Except in special cases, type is no longer set by hand. Computers with keyboards like typewriters assemble pages of type. The typesetting machines produce photographic film of the text automatically. From these, printing plates are made, either by moulding or photographically.

The plates are used on giant modern printing presses that are run by electricity. These can print thousands of books or newspapers every hour.

There are three main methods of printing – letterpress, photolithography, and gravure. Letterpress uses plates with a raised moulded surface. Photolithography uses plates with a flat surface. These are produced photographically. Gravure printing uses plates with an engraved surface, made by chemical etching.

The two main types of printing machine used are the sheet-fed and the web-fed. In sheet-fed machines, single sheets of paper are automatically fed into the machine and printed individually. In a web-fed machine, a continuous roll of paper is fed through the machine. Both types of machine can print up to four colours on both sides of the paper at once. The paper goes through a different set of plates for each colour. Some machines can also cut up the sheets and fold them into pages.

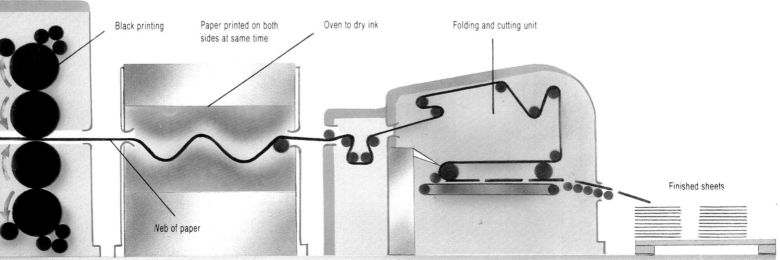

Black printing | Paper printed on both sides at same time | Oven to dry ink | Folding and cutting unit | Web of paper | Finished sheets

Famous Discoveries

c500BC	Static electricity	Thales of Miletus, Greece		1742	Centigrade temperature scale	Anders Celsius, Sweden
c240BC	How things float	Archimedes, Greece		1752	The nature of lightning	Benjamin Franklin, USA
c150	Earth-centred universe	Claudius Ptolemy, Greece		1772	Nature of combustion	Antoine Lavoisier, France
1304	Cause of rainbow	Theodoric of Freibourg, Germany		1774	Preparation of oxygen	Joseph Priestley, England
1543	Sun-centred solar system	Nicolaus Copernicus, Poland		1791	Metric system of units	France
1600	Earth's magnetism	William Gilbert, England		1798	Nature of heat	Count Rumford, England
1604	How objects fall	Galileo Galilei, Italy		1800	Wave nature of light	Thomas Young, England
1609	How the planets move	Johannes Kepler, Germany		1800	Electric current	Alessandro Volta, Italy
1609	Moons of Jupiter	Galileo Galilei, Italy		1802	Atomic theory	John Dalton, England
1616	Chemical element defined	Robert Boyle, Ireland		1807	Discovery of new elements using electricity	Humphry Davy, England
1643	Air pressure	Evangelista Torricelli, Italy		1808	How gases combine	Joseph Gay-Lussac, France
1662	Law of gases	Robert Boyle, Ireland		1811	Molecules in gases	Amedeo Avogadro, Italy
1666	Nature of white light	Isaac Newton, England		1820	Electromagnetism	Hans Oersted, Denmark
1666	Gravity	Isaac Newton, England				
1687	Laws of motion	Isaac Newton, England		1820	Force between current-carrying wires	André Ampère, France
1690	Wave theory of light	Christiaan Huygens, Holland				
1718	Fahrenheit temperature scale	Gabriel Fahrenheit, Germany		1827	Law of electric current	Georg Ohm, Germany

Archimedes

Galileo

Newton

Ampère

1831	**Electromagnetic induction**	Michael Faraday, England	
1833	**Laws of electrolysis**	Michael Faraday, England	
1841	**Heat and work**	James Joule, England	
1855	**Prediction of radio waves**	James Maxwell, Scotland	
1869	**Periodic table of elements**	Dimitri Mendeleyev, USSR	
1887	**Radio waves discovered**	Heinrich Hertz, Germany	
1887	**Speed of light**	Albert Michelson, USA	
1894	**Noble gases**	William Ramsey, Scotland	
1895	**X-rays**	Wilhelm Rontgen, Germany	
1896	**Radioactivity**	Antoine Becquerel, France	
1897	**Electron**	Joseph John Thomson, England	
1898	**Radium**	Pierre and Marie Curie, France	
1899	**Alpha and beta particles**	Ernest Rutherford, New Zealand	
1900	**Quantum theory**	Max Planck, Germany	
1903	**Theory of radioactivity**	Ernest Rutherford (New Zealand) and Frederick Soddy (England)	
1905	**Relativity**	Albert Einstein, Germany	
1905	**Photoelectric effect**	Albert Einstein, Germany	
1911	**Atomic nucleus**	Ernest Rutherford, New Zealand	
1911	**Superconductors**	Heike Kammerlingh Onnes, Holland	
1913	**Structure of the atom**	Niels Bohr, Denmark	
1915	**General relativity**	Albert Einstein, Germany	
1919	**Proton**	Ernest Rutherford, New Zealand	
1926	**Wave nature of matter**	Erwin Schoedinger, Austria	
1927	**Uncertainty principle**	Werner Heisenberg, Germany	
1929	**Expanding universe**	Edwin Hubble, USA	
1932	**Neutron**	James Chadwick, England	
1938	**Nuclear fission**	Otto Hahn, Germany	
1939	**Chemical bonding**	Linus Pauling, USA	
1964	**Quark**	Murray Gell-Mann, USA	
1974	**Black hole**	Stephen Hawking, England	
1986	**High-temperature superconductors**	Alex Muller (Switzerland) and Georg Bednorz (West Germany)	

Ohm

Faraday

Thomson

Einstein

Great Inventions

c4000BC	Wheel	Asia		1800	Electric battery	Alessandro Volta, Italy
c4000BC	Weighing instruments	Mesopotamia		1803	Steam train	Richard Trevithick, England
c3500BC	Potter's wheel	Mesopotamia		1820	Electromagnet	Hans Oersted, Denmark
236BC	Screw for lifting water	Archimedes, Greece		1822	Photograph	Joseph Niépce, France
600BC	Cast iron	China		1831	Transformer	Michael Faraday, England
c1000	Gunpowder	China		1831	Dynamo	Michael Faraday, England
1088	Water-powered clock	Han Kung-Lien, China		1831	Electric motor	Michael Faraday, England
1267	Magnifying glass	Roger Bacon, England		1835	Photographic negative	William Fox Talbot, England
1280	Spectacles	S di Popozo, Italy		1837	Electric telegraph	William Cooke and Charles Wheatstone (England)
c1450	Printing press	Johannes Gutenberg, Germany		1838	Morse code	Samuel Morse, USA
c1590	Microscope	Zacharias Janssen, Holland		1839	Bicycle	Kirkpatrick Macmillan, Scotland
c1593	Thermometer	Galileo Galilei, Italy		1843	Aneroid barometer	Lucien Vidi, France
c1608	Lens telescope	Hans Lippershey, Holland		1843	Iron-hulled ship with propeller	Isambard Kingdom Brunel, England
1642	Adding machine	Blaise Pascal, France		1843	Analytical engine	Charles Babbage, England
1643	Mercury barometer	Evangelista Torricelli, Italy		1852	Steam-powered airship	Henri Giffard, France
1657	Pendulum clock	Christiaan Huygens, Holland		1856	Steel furnace	Henry Bessemer, England
1668	Reflecting telescope	Isaac Newton, England		1856	Synthetic dyes	William Perkin, England
1674	Calculating machine	Gottfried von Leibniz, Germany		1859	Spectroscope	Gustav Kirchoff and Robert Bunsen, Germany
1698	Steam engine	Thomas Savery, England		1860	Gas-burning engine	Etienne Lenoir, Belgium
1764	Spinning machine	James Hargreaves, England		1862	Plastics	Alexander Parkes, England
1712	Steam-driven pump	Thomas Newcomen, England		1866	Dry cell battery	Georges Leclanche, France
1733	Mechanical loom	John Kay, England		1867	Dynamite	Alfred Nobel, Sweden
1752	Lightning conductor	Benjamin Franklin, USA		1876	Telephone	Alexander Graham Bell, USA
1769	Efficient steam engine	James Watt, England		1876	Four-stroke gas engine	Nikolaus Otto
1769	Steam-driven carriage	Nicolas Cugnot, France		1877	Phonograph	Thomas Edison, USA
1775	Submarine	David Bushnell, USA				
1786	Steam boat	John Fitch, USA				
1783	Hot-air balloon	Etienne and Joseph Montgolfier, France				

Year	Invention	Inventor
1879	Electric light	Thomas Edison, USA
1879	Refrigerator	Karl von Linde, Germany
1882	Sewing machine	Walter Hunt, USA
1883	Petrol engine	Gottlieb Daimler, Germany
1884	Steam turbine	Charles Parsons, England
1885	Motorcycle	Gottlieb Daimler, Germany
1885	Motor car	Karl Benz, Germany
1888	Pneumatic cycle tyre	John Dunlop, Scotland
1889	Telephone exchange	Almon Strowger, USA
1891	Moving pictures	Thomas Edison, USA
1891	Electrical storage battery	Gaston Plant, France
1892	Oil-burning engine	Rudolf Diesel, Germany
1894	Radio transmitter	Guglielmo Marconi, Italy
1897	Cathode-ray tube	Ferdinand Braun, Germany
1898	Tape recorder	Valdemar Poulsen, Denmark
1900	Hydrofoil boat	E. Forlanini, Italy
1903	Aeroplane	Wilbur and Orville Wright, USA
1904	Diode valve	John Ambrose Fleming, England
1907	Triode valve	Lee de Forest, USA
1907	Helicopter	Paul Cornu, France
1908	Geiger counter	Hans Geiger, Germany
1918	Sonar	Paul Langevin, France
1925	Television	John Logie Baird, Scotland
1926	Liquid-fuelled rocket	Robert Goddard, USA
1930	Jet engine	Frank Whittle, England
1930	Particle accelerator	John Cockcroft (England) and Ernest Walton (Ireland)
1931	Electron microscope	Max Knoll and Ernst Ruska, Germany
1931	Cyclotron	Ernest Lawrence, USA
1935	Nylon	Wallace Carothers, USA
1935	Radar	Robert Watson-Watt, England
1937	Radio telescope	Grote Reber, USA
1938	Scanning electron microscope	M. von Ardenne, Germany
1942	Nuclear reactor	Enrico Fermi, USA
1947	Transistor	John Bardeen, William Shockley and Walter Brattain, USA
1947	Instant camera	Edwin Land, USA
1948	Computer	Fredric Williams and Tom Kilburn, England
1948	Hologram	Denis Gabor, Hungary
1949	Rotary engine	Felix Wankel, Germany
1954	Communications satellite	Arthur Clarke, England
1955	Hovercraft	Christopher Cockerell, England
1955	Ultrasound scanning	I. Donald, England
1956	Video recorder	A. Poniatoff, USA
1957	First artificial satellite	USSR
1958	Integrated circuit	Jack Kilby, USA
1960	Laser	Theodore Maiman, USA
1961	First man in space	Yuri Gagarin, USSR
1962	First communications satellite launched	USA
1966	Optical fibres	K. Kao and G. Hockham, England
1969	First men on Moon	Neil Armstrong and Edwin Aldrin, USA
1971	Microprocessor	Ted Hoff, USA
1971	First space station	USSR
1981	*Space Shuttle*	USA

Factfinder

Absolute zero The coldest temperature −273.15°C. It is only possible in theory, but scientists have recorded temperatures one-millionth of a degree above it.

Acceleration The rate at which velocity changes with time. Acceleration is measured by the change of speed divided by the time taken.

Acid A sour-tasting substance which produces hydrogen ions when dissolved in water. Acids turn blue litmus red and react with certain metals to give hydrogen.

Acoustics The science that studies sound and hearing.

Alternating current An electric current that flows first in one direction and then in the opposite direction. The electricity supplied by the mains is alternating current.

Ampere The unit used to measure the size of an electric current. It is named after the French scientist André Ampère (1775–1836).

Amplifier An electronic device which magnifies the strength of a signal, such as a radio signal.

Archimedes' principle A statement concerned with the upward force on a floating body, discovered by the Greek scientist Archimedes (c287–212 BC). It is that the upward force on a floating body is equal to the weight of the fluid displaced.

Atmosphere The band of air around the earth. The highest layer, called the ionosphere, extends roughly 400 km above the surface.

Atom A very small particle, the smallest part of an element that can exist. (*See* molecule).

Barometer An instrument used for measuring atmospheric or air pressure. In the mercury barometer, the height of a column of mercury indicates the pressure. In an aneroid barometer, the pressure is measured by the amount it squashes the sides of a metal box containing a vacuum.

Base A substance that reacts with an acid to form water and neutralize the acid.

Boiling point The temperature at which a liquid boils and turns from liquid into gas. The boiling point of water is 100°C at sea level.

Carbohydrate A substance made up of carbon, oxygen and hydrogen. Starches and sugars are carbohydrates.

Catalyst A substance which speeds up a chemical change without being changed itself. For example, platinum speeds up the reaction of ammonia and oxygen to produce nitric acid.

Cathode-ray tube The picture tube in a television receiver. It consists of a cone-shaped glass vessel with a long neck. An electron gun in the neck fires electrons at the fluorescent screen, producing spots of light.

Celsius temperature scale A scale used to measure temperature in which the freezing point of water is 0° and the boiling point of water is 100°. It was named after the Swedish scientist Anders Celsius (1701–44).

Another name for the Celsius scale is the Centigrade scale.

Centripetal force The inward force that keeps a body, such as a satellite, moving in a circular path.

Chain reaction A process that proceeds in steps, with the completion of one step starting off the next step.

Charge-coupled device, CCD An electronic device which is used in place of a photographic plate in astronomy. It is extremely sensitive to light and is used to detect very faint stars.

Chemical change A change in which a new substance is produced. Burning is an example of a chemical change.

Chemistry The science of the composition of things. Organic chemistry is concerned with carbon compounds (mostly in living things), inorganic chemistry with all other compounds.

Chip A small piece of semiconductor material on which the components of an electronic circuit can be engraved. (*See* integrated circuit.)

Combustion Another word for "burning". This is a chemical reaction which occurs when a substance combines with oxygen and gives off light and heat.

Communications satellite A satellite, an object that circles or orbits the Earth, which is used to send messages between distant places

Complementary colours A pair of colours that produce white light when mixed together. Yellow and blue light are complementary, for example.

Compound A substance consisting of two or more elements in fixed proportion, which can be described by a formula. For example, water (H_2O) is a compound of hydrogen and oxygen.

Computer An electronic device for storing and manipulating large amounts of information. Their great advantage is the speed with which they do calculations and retrieve information.

Concave mirror A mirror whose surface is curved inwards, like a small cave.

Conduction The way heat and electricity travels through a solid substance.

Conductor A substance that allows electricity to flow through it. All metals are conductors.

Convection The way heat travels through a gas or liquid as currents of heated material. The hot gas or liquid rises to the top, the cold gas sinks to the bottom.

Convex mirror A mirror that is curved outwards. The outside of a shiny spoon forms a convex mirror.

Crystal A solid made up of groups of atoms or molecules arranged in a fixed, regular pattern. Each grain of common salt is a crystal.

Database A collection of information stored on a

computer. The database can be searched quickly for particular items, and the information displayed on a computer screen.

Decibel A unit used for measuring the loudness of sounds. A soft whisper is about 0 decibels. A jet taking off is about 120 decibels.

Density The mass of a substance in relation to its volume. It is usually stated as kilograms per cubic metre, or pounds per cubic foot.

Diffraction of light The way a thin beam of light spreads out around the edge of a shadow. This causes thin bands of light and dark along the edge of the shadow.

Direct current An electric current that flows in one direction, and does not reverse its flow as alternating current does. The electricity produced by a battery is direct current.

Distillation A method for purifying or separating liquids. The mixture is heated until vaporized, and the vapour is condensed. As liquids have different boiling points, they can be separated by this method.

Doppler effect The way the pitch or frequency of waves seems to change if the source of the waves is moving. For example, the pitch of a police car siren seems higher than normal when the car is approaching but lower than normal as the car moves away. Named after the Austrian physicist Christian Doppler (1803–53).

Dynamo *See* Generator.

Effort The force needed to do work. In a simple machine, such as a lever, the effort is increased by the machine so that it overcomes a greater force called the load.

Elasticity The ability of a material to return to its original shape after it has been stretched out of shape.

Electricity A form of energy possessed by electrons and protons. A body with more than its normal number of electrons is said to have a negative electric charge. A body with a less than normal number of electrons is said to have a positive electric charge. Charges that are stationary are called static electricity. Moving electric charges form an electric current.

Electrode A metal piece into and out of which an electric current passes, such as the terminals of a battery. The negative electrode is called the cathode; the positive electrode is called the anode.

Electrolysis The breaking down of a substance by passing electricity through it or through a solution of it. Electrolysis is used to manufacture many chemicals such as chlorine, and in the electroplating industry.

Electromagnetic induction The way a changing magnetic field can start, or induce, an electric current in a wire. Electromagnetic induction is used in generators and transformers.

Electromagnetic wave Waves of electricity and magnetism that can carry energy through empty space. Light, microwaves, ultraviolet rays, infra-red rays, X-rays, radio waves are all electromagnetic waves with different wavelengths. They all travel through empty space at the same speed, 300,000 metres per second.

Electromagnetism The related effects of electricity and magnetism. Electric currents have magnetic effects, and magnetic fields can produce electric currents.

Electron A tiny particle that circles the central nucleus of an atom, and has a negative electric charge. An electric current is a flow of electrons.

Electronics A branch of physics dealing with the use of electrons in science and industry.

Electron microscope An instrument for producing a much magnified picture of a small object. Electron microscopes use a beam of electrons instead of light to 'see' the object. The picture is produced electronically on a television screen.

Element A substance made up of one type of atom. There are 92 elements in nature. All other substances are compounds.

Elementary particles Small particles of matter and energy that make up atoms. The electron is an elementary particle. Scientists think that some elementary particles, such as the proton and neutron, are made up of still smaller particles called quarks.

Energy The ability to do work. There are many forms of energy, such as heat, light or electrical energy. One form of energy can be changed into another form but energy cannot be lost or gained.

Fahrenheit temperature scale A scale used to measure temperatures in which the freezing point of water is 32° and the boiling point of water is 212°. The scale is named after the German scientist Gabriel Daniel Fahrenheit (1686–1736).

Fluorescence The glow caused when light is absorbed at one wavelength and sent out at another. In a neon tube, ultraviolet is turned into visible light by fluorescent substances in the tube.

Focus The point at which light rays meet to form a sharp image after passing through a lens, or being reflected from a curved mirror. It is also called the focal point. The distance between the focus and the centre of the lens or mirror is called the focal length of the lens or mirror.

Force A push or pull that makes an object move, or change shape or direction. Examples are gravity and magnetism.

Frequency The number of times something is repeated in a set time. In the movement of waves such as radio waves, the frequency of vibrations or peaks in the wave is measured in hertz (the number of cycles per second).

Friction The force that slows the movement, and produces heat, when two surfaces are rubbed together. There is greater friction between rough surfaces than between smooth, or oiled, surfaces.

Fulcrum The point about which a lever turns or pivots.

Galvanometer An instrument which detects and measures very small electric currents.

Gamma rays A powerful type of electromagnetic radiation given out when certain atoms disintegrate.

Gas A substance that spreads itself out to take up all the space available. A gas has no definite volume or shape.

Geiger counter An instrument which detects and measures radioactivity. It is named after Hans Geiger (1882–1945), the German scientist who invented it.

Generator A machine that converts mechanical energy into electrical energy. A dynamo produces direct current (d.c.) electricity. An alternator produces alternating current (a.c.) electricity.

Gravity The force that draws any two bodies together. Gravity depends upon mass. The large mass of the earth creates a strong gravitational force, so objects fall downwards towards the earth. The gravity between two bodies decreases as the bodies get further apart.

Greenhouse effect The way a greenhouse warms up when in sunlight. Sunlight passes through the glass walls of the greenhouse and is converted to heat which cannot escape. The greenhouse effect of the upper atmosphere causes the temperature of the earth's atmosphere to be warmer than it would otherwise be.

Gyroscope An instrument used in navigation. It is a wheel which spins inside a framework. The wheel can turn freely in all three dimensions and remains in the same position whatever the movements of the aircraft or ship.

Hardware The physical parts of a computer system, such as the printer, the display screen, and the computer itself. Software is the computer programs.

Heat A form of energy due to the movement of the atoms and molecules in a body. The amount of heat in a body is usually measured in joules, although heat units like the calorie or the British thermal unit are sometimes used.

Helium A colourless gas used for filling airships and in some fluorescent lamps. It is found in the sun and other stars.

Hologram A three-dimensional picture made using laser light.

Hovercraft A propeller-driven vehicle which moves on a cushion of air. Hovercraft can travel over land or sea.

Hydrocarbon A chemical compound that contains carbon and hydrogen. Examples are petroleum and natural gas.

Hydrofoil A type of boat mounted on underwater foils or wings. When it has reached a certain speed, the hull rises out of the water.

Hydrogen A colourless gas which burns easily. It is the simplest chemical element. It is lighter than air.

Image A picture or appearance of an object formed by light that has passed through a lens, or been reflected from a mirror.

Indicator A substance that changes colour in the presence of an acid or base. An example is litmus which is red in acid and blue in a base.

Inertia The tendency for an object to stay in the same state of motion. For example, a body at rest stays still and a body moving at a constant speed in a straight line continues moving in the same way because of inertia. A force is needed to overcome inertia and change the motion.

Information technology The methods of sending, obtaining, and storing information by electronic means. It involves the use of computers, databases, and modems for connecting computers together.

Infra-red rays A type of electromagnetic radiation with wavelength just longer than that of red light. It can be felt as heat.

Insulator A material that does not conduct heat or electricity. Many non-metals, such as rubber and plastics, are insulators.

Integrated circuit A complete electronic circuit built on a small piece, called a chip, of semiconductor material such as silicon. Integrated circuits are used in computers, radios, television sets, and most modern electronic devices.

Intensity The amount of heat, light, sound or electrical energy present. For example, a bright light or a loud sound has a high intensity.

Interference of light The way two beams of light of the same wavelength can produce bands of light and dark. This happens because the waves in the two beams are sometimes out of step, and cancel each other out, producing a dark band. Where the beams are in step, a bright band is produced.

Ion An atom, or group of atoms, which carries an electric charge. The charge results from a loss of electrons (giving a positive charge) or a gain (giving a negative charge).

Isotope An atom that is chemically the same as the normal atoms of the element but has a different number of neutrons in its nucleus.

Joule A unit used to measure the amount of energy or work done. One joule is the work done when a weight of one newton is lifted one metre. It is named after James Joule (1818–89), a British physicist.

Kelvin temperature scale A scale used to measure temperatures in which absolute zero is 0° and the freezing point of water is 273.15°. One degree kelvin is equal to one degree on the Celsius scale. It is named after the British scientist Lord Kelvin (1824–1907).

Kilogram A unit used to measure mass in the metric

system. One kilogram is 1,000 grams or about 2.2 pounds.

Kilometre A unit used to measure length in the metric system. One kilometre is 1,000 metres or 0.6214 miles.

Kinetic energy The energy a moving body possesses. Wind and flowing water have kinetic energy, for example.

Laser A device that produces a narrow powerful beam of light. A laser is a light amplifier that increases an initial weak pulse of light into an intense narrow beam. Lasers are used in medicine and industry.

Lens A piece of glass or transparent material that has curved surfaces. Light passing through a lens is bent and can form an image. Lenses are used, for example, in cameras, microscopes, and telescopes.

Lever A simple machine used for lifting heavy weights. It consists of a strong bar that turns about a pivot, like a seesaw.

Liquid A form of matter which can flow and takes up the shape of its container. Water, milk, and fruit juice are liquids.

Litmus A substance obtained from plants. In contact with an acid, it turns red; with an alkali, it turns blue.

Load The weight lifted or moved by a machine.

Machine A device that is used to do work more easily. Simple machines include the lever, the screw, the wheel and axle, the pulley, and the inclined plane or slope.

Magnet An object which attracts iron and attracts or repels other magnets. The magnetic force is strongest at two points called the north and south poles. When free to move, a magnet turns so that the north pole points north and the south pole points south, as in a compass.

Magnetic field The space around a magnet or an electric current where its magnetic effect can be felt.

Mass The amount of matter in an object. Mass is different from weight because weight depends on gravity but mass is always the same.

Mechanical advantage The amount by which a machine can magnify a force. It is the load (the weight lifted or moved by the machine) divided by the effort (the force needed to lift the load).

Melting point The temperature at which a substance melts, or changes from a solid to a liquid form.

Memory The part of a computer that stores the set of instructions, or program, and the information the computer needs during its work. There are two kinds of memory inside a computer: ROM, or read-only memory which is used to store permanent information; RAM, or random access memory, which remembers the program and information not needed permanently. Other memories, such as disk memories, can also be connected to the computer.

Metre A unit used to measure distances in the metric system. One metre is about 39.37 inches.

Microprocessor An integrated circuit that contains most of the parts of a computer on a small piece of silicon. They are used in small computers and in many devices around the home, such as cameras, sewing and washing machines. In industry they control robots and automatic machines.

Microwave A form of electromagnetic radiation of short wavelength. Microwaves are used in communication (eg radio) and in cookery.

Mixture A material made by adding together two or more substances. The substances in a mixture can be separated out by dissolving, heating or other physical means. Air is a mixture of gases, for example.

Modem A device used to connect a computer to a telephone line so that computer information can be sent along the line. The modem changes the computer signals, which are called digital signals, into sounds that can be transmitted by telephone lines.

Molecule The smallest particle of a chemical substance, consisting of one or more atoms combined. A molecule cannot be broken up and still remain the same substance.

Momentum The impetus of a moving object. It is equal to the mass of the object multiplied by its speed.

Neutrino A tiny particle that can travel easily through solid material.

Neutron A particle found in the nucleus of all atoms (except hydrogen). Unlike protons and electrons, neutrons have no electric charge. A neutron weighs the same as a proton, and about 2,000 times more than an electron.

Nitrogen A colourless gas with no smell which makes up most of the air.

Nuclear fission Fission is another word for splitting. In nuclear fission, the nucleus of an atom splits in two, releasing energy.

Nuclear fusion The joining, or fusing, of the nuclei of two light atoms to make a heavier nucleus. This process releases large amount of energy. The sun produces its energy by fusing hydrogen nuclei to make helium.

Nuclear power Energy obtained from the nucleus of certain atoms, by nuclear fission. In a nuclear power plant, the energy is released in a nuclear reactor and changed into electricity.

Nucleus The centre of an atom. It contains protons and neutrons and is positively charged.

Nylon An artificial plastic and fibre. The raw materials come from oil or coal. Many different types of nylon are made, including nylon thread.

Ohm A unit used to measure electrical resistance. It is named after G.S. Ohm (1787–1854), a German physicist.

Optical fibre A very thin, bendable glass thread which

can transmit light by internal reflections. It is used in surgery as well as in communications.

Orbit The path of a planet or satellite as it moves around another body in space.

Oxygen A colourless, tasteless gas that is found in air. Oxygen is a chemical element. It is essential for life, and for burning.

Ozone A form of oxygen which has three atoms in each molecule instead to two.

Ozone layer A layer of the earth's atmosphere containing ozone, which protects the earth from too much ultraviolet radiation.

Parallel circuit An electrical circuit in which the components are connected side-by-side. The current flowing in the circuit is shared by the components.

Particle A very small piece of a material. In modern physics, the word is used to describe the components of an atom, such as protons or neutrons.

Particle accelerator A large machine used by scientists to study the small particles that make up atoms. It speeds up, or accelerates, particles such as protons or electrons and shoots them at a target.

Petroleum A liquid fuel containing hydrocarbons, which is found trapped in between rocks below the earth's surface.

Phosphorescence A cold glow given out by some substances. For example, fireflies and glow-worms phosphoresce.

Photon A packet of light energy. In some situations, a beam of light behaves as if it was a stream of small particles which scientists call photons.

Physical change A change, such as melting or boiling, that does not produce a new chemical substance.

Physical chemistry The science that studies the physical changes that occur during chemical processes.

Physics The science that studies matter, the forces of nature and the different forms of energy, such as heat, light and motion.

Plastics Artificial materials in which the molecules are joined together in a long chain (or polymer). They can be shaped by pressure and heat. Many types of plastic are made, with different properties for different purposes.

Plutonium A heavy, radioactive metal used in nuclear reactors and nuclear weapons. It is made from uranium.

Potential energy The energy that an object has because of its position. An object on a high shelf has potential energy that is released as it falls to the ground.

Pressure The force or weight acting on a unit area of surface. Atmospheric pressure is the pressure of the air on a unit area of the earth's surface.

Primary colours Three colours which can be mixed together to produce any other colour. With coloured lights, the primary colours are red, green and blue. With paints, the primary colours are red, yellow and blue.

Program The list of instructions fed into a computer to tell it how to carry out a task.

Proton A particle found in the nucleus of all atoms. It has a positive electrical charge equal in size to the negative charge of an electron.

Quantum theory A modern theory that helps scientists describe how very small objects, such as atoms, are made up and behave.

Quark A tiny particle thought to exist inside protons and neutrons. Quarks have never been seen on their own but scientists are confident they exist.

Radar A method of detecting and locating the position of objects. Microwaves, electromagnetic waves of short wavelengths, are reflected by the object and recorded on the screen of a cathode-ray tube.

Radiation The transfer of energy by electromagnetic waves, such as light, radio, X-rays etc. Heat radiation is the transfer of heat by waves. This is how the earth is warmed by the sun.

Radioactivity The breaking up of the unstable nucleus of an element, such as radium, giving out radiation, such as alpha and gamma rays.

Radiocarbon dating A method for finding the age of a piece of wood, or other once-living material, by measuring the amount of radioactive carbon in the wood or material. Archaeologists use the method to find the age of items they dig up.

Reflection The bouncing of light or other rays from a surface.

Refraction The bending of light rays as they pass from one material to another. Refraction causes a straw in a glass of water to appear bent.

Relativity A theory that describes how objects behave when moving at very high speeds, near the speed of light. It was discovered by Albert Einstein in 1905.

Resistance The force acting against a change in motion. For example, water resists a ship's motion. Electrical resistance is the force acting to slow the flow of a current through a conductor.

Resonance The way in which a small vibration can cause a large effect. For example, a singer can make a glass vibrate slightly by singing loudly. If the right note is sung, the glass vibrates violently because of resonance, and may break.

Robot A machine which can do a job that is usually done by a human being. Robots are used on factory assembly lines to do one particular job that is continually repeated.

Salt A substance formed when an acid is mixed with a

base. Common salt, which is found in sea water, is sodium chloride. It can be made by mixing hydrochloric acid with sodium hydroxide, a base.

Satellite An object that circles around another much larger body. The moon is a satellite of the earth.

Semiconductor A material that can conduct electricity but not as well as a conductor. Semiconductors, such as silicon, are used to make integrated circuits and transistors.

Series circuit An electric circuit in which the components are connected end-to-end, so that the current flows through all the components one after the other.

Silicon The substance used for making microchips (silicon chips), used in computers, etc. It is the second most abundant element in the earth's crust, occurring in many minerals, such as sand.

Software The program (list of instructions) and data (information) which are fed into a computer. The computer itself and all machinery connected to it are called hardware.

Solution A liquid in which a substance is dissolved. Sea water is a solution of common salt and other substances in water.

Space probe An unmanned spacecraft sent to explore a distant place in space. Space probes have been sent to all the planets, except Pluto, and have sent back pictures of the planets.

Space Shuttle The first reusable space vehicle. An American craft, it is launched into space by rockets, but lands like an aircraft.

Spectrum The rainbow-coloured band of light produced when white light is passed through a prism. The colours are arranged in order of the wavelength of their waves; red is longest and violet is shortest.

Speed The rate at which something moves. The speed in kilometres per hour is calculated by dividing the distance travelled, in kilometres, by the time taken in hours.

Sputnik A Soviet space satellite. Launched 4 October 1957, *Sputnik* 1 was the first artificial satellite to orbit the earth.

Static electricity Electric charges that are not moving. Static electricity builds up on a cat's fur when it is combed, causing the fur to stand on end and crackle.

Stationary orbit An orbit, or flight path, around the earth in which a satellite is moving at exactly the same speed as the earth's rotation. So the satellite always stays above the same point on the earth's surface.

Superconductor A substance which loses its electrical resistance at very low temperatures. Superconductors are usually metals. Researchers have recently discovered ceramic superconductors that do not require such extreme low temperatures.

Surface tension The way the surface of a liquid such as water seems to be covered by a thin elastic film. This causes small droplets to become ball-shaped. Some insects can walk on water because the surface tension holds them up.

Theory A set of ideas that scientists use to explain how the world works, and to make predictions. Quantum theory, for example, makes predictions about the behaviour of atoms and small particles.

Thermodynamics The branch of science concerned with heat and mechanical energy, and how one can be converted into the other.

Transformer A device used to change the voltage of an alternating electric current. Transformers are used in electric power stations to increase the voltage of the electricity produced so that it can be sent along high-voltage cables.

Transistor A semiconductor electronic device which controls the flow of an electric current. It is used as an amplifier in radios, television sets, and computers.

Ultrasound Sound waves of a very high frequency which are beyond human hearing.

Ultraviolet rays A type of electromagnetic radiation with a wavelength shorter than violet light. Ultraviolet rays occur in sunlight and cause sunburn.

Uranium A heavy, grey metal. It is radioactive and is used as fuel in a nuclear reactor.

Vacuum An empty space. As it contains no matter, there is no pressure in a vacuum.

Velocity The speed of an object in a given direction.

Voltage The electrical pressure in a circuit, which drives the electrical current around the circuit. The pressure is measured in volts, named after an Italian scientist Alessandro Volta (1745–1827).

Voltaic cell A type of electric cell invented by Alessandro Volta in 1800. It consists of two terminals of different metals dipping into salt water.

Wavelength The distance between the peak of one wave and the peak of the next wave.

Waves Regular disturbances that spread out from their source. Sound waves are disturbances of the molecules of the air caused by a vibrating body. Electromagnetic waves are disturbances of the magnetic and electric fields in space.

Weight The effect of gravity pulling downwards on something. It is the force exerted by gravity.

Work The amount of energy used when a force moves an object. The amount of work done is calculated by multiplying the force by the distance the object moves.

X-rays Electromagnetic radiation of very short wavelength. They can pass through many materials, and affect a photographic plate or film.

Index